Evaluation Methodologies for Aid in Conflict

Knowledge and rigorous evidence around the role of external development partners in situations of conflict and fragility is still lacking. There is little accountability for the billions in aid being spent in places such as Afghanistan, Iraq and the Democratic Republic of Congo.

This book analyses evaluation theory and practice in order to help fill this knowledge gap and advocates a realistic and rigorous approach to evaluating international engagement. Through a series of case studies, this book highlights both the promise, and potential pitfalls, of taking a more evaluative approach to understanding aid in conflict regions. These illustrate the methodological and analytical approach taken by researchers working to understand the results and effectiveness of conflict prevention and peacebuilding support. While well-grounded in current theoretical and methodological debates, the book provides valuable practical information by examining how and why different choices were made in the context of each evaluation. The book shows what future steps may be envisaged to further strengthen evaluations of support for conflict prevention and peacebuilding. The analysis draws on a wealth of perspectives and voices to provide researchers and students in development studies and conflict and peace studies as well as development evaluators with a deep and broad understanding of evaluation methods and approaches.

Ole Winckler Andersen is Head of the Evaluation Department, Danida, Ministry of Foreign Affairs, Denmark.

Beate Bull is Senior Adviser at the Evaluation Department, Norwegian Agency for Development Cooperation, Norway.

Megan Kennedy-Chouane is Policy Analyst at the Organisation for Economic Co-operation and Development (OECD), France.

Routledge Explorations in Development Studies

The Domestic Politics of Foreign Aid
Erik Lundsgaarde

Social Protection in Developing Countries
Reforming Systems
Katja Bender, Markus Kaltenborn and Christian Pfleiderer

Formal Peace and Informal War
Security and Development in Congo
Zoë Marriage

Technology Development Assistance for Agriculture
Putting Research into Use in Low Income Countries
Norman Clark, Andy Frost, Ian Maudlin and Andrew Ward

Statelessness and Citizenship
Camps and the Creation of Political Space
Victoria Redclift

Governance for Pro-Poor Urban Development
Lessons from Ghana
Franklin Obeng-Odoom

Nationalism, Law and Statelessness
Grand Illusions in the Horn of Africa
John R. Campbell

HIV and East Africa
Thirty years in the shadow of an epidemic
Janet Seeley

Evaluation Methodologies for Aid in Conflict
Ole Winckler Andersen, Beate Bull and Megan Kennedy-Chouane

Digital Technologies for Democratic Governance in Latin America
Opportunities and Risks
Anita Breuer and Yanina Welp

Evaluation Methodologies for Aid in Conflict

Edited by
Ole Winckler Andersen
Beate Bull
Megan Kennedy-Chouane

LONDON AND NEW YORK

First published 2014
by Routledge
2 Park Square, Milton Park, Abingdon, Oxon, OX14 4RN

and by Routledge
711 Third Avenue, New York, NY 10017

Routledge is an imprint of the Taylor & Francis Group, an informa business

© 2014 selection and editorial material Ole Winckler Andersen, Beate Bull and Megan Kennedy-Chouane; individual chapters, the contributors

The right of Ole Winckler Andersen, Beate Bull and Megan Kennedy-Chouane to be identified as authors of the editorial material, and of the individual authors as authors of their contributions, has been asserted by them in accordance with sections 77 and 78 of the Copyright, Designs and Patents Act 1988.

All rights reserved. No part of this book may be reprinted or reproduced or utilised in any form or by any electronic, mechanical, or other means, now known or hereafter invented, including photocopying and recording, or in any information storage or retrieval system, without permission in writing from the publishers.

British Library Cataloguing in Publication Data
A catalogue record for this book is available from the British Library

Library of Congress Cataloguing in Publication data
  Evaluation methodologies for aid in conflict / edited by Ole Winckler Andersen, Beate Bull, Megan Kennedy-Chouane.
    pages cm
  Includes bibliographical references and index.
  1. Postwar reconstruction – Case studies. 2. Peace-building – Case studies. 3. Nation building – Case studies. 4. Economic assistance – Case studies. 5. Economic development – Case studies. I. Winckler Andersen, Ole, editor of compilation. II. Bull, Beate, 1968- editor of compilation. III. Kennedy-Chouane, Megan, editor of compilation.
  HV639.E83 2014
  362.88–dc23
  2013023609

ISBN13: 978-0-415-87080-1 (hbk)
ISBN13: 978-0-203-79800-3 (ebk)

Typeset in Times
by Out of House Publishing

Printed and bound by CPI Group (UK) Ltd, Croydon, CR0 4YY

Contents

List of illustrations		vii
List of contributors		viii
Foreword		xii
CHRISTIAN FRIIS BACH		

1 **Introduction**   1
   OLE WINCKLER ANDERSEN AND MEGAN KENNEDY-CHOUANE

2 **Evaluation approaches in situations of conflict and fragility**   15
   EVA BROEGAARD, BEATE BULL AND JENS KOVSTED

3 **Critical reflections on the South Sudan evaluation of conflict prevention and peacebuilding activities**   38
   CHRIS BARNETT AND JON BENNETT

4 **Battlefields of method: evaluating Norwegian peace efforts in Sri Lanka**   61
   JONATHAN GOODHAND, BART KLEM AND GUNNAR M. SØRBØ

5 **The case of Congo: an evaluation approach focusing on context**   85
   EMERY BRUSSET AND IVO HOOGHE

6 **Assessing development cooperation in northeast Afghanistan with repeated mixed-method surveys**   105
   JAN R. BÖHNKE, JAN KOEHLER AND CHRISTOPH ZÜRCHER

7 **Impact evaluation for peacebuilding: challenging preconceptions**   130
   MARIE GAARDER AND JEANNIE ANNAN

8 **Evaluating statebuilding support: learning from experience or judging from assumptions?** 154
JÖRN GRÄVINGHOLT AND JULIA LEININGER

9 **Systems thinking in peacebuilding evaluations: applications in Ghana, Guinea-Bissau and Kosovo** 175
DIANA CHIGAS AND PETER WOODROW

Index 198

Illustrations

Figures

9.1	Polarisation and politicisation of public life in Ghana	180
9.2	Chieftaincy conflicts in Ghana	180
9.3	Conflict analysis of Guinea-Bissau	185
9.4	Theory of change of peacebuilding programming in Kosovo	188
9.5	What actually happened in Kosovo	190

Tables

6.1	Important variables in quantitative analysis	116
8.1	Sample of analysed evaluation studies	158

Boxes

6.1	The framework for the evaluation as derived from the conflict assessment	107
6.2	A theory of change for aid in northeast Afghanistan	110
6.3	Some findings: the impact of aid in Afghanistan	121
8.1	Taking the conventional approach to evaluation to its limits	160

Contributors

Ole Winckler Andersen has worked for the Danish Ministry of Foreign Affairs for the past 20 years. From 2007 to 2013 he was Head of the Evaluation Department, during which period the department was engaged in evaluations in South Sudan, Somalia, Afghanistan and Nepal. He has been a member of several management committees for international development evaluations, and has contributed to books and international journals on development evaluation.

Jeannie Annan is the Director of Research and Evaluation at the International Rescue Committee and a Visiting Scientist at the Harvard School of Public Health. Her research examines the impact of programmes that prevent and respond to violence against children and women in Uganda, Liberia, Côte d'Ivoire, DRC and on the Thai-Burmese border. She also serves on the Board of Commissioners of the International Initiative for Impact Evaluation (3ie).

Chris Barnett is presently the Director of the Centre for Development Impact, and works at both the Institute of Development Studies (located at the University of Sussex) and Itad (a consultancy specialising in monitoring and evaluation). He is the Project Director for the independent *Impact Evaluation of the Millennium Villages in Ghana*, as well as team leader for a four-year assignment to evaluate a major civil society fund in Malawi. He has published work on evaluation methodologies, feedback loops and innovation prizes.

Jon Bennett has 35 years' experience living and working in 'fragile' states. He has evaluated OECD DAC donor and UN programmes in Africa and Asia. He was the founding Director of the Internal Displacement Monitoring Centre (Geneva) and from 2004 to 2005 was UN Team Leader for the postwar recovery assessment in Sudan. He has published four books and most recently been the team leader on the *Evaluation of UNDP Support to Conflict-affected Countries* (2013) and the evaluation in South Sudan (2011) discussed in Chapter 3 of this book.

Jan R. Böhnke has worked as an evaluation researcher in health and development in post-conflict states. Currently, he is a Research Fellow at the University of York, UK, working on the use of multivariate statistical models in mental

List of contributors   ix

health evaluations. He is responsible for the survey design and quantitative analyses of the *North East Afghanistan Longitudinal Study* and was one of the team members of the Afghanistan evaluation discussed in Chapter 6 of this book.

Eva Broegaard has worked with Danida's Evaluation Department, where she managed evaluations in Africa, Latin America and Asia – including Afghanistan, Nepal and other situations of conflict and fragility. She also teaches evaluation methodology at graduate and postgraduate level and has co-authored several books and papers on evaluation.

Emery Brusset is the director of Channel Research and has been the team leader and manager of a number of evaluations in fragile contexts, including the DRC evaluation discussed in Chapter 5 of this book. A graduate from Yale and the London School of Economics, he was a UN staff member and has contributed to books on real time evaluation and evaluations of peace operations.

Beate Bull worked as a senior advisor in the Evaluation Department in Norad from 2005 to 2013, managing several evaluations in conflict-affected countries, including leading the work with the OECD DAC guidance on evaluating in situations of conflict and fragility for Norad. She has published peer-reviewed articles and has also worked for the UNDP and UNDPKO in East Timor (2001–2004), and for UNV (in East Timor, 1999). Her experience also includes work in the Great Lakes region for the Norwegian Foreign Ministry.

Diana Chigas joined CDA in 2003 as Co-Director of the Reflecting on Peace Practice Project (RPP). She is also Professor of the Practice of Negotiation and Conflict Resolution at the Fletcher School of Law and Diplomacy. Prior to joining CDA, Diana worked as a facilitator, trainer and consultant in negotiation, dialogue and conflict resolution. Her work has included development of strategies on preventive diplomacy, and facilitation of dialogue in El Salvador, South Africa, Ecuador and Peru, Georgia/South Ossetia and Cyprus. She has performed evaluations of peacebuilding and conflict prevention programming in Kosovo and Latin America.

Marie Gaarder is a Manager in the World Bank's Independent Evaluation Group (IEG). Prior positions include Deputy Executive Director of the International Initiative for Impact Evaluation (3ie) and Director of the Evaluation Department, Norad, where she contributed to the OECD DAC guidance on evaluating peacebuilding activities and supervised evaluations of Norway's efforts in Afghanistan and in Sri Lanka and of the Training for Peace programme. Her recent research includes impact evaluation of research dissemination, systematic reviews of the health effects of cash transfer programmes, and a comparative study of efforts to institutionalise government evaluations.

Jonathan Goodhand is a Professor in Conflict and Development Studies in the Department of Development Studies, School of Oriental and African Studies, University of London. His primary research interests are the political economy of armed conflict, NGOs and peacebuilding and 'post-conflict' reconstruction, with a particular focus on Afghanistan and Sri Lanka. He co-authored the evaluation of Norwegian peace efforts in Sri Lanka (2011) discussed in Chapter 4 in this book and has a number of other publications on conflict and peacebuilding.

Jörn Grävingholt is Senior Researcher at the German Development Institute in Bonn. He has published widely on governance, democracy promotion and statebuilding policies of OECD countries and conducted field research and evaluations in Russia, Central Asia and South Asia.

Ivo Hooghe has been working at the Office of the Special Evaluator (FPS Foreign Affairs, Belgium) since 2006. In recent years he was involved in the management of peacebuilding evaluations in the DRC, Burundi and South Sudan and he contributed to the OECD DAC guidance on evaluating in situations of conflict and fragility.

Megan Kennedy-Chouane is a policy analyst at the OECD, where she managed the development of the OECD DAC guidance on evaluating in situations of conflict and fragility. She has published in the OECD Papers on evaluating conflict prevention and peacebuilding assistance and co-authored several papers on development evaluation. Previously, she was a Thomas J. Watson fellow and worked in the non-profit sector with a focus on children and youth in development.

Bart Klem is a researcher and lecturer in Political Geography at the University of Zurich, Switzerland. Alongside his academic work, he has executed several evaluations in the field of development and conflict, including the evaluation of Norwegian peace efforts in Sri Lanka (2011) discussed in Chapter 4 of this book.

Jan Koehler is researcher at the Governance in Areas of Limited Statehood research centre at Free University, Berlin. A social anthropologist by training he has worked in and on fragile states and conflict zones over the past 20 years, focusing on the Caucasus region, Central Asia and Afghanistan. He is team leader for the impact assessment of the North Afghanistan Stability Programme financed by the German Foreign Office and team member for the longitudinal impact assessment in Northeast Afghanistan discussed in Chapter 6 of this book.

Jens Kovsted is a development economist and evaluation specialist. Educated at the Universities of Copenhagen and Cambridge, he has been responsible for several impact evaluations of government programmes and policies. He has published peer-reviewed books and articles on evaluation, financial sector regulation, macroeconomic policies, and health (in particular HIV/Aids).

Julia Leininger is Senior Researcher at the German Development Institute in Bonn, Germany. Her research focuses on (de-)democratisation and international democracy promotion in fragile states, with particular emphasis on sub-Saharan Africa. She works as a policy advisor, and has published several books and journal articles. Most recently, she co-authored an evaluation of international statebuilding support in fragile states.

Gunnar M. Sørbø is Senior Researcher and former Director of Chr. Michelsen Institute (CMI). An anthropologist by profession, his professional profile and research interests include development policy and planning as well as conflict studies and conflict management. He is an experienced team leader for policy-oriented reviews and evaluations including an evaluation of Norwegian peace efforts in Sri Lanka (discussed in Chapter 4 of this book) and an evaluation of Danish support to promote human rights and democracy. He is the author of a number of works, including several recent publications on Sudan.

Peter Woodrow joined CDA as Co-Director of the Reflecting on Peace Practice Program (RPP) in 2003 and is currently Executive Director. He is an experienced mediator, facilitator, trainer and consultant. He has also developed and implemented international programmes in peacebuilding, consensus-building, problem-solving, decision-making and inter-ethnic conflict resolution in Asia, Africa and Eastern Europe. He has performed evaluations in Ghana, Guinea-Bissau and Liberia, and of global programmes.

Christoph Zürcher is a Professor at the Graduate School of Public and International Affairs at the University of Ottawa. Previous teaching and research appointments include the University of Konstanz, Germany, the Institut d'études Politiques d'Aix-en-Provence, Stanford University and Free University in Berlin. His research and teaching interests include conflict research, statebuilding and interventions, international governance and development. He was a member of the team of researchers which conducted the Afghanistan evaluation discussed in Chapter 6 of this book.

Foreword

Fragile and conflict-affected states lie at the heart of the global development agenda and our mutual efforts to reduce poverty and promote stability and human rights. Today it is estimated that more than half of the world's poor live in fragile states, and this number will grow if we do not take concerted action.

With the endorsement in 2011 of the New Deal for Engagement in Fragile States there is now a stronger basis for supporting country-led transitions from fragility and conflict to peace and development. The group of fragile states, the g7+, is in the driver's seat of this exciting new process. In the coming years, the real challenge of the New Deal lies in its implementation – a main priority for the International Dialogue on Peacebuilding and Statebuilding, which I have the honour of co-chairing with the Minister of Finance of Timor-Leste, Emilia Pires. All efforts to this effect are important for making the case for peacebuilding and statebuilding in the post-2015 framework.

Independent analysis and evaluations of efforts in fragile states are of particular importance, and I welcome the growing number of evaluations that have been completed in recent years. This work has shown us that evaluations in fragile or conflict settings are associated with particular challenges, but also that evaluations can be an important tool for improving our efforts. In fragile states, where contexts are constantly evolving, a vital part of any engagement is a proper assessment of results and impact and continuous learning from experiences.

This book is an important step in that direction. It compares the experiences of a number of completed evaluations in settings of fragility and conflict, and analyses the evaluation methods applied in these settings. A key message is that the complexity of these settings requires adjustments in the methods we usually apply in development evaluation. Another main message is how important it is to understand the country context and to support country-led and country-owned processes, which is in line with the basic principles of the New Deal.

I therefore warmly welcome this new book and I am sure it will spur further analyses and dialogue on how we can learn from our joint experiences and improve the quality of evaluations in settings of fragility and conflict. We have no choice but to engage to solve the deep-rooted problems in fragile countries. This book will help us to better understand how to do so.

Christian Friis Bach
Co-Chair of the International Dialogue on Peacebuilding and Statebuilding
Minister for Development Cooperation of Denmark

1 Introduction

Ole Winckler Andersen
Danish Ministry of Foreign Affairs[1]

Megan Kennedy-Chouane
Development Co-operation Directorate, OECD[2]

> There are known knowns; there are things we know we know. We also know there are known unknowns; that is to say, we know there are some things we do not know. But there are also unknown unknowns – the ones we don't know we don't know.
> United States Secretary of Defense, Donald Rumsfeld, 12 February 2002

1 A primer

International interventions in foreign conflicts, both military and humanitarian, are hotly debated. Hundreds of millions of dollars are being spent each year to try to support recovery from conflict, peace, stability and economic development in places such as Afghanistan, the Democratic Republic of Congo and South Sudan. Yet many of the strategies, policies and programmes currently pursued are based on weak – or no – evidence that they actually help. In most cases, international partners have only a vague understanding of how their aid for conflict prevention and peacebuilding is actually affecting local populations and the long-term prospects of peace. And not knowing matters a lot in these settings because the consequences of making the wrong decisions, based on weak or unreliable evidence, are potentially so dramatic. That is why this book focuses on dissecting the evaluation process itself to explore how we know, and whether we actually know, what we think we know.

The book examines the methodological and analytical approaches taken by evaluators working to understand the results of international conflict prevent and peacebuilding support. These analyses highlight the real-life trade-offs but also the importance of maintaining methodological rigour while adapting evaluation approaches to conflict settings. In so doing, the authors point the way towards potential avenues to help strengthen the knowledge base through better evaluations.

2 Need for learning

The aid to conflict prevention and peacebuilding has increased significantly in the past decade. US$46.7 billion in net official development assistance (ODA) went to 45 fragile states in 2011,[3] or roughly 37 per cent of all ODA.[4] In spite of an acknowledged general professionalisation of these interventions, lack of progress in fragile states is widespread and a number of studies have pointed to the need for more learning and systematic evaluation of aid interventions in fragile states.

Across the globe, some 1.5 billion people live in countries affected by persistent political and criminal violence and weak or dysfunctional state institutions where life is not improving (World Bank 2011).[5] While progress is being made to reduce poverty and achieve common development goals, like the Millennium Development Goals (MDGs), people living in fragile states cannot expect their countries to achieve the MDGs by 2015. As has been documented in several analyses, the fragile states score significantly lower than other developing countries on most social indicators (OECD 2012b). The slow progress on social and economic indicators (e.g., poverty reduction, infant mortality, hunger) has led to a greater emphasis on creating an enabling environment for development by giving more attention to peacebuilding, statebuilding and armed violence prevention (OECD 2012b). In addition to the lack of progress, in spite of the high levels of aid, these countries often slip back into conflict.

The learning and accountability gaps all too common in development cooperation are multiplied and deepened in these settings.[6] High risk, fluidity and complexity make the political and operational realities of these settings particularly difficult for external development partners. Simultaneously there is strong political demand for analyses of 'what works' and 'what doesn't' in these contexts. Some lessons learned do exist, and experience has shown that aid can support progress towards positive change. For this role to be realised, however, external assistance needs to be targeted towards peacebuilding and statebuilding goals, its allocation optimised across countries, and its quality improved.[7]

It is widely accepted that approaches to development work and evaluations have to be adapted to settings of violent conflict and state fragility (Anderson et al. 2007; OECD 2012a). However, donors have only partly adjusted their aid to reflect this.[8] In addition, development agencies often find themselves operating in 'emergency mode', with high staff turnover and unrealistic spending targets. Relations with national partners can be extremely challenging, due to low capacities, lack of legitimate, accountable institutions or political instability. As a result, systematic learning, analysis and accountability for results have been weaker in these contexts, compared to other areas of development cooperation. This reflects the challenging context, but also symptomatic of development agencies' relative weaknesses in effectively tackling problems that require long-term, multifaceted and flexible solutions.

The increasing interest in providing support to these countries has created broader interest in understanding the mechanics of peace. The perception of failure – countries sliding back into conflict after a period of stability or stagnating in long-term crisis – has also motivated a deeper investigation of the role of external actors and a nuancing of the conflict continuum, moving away from rigid definitions of conflict/post-conflict periods. The pressure inside development agencies and international organisations has resulted in a number of analyses, which try to understand how development in these contexts can be understood and influenced and, in particular, in recent years there has been a demand for more evaluations of interventions in these contexts.

3 Fragile settings and types of interventions: implications for evaluation

Evaluation is broadly understood as the systematic and objective assessment of a programme or policy, its design, implementation and results (OECD 2002). Definitions of what should be understood with 'evaluation' in a conflict prevention and peacebuilding context and how this differs from evaluation in other fields, has been debated in the literature.[9] In particular, how core evaluation criteria (relevance, sustainability, effectiveness, impact and efficiency) may be understood in the context of conflict and fragility has been discussed.[10]

Two main issues complicate the development of robust evaluations of interventions in the field of conflict prevention and peacebuilding: the context of fragility itself and the types of interventions being undertaken by international actors in these settings. These issues make it difficult for those involved in an evaluation to reach agreement on what is to be analysed and how. The diversity across so-called fragile contexts also has major implications for both the external and internal validity of evaluation findings, as will be discussed further in Chapter 2.

First, as indicated earlier, the fragile states and contexts vary significantly and there is an ongoing discussion on how to define fragility.[11] The definitional challenge is compounded by the fact that fragile states terminology has been much maligned as stigmatising and analytically imprecise. The term 'fragile' is usually considered pejorative and some view it as an 'inherently political label reflecting Weberian ideals of how a "successful" state should function…[which] arguably does not adequately differentiate between the unique economic and sociopolitical dimensions of states' (GSDRC 2012). Fragility may therefore be viewed as a continuum of state performance, rather than an either or category. Many instead refer to 'situations of fragility' to account for this nuance and highlight issues of social and political fragility and conflict that may extend beyond the state apparatus. The group of 47 countries in situations of crisis and acute fragility includes a wide range of countries from essentially 'post-conflict' situations in Liberia, Nepal and Sri Lanka, to war and protracted violent conflict in Somalia, Iraq and Afghanistan. Other countries are mainly characterised by low capacities of the state and its inability or unwillingness to protect basic human rights and provide core services to its people. Still others, including South Sudan and Palestine, are characterised by a focus on state formation in the context of ongoing violent conflict. Regional and cross-border conflicts characterise other conflicts, particularly central Africa and the Great Lakes region.

The notion of peacebuilding is also debated.[12] Peacebuilding is used to refer both to the process of supporting stabilisation and the reduction of violence, as well as the longer-term transformation towards resilient cultures capable of resolving disputes without violence, meeting preconditions for sustainable development. Two groups of definitions of peacebuilding therefore exist. A broader definition, which seems to be close to statebuilding, and a narrower one, which focuses on stopping violence. This second definition is close to a definition of conflict prevention. The first definition will have a main focus on society/institutional (macro or impact) level while the second will have its focus on the more immediate outcome (micro) level.[13] In addition, conflict prevention and peacebuilding cover a wide range of different types of interventions, such as election support, support to parliament, good governance, demobilisation of ex-combatants, etc. Many publications (and analyses) no longer make a distinction between the three areas (conflict prevention, peacebuilding and statebuilding).

The focus of this book being on evaluation methods, we will not go further into these definitional debates. Most chapters will use the definition that was provided in the evaluation's Terms of Reference, or the author's own definition. For readers that are new to this field, the Organisation for Economic Co-operation and Development (OECD) working definition provides a useful place to start (OECD 2011a, 2012a). This definition covers activities designed to prevent conflict through addressing structural and proximate causes of violence, promoting sustainable peace, delegitimising violence as a dispute resolution strategy, building capacity within society to peacefully manage disputes and reducing vulnerability to triggers that may spark violence.[14]

It is possible to identify five specific characteristics of fragility that directly impact evaluation of conflict prevention and peacebuilding interventions (as well as their design and implementation) (OECD 2012a):

1. Fragile and conflict-affected situations are inherently high-risk environments – for the people who live there, for their governments and for those who provide assistance. As a consequence, planning horizons and priorities are short term – typically focusing on ensuring access to basic necessities. Interventions tend to be carried out with a sense of urgency that does not lend itself well to planning, collection of baseline activities or reflective analysis.
2. Situations of conflict and fragility are characterised by complex political economies[15] in which development partners can be parties (or perceived to be parties) in an ongoing conflict.
3. Fragile and conflict-affected situations are most often characterised by weak or absent national and local capacities and institutions. The state may be engaged in the conflict and/or be the coveted object of the conflict.
4. Situations of conflict and fragility are characterised by the fact that they are confronted with a combination of internal and external stresses that heighten the threat of violent conflict. This affects the safety, incentives and behaviour of all involved.
5. Finally, aid provided in conflict-affected and fragile situations is often part of broader geopolitical or economic agendas (e.g., the war on terrorism, ensuring access to scarce resources such as oil, fighting transnational organised crime and curbing immigration flows). The politics of conflict influence how external actors engage with the conflict (or not) at a given point in time.

While the same can be said of other forms of development cooperation, the stakes are higher and the level of engagement more visible when it comes to conflict-affected and fragile situations. This may in part explain the high volatility of aid to fragile states, as political agendas and economic drivers of decision making shift.

Second, the types of interventions taking place and their intended objectives and modes of operation are often not clear, which makes it difficult to benchmark relevant measures by which to evaluate. There is often confusion around the distinction between conflict prevention and peacebuilding, and other interventions with a humanitarian or an economic development focus.[16] Conflict prevention and peacebuilding interventions aim to achieve peace. Peace is not just the absence of 'hot' conflict, but connotes a broader state of wellbeing, certainty and sustainability of the peace and the outlook of affected people. It has been suggested that successful donor contributions to peace must 'include comprehensive efforts to identify and support structures which will tend to consolidate peace and advance a sense of confidence and well-being among people' (United Nations 1992). This includes balancing support over changing short- and long-term priorities that range from the very direct (e.g., disarming the previously warring parties and restoring order) to creating long-term structures for peaceful coexistence and development (e.g., advancing efforts to protect human rights, reforming or strengthening governmental institutions and promoting formal and informal livelihood support structures). Peacebuilding is a profoundly transformative process. Peace goes beyond a cessation of hostilities or reduction in overt violence. While all development processes involve changes in power relations, cultures and ways of life, peace has been defined as a set of values, attitudes and modes of behaviour (United Nations General Assembly 2008). Recently, peacebuilding practitioners have put forth a typology of peacebuilding work, distinguishing between technical and transformative approaches to supporting peace (Fisher and Zimina 2008). Interventions in settings of violent conflict are therefore often based on the premise that cultures can be changed and an implicit assumption that external actors can have some influence. Moving towards a 'culture of peace' thus involves creating fundamental transformations. Analysing such activities is unfamiliar for many development evaluators, and it is not always clear what methods and tools will be well-suited to analysing such work.

Not all assistance provided in settings of conflict or fragility is actively aimed at supporting peace, and many 'traditional' development and humanitarian activities are also carried out in fragile states. Donors have recognised and are increasingly trying to operationalise strategic links between the 'three Ds': development, diplomacy and defence, to work across various parts of government in order to more effectively contribute to long-term peace and statebuilding processes within their overall foreign policy agenda, which also includes pursuit of national interests, diplomatic and trade relations, and security agendas.

Thus, it can be argued that evaluation of conflict prevention and peacebuilding interventions are different from evaluations of other types of policies or programmes in a number of ways (Elkins 2010: 310).[17] First, the context is different (security problems, weak capacity, difficult to find local partners, local partners sometimes risk their lives when working for international organisations (Elkins 2010: 313), no or weak civil society, systems are not in place, etc.). Second, the objectives of the interventions are different, and different intervention approaches and modalities of assistance are applied. These differences characterise the conflict prevention and peacebuilding interventions, but obviously also have implications for how to evaluate these interventions.

As will be discussed in more detail in Chapter 2, many of the challenges related to evaluations of conflict prevention and peacebuilding described here may also be found in evaluations of other types of international activities (such as health or education programmes) but may be more pronounced in these contexts. Specifically, the purpose of the interventions, including the associated theories and assumptions,[18] are not always clearly defined or must be reconstructed for the purpose of the evaluation. Underlying objectives and assumptions may also be difficult to define due to the fact that they are in flux and change as the conflict situation itself evolves. Another main challenge is the lack of baselines and monitoring data.[19] A third is the widespread use of cases, with limited rigorous sampling, which can weaken the generalisability of conclusions. The lack of both a clear theory of change combined with often low-quality data, can be challenges in other complex evaluations, but it seems that the challenges are more severe in these evaluations not least due to the absence of relevant government institutions charged with regular data collection (e.g., census data). The evaluations will therefore often have to base their findings and conclusions on interviews with resulting risk of different bias problems. It has, however, to be acknowledged that a lot of work has been invested in developing better analytical tools, which can be used for conflict assessments.[20]

4 The peacebuilding knowledge base

There are many attempts to understand the dynamics of societies at war and the transition to peace and sustainable development, as well as to assess the results of particular conflict prevention and peacebuilding interventions. Different groups of operational and academic analysis can be identified. Here, we group these into three main types in order to give a picture of the current knowledge base around conflict prevention and peacebuilding activities. These groups are not mutually exclusive, however, and overlaps exist between them. There is also constant interaction and feedback with work in each area influencing others.

Academic research on state fragility, conflict, peacebuilding, etc., has increased significantly since the beginning of the 1990s, where discussions were initiated on the experiences of peacebuilding (Paffenholz and Reychler 2007: 33–35).[21] Since then, several assessments of the status of this research have been made.[22] New journals have been established and an impressive number of conferences have been organised. Often the peace research has not been based on clear and systematic use of assessment methods, but an increasing number of academic studies have tried to use more rigorous, including quantitative, methods.[23]

A related area of research comprises studies and analyses on the need for a more systematic use of evaluations.[24] However, most of these do not systematically discuss the particular practical and methodological challenges of evaluations of conflict prevention and peacebuilding.[25] While several studies mention the significant methodological development that has taken place within the field of evaluation of more traditional development interventions, there are few attempts to relate in detail the two fields.[26] Instead most of these analyses provide a more general introduction to evaluation and evaluation methods, including to key evaluation questions and indicators.[27] They may also discuss the need for analyses of the context and the particular conflict, but these discussions are not or only partly related to discussions within evaluation research on theory of change, programme theory, etc.[28] Few of these publications have tried to address the methodological challenges mentioned above.[29] Instead it is argued in several analyses that, although there is an increasing understanding of the need for a methodological debate, this debate is still in its early stages.[30] One reason for this seems to be that evaluation is a new area for many who are active in conflict prevention and peacebuilding, and therefore papers on evaluations tend to have an introductory character instead of examining the particular challenges associated with these contexts.[31]

The second type of analyses are carried out by practitioners including international organisations, policy groups, donor agencies and non-governmental organisations, such as analyses published by for instance OECD[32] and the World Bank Group.[33] Most analyses in this group have a normative character and are only partly based on systematic information about the effects of the interventions. As will be discussed in several of this book's chapters, the OECD's DAC Network on Development Evaluation and the International Network on Conflict and Fragility (INCAF) have developed guidance on evaluating conflict prevention and peacebuilding activities (OECD 2012a).

Finally, the third type of analyses consists of an increasing number of evaluations of interventions in fragile states, including at the project or programme level. A search on the Internet in late 2012 found that a number of evaluations have been carried out over the past five years, some of which are discussed in later chapters. The OECD DAC Evaluation Resource Centre (DEReC) contains some 50 evaluation reports in the 'conflict, peace and security' sector. An analysis of development agencies' evaluation plans has also shown that the number of studies being carried out in the areas of peacebuilding and fragility has increased in recent years.[34] Two workshops jointly organised by FiEnt and Swiss Peace in 2012 highlighted a number of evaluative efforts underway in different parts of the peacebuilding field and pointed to continuing challenges in the field (Bachtold et al. 2013).

In spite of the strengthened efforts in recent years, a number of gaps and weaknesses remain in this knowledge base not only about the individual conflict context, but specifically – and of particular relevance to the evaluation discussion – there are major concerns about how readily lessons and knowledge from one conflict context can inform efforts in other settings. Issues of external validity and the particularities of each fragile context have to some extent undermined the emergence of a coherent base of 'good practice' knowledge beyond the most basic principles (such as 'do no harm'). Further, there are concerns that much of the 'common wisdom' that has emerged may be based more on unquestioned shared assumptions than on solid evidence about the real effects of conflict prevention and peacebuilding interventions. That is, much of what we think we know, we may not really know for sure – even though this knowledge is used to make decisions with potentially serious consequences.[35]

5 Structure of the book

This book emerged from the real and pressing need to improve the quality of evaluations of aid interventions in settings of conflict and fragility by focusing on evaluation approaches and methodologies. Thus, the purpose is not to discuss the interventions as such but, based on the experiences of a number of recent evaluations, to contribute to and stimulate a discussion of how evaluation approaches and methodologies can be used and further developed and refined within this particular area.

The book focuses in particular on two key issues. First, the book discusses some of the practical and methodological challenges that recent evaluations of conflict prevention and peacebuilding have faced during their implementation and how these evaluations dealt with these challenges.

Second, although there is a widespread debate on evaluation of complex interventions and assessments of impact in other sectors, this debate seems so far not to have had a significant influence on the debate of adequate evaluation methodologies when it comes to evaluations of conflict prevention and peacebuilding.[36] The book raises the question whether evaluations of conflict prevention and peacebuilding interventions could learn more from evaluation methodologies, which have been applied in other sectors, and provides examples of the use of complex evaluation methodologies, impact evaluation and systems analysis.

Both issues are related to discussions about how to learn from evaluations and about the internal and external validity of the evaluations of interventions in settings of conflict and fragility. They are also linked to the politics of evaluation – that is who is commissioning and carrying out evaluations of conflict prevention and peacebuilding interventions, why and how? As we will see in the next chapters, the context of evaluation can have significant implications for both the applied methods and results.

Chapter 2 begins with outlining an analytical and methodological framework for analysing complex interventions. The chapter provides a methodological perspective based on recent discussions on development evaluation. It sets the stage for the following chapters by exploring core methodological concepts.

In the following country case chapters (3 to 6) on South Sudan, Sri Lanka, Democratic Republic of Congo and Afghanistan, the authors describe the context of the conducted evaluations and key issues examined and then discuss the methodological challenges with which these evaluations have been confronted. These chapters provide the reader with an in-depth look at the evaluation, drawing on real-life examples, and a critical reflection on how different methodological challenges were addressed by the evaluation teams.

Chapters 7–9 provide broader analyses of methodological issues from three different perspectives. Chapter 7 looks at the application of rigorous methods for assessing impact in settings of fragility, drawing on a review of a number of impact evaluations. Challenges related to evaluating statebuilding support are discussed in Chapter 8, based on a meta-evaluation of studies in this field. Finally the use of systems analysis and its application to evaluations in fragile context are described in Chapter 9.

Notes

1 Organisation provided for identification purposes only. The opinions expressed and arguments employed herein do not necessarily reflect the official views of the Danish Ministry of Foreign Affairs.
2 Organisation provided for identification purposes only. The editor participated in this project in a personal capacity; the opinions expressed and arguments employed herein do not necessarily reflect the official views of the organisation or of the governments of its member countries.
3 See OECD (2013) for a list of the 47 countries, which are currently classified as fragile or having conflict. The OECD Development Assistance Committee (DAC) Principles for Good Engagement in Fragile States (OECD 2007) outline that in fragile situations governments have 'weak capacity to carry out basic functions of governing their populations and territory, and lack the ability to develop mutually constructive and reinforcing relations with society'. Analysts and donors hold different notions of what is meant by 'fragile' and 'conflict-affected' and other classifications do exist (see, for example, discussions in Sanín (2011) and Grävingholt et al. (2012)).
4 OECD (2011b). Half of ODA to fragile states went to just five countries in 2009. With wars and major development interventions in Afghanistan and Iraq, this concentration has been increasing over the past decade and aid projections confirm this trend will continue. The OECD DAC has also pointed to neglect of certain fragile countries; about 20 fragile states are considered underaided.
5 See also Collier (2007). Analyses also show that the number of poor living in fragile states has increased and will continue to do so both in relative and absolute terms (see, for example, Chandy and Gertz (2011) and Summer (2012)).
6 See Savedoff et al. (2006).
7 Studies from the OECD Development Assistance Committee (DAC) also show that assistance to fragile states tends to be of 'lower quality' with high volatility and fragmentation (OECD 2011a). The insufficient progress has also (at least partly) been explained by the lack of a general implementation of 'Principles for Good International Engagement in Fragile States and Situation' as documented in two Monitoring Surveys. Development actors have identified unresolved tensions between the Paris Declaration principles of ownership and alignment and the Fragile States Principles and Good Humanitarian Donorship principles. The Paris Declaration and Accra Agenda for Action call on development partners to use country systems, align with national priorities and work with governments. However, the application of these principles is challenged in contexts where national governments are unwilling or unable to perform the basic functions of a state and provide for their people. Various actors (development, military, diplomatic,

private sector) may have overlapping or competing goals. The result is a proliferation of policy agendas and too many priorities – some of which contradict or compete with one another (we cannot do everything at once, even if we think everything is important). Operationalising various policy recommendations and good practice principles in a situation of high pressure, low information availability and complexity is challenging to say the least.

8 Only two of the ten principles are considered broadly or partly on track.
9 See, for example, Church (2008: 3).
10 See, for example, Church (2008: 3) for a discussion of 'value', which comes close to 'effect' in OECD DAC jargon. See also the discussion in Church (2008: 4) on a potential adaption of the usual evaluation concepts to a peacebuilding setting.
11 Definitions and concepts are given different interpretations by different actors. See for instance the discussion on the concept of 'fragile states' in Paris (2011) and references here. Another approach is the attempt to classify different types of fragile states by using indexes (see, for example, the discussion in Sanín 2011). Both authors agree that 'labels' are often used instead of well-defined concepts. See also Woodrow and Chigas (2009). See OECD DAC for a glossary of key terms.
12 See, for example, Heathershaw (2008), Chetail (2009). See also the discussion in Scharbatke-Church (2011) for a presentation of different definitions of peacebuilding.
13 See, for example, Church (2008: 3).
14 Blum (2011) provides further discussion.
15 The political economy of a state here refers to the way in which political and administrative institutions, the political environment, and the economic system influence each other. A political economy analysis focuses, for instance, on issues such as the influence of elections on the choice of economic policy, determinants of electoral outcomes, the political business cycles, central bank independence and redistributive conflicts in fiscal policy, but also on wider-ranging topics such as the origins and rate of change of political institutions and the role of culture in explaining economic outcomes and developments.
16 For instance Elkins (2010) makes a distinction between the three types of interventions based on Cammack et al. (2006).
17 Elkins (2010: 310). See also Cammack et al. (2006).
18 The question of how to measure success of peacebuilding operation is discussed in, for example, the first chapter of Diehl and Druckman (2010: 1) using Somalia as an example. They also discuss the distinction between the micro and macro (higher order) level. Diehl and Druckman (2010: 4–6) has a long discussion of the implication of not having clear (and measurable) objectives or when there are many stakeholders.
19 See, for example, Paffenholz (2011: 2).
20 See, for instance, Bornstein (2010) and Paffenholz (2011).
21 See also Goodhand (2006: ch. 2); Diehl and Druckman (2010: ch. 1); and Paris (2011).
22 See Diehl and Druckman (2010: 4–9).
23 See, for example, Höglund and Öberg (2011), which contains a comprehensive discussion of several relevant methods that could also be used in evaluations. There is also an increasing number of examples of attempts to make impact evaluations within this field with the use of rigorous methods (see, for example, Fearon et al. 2009; Flores and Nooruddin 2009; Chauvet et al. 2010). This book's authors do also indicate that the distinction between research and evaluation can be difficult to make.
24 See, for example, Paffenholz and Reychler (2007) and Church and Shouldice (2002) for short introductions to the development of evaluation within peacebuilding. See also Çuhadar-Gürkaynak et al. (2009), Diehl and Druckman (2010) and Scharbatke-Church (2011). Scharbatke-Church (2011: 468) mentions also that many are sceptical about using traditional methods in peacebuilding evaluation.
25 See, for example, also Diehl and Druckman (2010: 18–22), which discusses various evaluation approaches and methodologies, but without going into detail.

26 See, for example, Paffenholz and Reychler (2007: 8–50). See also Diehl and Druckman (2010), which features very few references to literature on evaluation methodology. New developments in evaluation methodology and theory have, however, taken place. This applies in particular for theories of change, complex evaluation and impact evaluations.
27 See, for example, Church and Rogers (2006). Compare also with Paffenholz (2011: 15–16) and Scharbatke-Church (2011). See also Diehl and Druckman (2010).
28 See, for example, Diehl and Druckman (2010: ch. 6), which contains many valid and relevant considerations, but does not reference discussions on evaluation approaches and methodologies. The closing chapter in the book does, however, have discussions that are similar to discussions on programme theory within the evaluation community. See also Elkins (2010) for a discussion of evaluation challenges in 'Peace-precarious situations'.
29 For example, Diehl and Druckman (2010).
30 See, for instance, Paffenholz (2011: 1).
31 See Paffenholz (2011: 1).
32 See, for example, OECD (2011a: 15), which actually recommends regular evaluations of the effectiveness of the interventions.
33 See also Manor (2007) and World Bank (2011). In particular World Bank (2011) contains a systematic overview but does not discuss the challenges related to evaluation. The report is, however, based on research at a number of research institutions.
34 See plans database and analyses from the DAC Network on Development Evaluation: www.oecd.org/dac/evaluation/evaluation-plan-inventory.htm.
35 Others have pointed to the dangers of the so-called 'unknown knowns' (Zizek 2004) that is knowledge which one knows but refuses to see or admit.
36 See, for example, Paffenholz (2011: 1–2).

Bibliography

Anderson, M. B., Chigas, D. and Woodrow, P. (2007) 'Encouraging Effective Evaluation of Conflict Prevention and Peacebuilding Activities: Towards DAC Guidance', *OECD Journal on Development* 8(3). www.oecd-ilibrary.org/development/oecd-journal-on-development/volume-8/issue-3_journal_dev-v8-3-en, accessed 26 March 2013.

Bachtold, S., Dittli, R. and Servaes, S. (2013) *Help or Hindrance? Results-orientation in Conflict-affected Situations*, Working Paper (1/2013). Bern: Swiss Peace Foundation.

Barnett, M., Kim, H., O'Donnell, M. and Sitea, L. (2009) 'Peacebuilding: What is in a Name?' *Global Governance* 13: 35–58.

Baudienville, G. with inputs from Domingo, P., Ray, D. B., Rao, S. and Hedger, E. (2010) *Aid Instruments in Fragile and Conflict-affected Situations: Impacts on the State- and Peace-Building Agenda*, London: Overseas Development Institute.

Blum, A. (2011) *Improving Peacebuilding Evaluation – A Whole-of-field Approach*, Special Report, Washington, DC: United States Institute of Peace. www.usip.org/files/resources/Improving_Peacebuilding_Evaluation.pdf, accessed March 2013.

Bornstein, L. (2010) 'Peace and Conflict Impact Assessment (PCIA) in Community Development: A Case Study from Mozambique', *Evaluation* 16(2): 165–176.

Cammack, D., McLeod, D. and Rocha Menocal, A., with Christiansen, K. (2006) *Donors and the 'Fragile State' Agenda: A Survey of Current Thinking and Practice*, London: Overseas Development Institute (ODI).

Chandy, L. and Gertz, G. (2011) 'Poverty in Numbers: The Changing State of Global Poverty from 2005 to 2015', *Policy Brief 2011–01*, Washington, DC: Brookings Institute.

Chauvet, L., Collier, P. and Duponchel, M. (2010) 'What Explains Aid Project Success in Post-Conflict Situations?' *Policy Research Working Paper 5418*, Washington, DC: World Bank.

Chetail, V. (ed.) (2009) *Post-Conflict Peacebuilding: A Lexicon*, Oxford: Oxford University Press.

Church, C. (2008) 'Peacebuilding Evaluation: From Infancy to Teenager', *New Routes* Editorial, 3–7.

Church, C. and Rogers, M. (2006) *Designing for Results: Integrating Monitoring and Evaluation in Conflict Transformation Programs*, Washington, DC: Search for Common Ground.

Church, C. and Shouldice, J. (2002) *The Evaluation of Conflict Resolution Interventions: Framing the State of Play*, Letterkenny: INCORE International Conflict Research, Browne Printers Ltd.

——(2003) *The Evaluation of Conflict Resolution Interventions. Part II Emerging Practice and Theory*, Letterkenny: INCORE International Conflict Research, Browne Printers Ltd.

Collier, P. (2007) *The Bottom Billion*, Oxford: Oxford University Press.

Çuhadar-Gürkaynak, E., Dayton, B. and Paffenholz, T. (2009) 'Evaluation in Conflict Resolution and Peacebuilding', in D. J. D. Sandole, S. Byrne, I. Sandole-Staroste and J. Senehi (eds) *Handbook of Conflict Analysis and Resolution*, London and New York: Routledge, pp. 286–299.

Denkurs, T. (2012) 'Challenging the International Peacebuilding Evaluation Discourse with Qualitative Methodologies', *Evaluation and Program Planning* 35: 148–153.

Diehl, P. and Druckman, D. (2010) *Evaluating Peace Operations*, London: Lynne Rienner Publishers Inc.

Dziedzic, M., Sotirin, B and Agoglia, J. (eds) (2008) *Measuring Progress in Conflict Environments*, Carlisle, PA: US Army Peacekeeping and Stability Operations Institute.

Elkins, C. (2010) 'Evaluating Development Interventions in Peace-Precarious Situations', *Evaluation* 16(3): 309–321.

Fearon, J., Humfreys, M. and Weinstein, J. (2009) 'Can Development Aid Contribute to Social Cohesion after Civil War? Evidence from a Field Experiment in Post-Conflict Liberia', *American Economic Review, Papers and Proceedings* 99(2): 287–291.

Fisher, S. and Zimina, L. (2008) 'Just Wasting Our Time? Open Letter', in *Berghof Handbook for Conflict Transformation*, Berlin: Berghof Foundation. http://humansecuritygateway.com/documents/BRCCCM_ProvocativeThoughtsForPeacebuilders.pdf, accessed March 2013.

Flores, T. E. and Nooruddin, I. (2009) 'Financing the Peace: Evaluating World Bank Post-conflict Assistance Programs', *The Review of International Organizations*, 4(1): 1–27.

Goodhand, J. (2006) *Aiding Peace? The Role of NGOs in Armed Conflict*, Boulder and London: Lynne Rienner Publishers.

Grävingholt, J., Ziaja, S. and Kreibaum, M. (2012) 'State Fragility: Towards a Multi-Dimensional Empirical Typology', Discussion Paper 3/2012. Bonn: German Development Institute.

GSDRC Applied Knowledge Services (2012) *Definitions and Typologies of Fragile States*, www.gsdrc.org/go/fragile-states/chapter-1-understanding-fragile-states/definitions-and-typologies-of-fragile-states, accessed January 2013.

Heathershaw, J. (2008) 'Unpacking the Liberal Peace: The Dividing and Merging of Peacebuilding Discourses', *Journal of International Studies*, 36(3): 597–621.

Hoffmann, M. (2003) 'PCIA Methodology: Evolving Art Form or Practical Dead End?' in *Berghof Handbook for Conflict Transformation*, Berlin: Berghof Foundation. www.berghof-handbook.net/profile, accessed January 2013.

Höglund, K. and Öberg, M. (eds) (2011) *Understanding Peace Research. Methods and Challenges*, London and New York: Routledge.

Kennedy-Chouane, M. G. (2011) 'Improving Conflict Prevention and Peacebuilding Assistance Through Evaluation', *OECD Journal: General Papers*, Volume 2010(1): 99–107.

Lanz, D., Wählisch, M., Kirchhoff, L. and Siegfried, M. (2008) *Evaluating Peace Mediation*, Brussels: Initiative for Peacebuilding. www.oecd.org/derec/ec/Swiss%20Peace%20-%20evaluating%20peace%20negotiations.pdf, accessed July 2013.

Manning, R. and Trzeciak-Duval, A. (2010) *Situations of Fragility and Conflict: Aid Policies and Beyond* (unpublished) http://1818france.org/2011/TrzeciakManning.pdf, accessed 14 March 2013.

Manor J. (ed.) (2007) *Aid That Works*, Washington, DC: World Bank.

Marcus, M., McKechnie, A., King, M., Coppin, E. and Denney, L. (2012) *Innovative Aid Instruments and Flexible Financing*, London: Overseas Development Institute.

OECD (2002) *Glossary of Key Terms in Evaluation and Results-based Management*, Paris: OECD Publishing. www.oecd.org/dac/2754804.pdf, accessed July 2013.

——(2007) *Principles for Good Engagement in Fragile States and Situations*, Paris: OECD Publishing. www.oecd.org/dac/incaf/38368714.pdf, accessed July 2013.

——(2011a) *International Engagement in Fragile States: Can't We Do Better? Conflict and Fragility*, Paris: OECD Publishing, doi: 10.1787/9789264086128-en.

——(2011b) *Ensuring Fragile States Are Not Left Behind – 2011 Factsheet on Resource Flows in Fragile States*, Paris: OECD Publishing. www.oecd.org/dataoecd/5/11/49108935.pdf, accessed July 2013.

——(2011c) *Supporting Statebuilding in Situations of Conflict and Fragility: Policy Guidance*, DAC Guidelines and Reference Series, Paris: OECD Publishing, doi: 10.1787/9789264074989-en.

——(2012a) *Evaluating Peacebuilding Activities in Settings of Conflict and Fragility: Improving Learning for Results*, DAC Guidelines and Reference Series, Paris: OECD Publishing, doi: 10.1787/9789264106802-en.

——(2012b) *Achieving the MDGs – Addressing Conflict, Fragility and Armed Violence, International Dialogue*, Paris: OECD Publishing. www.oecd.org/document/19/0,3746,en_21571361_43407692_46008211_1_1_1_1,00.html, accessed March 2012.

——(2013) *Ensuring Fragile States Are Not Left Behind – 2013 Factsheet on Resource Flows in Fragile States*, Paris: OECD Publishing. www.oecd.org/dac/incaf/factsheet%20213%20resource%20flows%20final.pdf, accessed July 2012.

Paffenholz, T. (2005) 'Third-generation PCIA: Introducing the Aid for Peace Approach', *Berghof Handbook for Conflict Transformation*, Berlin: Berghof Foundation. www.berghof-handbook.net/documents/publications/dialogue4_paffenholz.pdf, accessed 14 May 2013.

——(2011) *Peacebuilding Evaluation: Assessing the Relevance and Effectiveness of Peacebuilding Initiatives: Lessons Learned from Testing New Approaches and Methodologies*, paper prepared for the Annual Convention of the International Studies Association. Montreal, 16–19 March 2011.

Paffenholz, T. and Reychler, L. (2007) *Aid for Peace: A Guide for Planning and Evaluation in Conflict Zones*, Baden-Baden: NOMOS.

Paris, R. (2011) 'Ordering the World: Academic Research and Policymaking on Fragile States', *International Studies Review* 13: 58–71.

Sanín, F. G. (2011) 'Evaluating State Performance: A Critical View of State Failure and Fragility Indexes', *European Journal of Development Research* 23(1): 20–42.

Savedoff, W. D., Levine, R. and Birdsall, N. (2006) *When Will We Ever Learn? Improving Lives Through Impact Evaluation*, Evaluation Gap Working Group www.cgdev.org/files/7973_file_WillWeEverLearn.pdf, accessed May 2013.

Scharbatke-Church, C. (2011) 'Evaluating Peacebuilding: Not Yet All it Could Be', in *Berghof Handbook for Conflict Transformation*, Berlin: Berghof Foundation, pp. 459–482. www.berghof-handbook.net/profile, accessed January 2013.

Summer, A. (2012) 'Where Do The World's Poor Live? A New Update', IDS Working Paper, Volume 2012, No 393.

United Nations (1992) *An Agenda for Peace*, UN Doc A/47/277-S/24111, June.

United Nations General Assembly (2008) *Culture of Peace*, resolution adopted by the General Assembly at the fifty-second session, agenda item 156 (A/RES/52/13) www3.unesco.org/iycp/kits/res52-13_en.htm, accessed 24 May 2013.

Woodrow P. and Chigas, D. (2009) *A Distinction with a Difference: Conflict Sensitivity and Peacebuilding*, Cambridge, MA: CDA Collaborative Learning Projects.

World Bank (2011) *World Development Report 2011: Conflict, Security, and Development*, Washington, DC: World Bank.

Zizek, S. (2004) 'What Rumsfeld Doesn't Know that he Knows about Abu Ghraib', *In These Times*, 21 March (published online). www.lacan.com/zizekrumsfeld.htm.

2 Evaluation approaches in situations of conflict and fragility

Eva Broegaard
Advice & Analysis[1]

Beate Bull
Norad[2]

Jens Kovsted
Novo Nordisk[3]

1 Introduction

The field of evaluation in situations of conflict and fragility is still young, but in the process of maturing. As illustrated in Chapter 1, the field has developed gradually alongside shifts in international conflict prevention and peacebuilding, including the increase in resources allocated to development assistance in settings of conflict and fragility. This surge in international interventions in these settings has led to mounting demands for evaluations, and subsequently to rising expectations about the quality and type of knowledge that these evaluations are expected to produce. As donor involvement in situations of conflict and fragility remains challenging, evaluations are typically seen not just as serving accountability purposes, but also as a means to support continued learning. Thus, whether conclusions and lessons have broader relevance is a core concern for the evaluative work.

As mentioned in Chapter 1, many practitioners in the conflict prevention and peacebuilding field remain sceptical about the merits and usability of traditional evaluation methods to their work (Çuhadar-Gürkaynak et al. 2009). Some have even argued that the complexity of conflict prevention and peacebuilding work makes outcome and impact evaluation nearly impossible,[4] and that evaluation tools are incapable of measuring intangible changes that occur from activities aiming to resolve conflict and build peace. Others acknowledge the particular difficulties entailed, but argue that it is nonetheless in principle possible to identify both case-specific and more generic knowledge, if certain prerequisites are ensured (Stern and Druckman 2000).

Evaluation of conflict prevention and peacekeeping is not a new field. However, prior to the mid 1990s much of this work consisted of monitoring ceasefires or buffer zones between warring parties (Rietjens et al. 2011). With the new, more complex peacebuilding agenda that emerged in the 1990s, several evaluative initiatives began to reflect on the peacebuilding field's own learning. This resulted in the publication of a wave of synthesis or summary studies around 2003–2004, taking stock of the existing information on conclusions, use and terminology etc., including the Utstein study (Smith 2004), the Reflecting on Peace Practices Project (Anderson and Olson 2003) and the INCORE study (Church and Shouldice 2003). The Utstein study looked at 336 peacebuilding projects and, among other findings, highlighted the dearth of rigorous evaluations in the fields of peace and conflict prevention[5] and a 'strategic deficit' in the evaluations conducted.[6] Since then a number of evaluations of conflict prevention and peacebuilding interventions have been conducted – as mentioned in Chapter 1 and the other chapters of this book – but despite concerted efforts to increase the quality of evaluations, notably under the umbrella of OECD Development Assistance Committee (DAC), much remains to be done. The evaluations to date have to a large degree ended up mapping the field, resulting in evaluations that describe the actors, aid coordination mechanisms and channels, and how interaction with the context takes place, rather than understanding what factors are at play to cause the observed (lack of) positive impact. They rarely produce new knowledge about the causal effects of the interventions in terms of achieving the intended objectives or avoid prolonging conflict (Norad 2011: 14).[7] Thus, there is not only an understandable call for more knowledge about whether the substantial amounts of aid channelled at these situations is leading to sufficient positive change to be worthwhile, but the debate about which evaluation methods are most suitable for producing such knowledge in settings of conflict and fragility is also ongoing.

This chapter provides an introduction to current debates on development evaluation methodology relevant in the field of conflict prevention and peacebuilding as well as challenges and perspectives on strengthening evaluative knowledge about aid in these settings. The aim is to provide the reader with background information related to the different evaluations and approaches presented in the subsequent chapters. The chapter is divided in four sections following this introduction. In Section 2 we introduce four key issues from the current evaluation debate: (i) the nature of knowledge; (ii) theory-based evaluation (iii) the use of conflict theory; and (iv) the impact evaluation debate. Section 3 discusses the important principle of not doing harm in these evaluations, while Section 4 provides considerations on sampling and data collection in these complex settings. Section 5 gives a brief summing up and points forward to the different evaluation experiences covered by this book.

2 Evaluative knowledge: considerations on methodology

As mentioned in the introduction, a rich methodological debate has taken place during the past ten years or so. The following cannot do full justice to this debate, but will provide a brief introduction to some of the key issues of relevance for evaluations in settings of conflict and fragility.

2.1 Evaluation and the nature of knowledge

In social science the issue of the nature of knowledge has engendered important and at times divisive debate. It is often seen as a clash between social realism and social constructionism, between views of knowledge as the external and 'objective' study of 'social facts', or as constructed through investigative processes that are an integral part of the field of study. Both perspectives have been present in discussions and research of development efforts in situations of conflict and fragility and can be relevant to evaluation within this field. This concerns whether evaluations can deliver 'objective' assessments and 'solid' knowledge, or rather will always represent one narrative among a plethora of possible narratives.

While the development evaluation literature also to some degree reflects these debates (see, for instance, Bamberger et al. 2006), specific evaluations rarely position themselves in relation to a theory of knowledge. However, concerns on the nature and role of evaluative knowledge can nevertheless be seen to form an important undertow in the general evaluation debates as well as in individual evaluations. Below, some of the positions found in the debate on development and evaluation with emphasis on situations of conflict and fragility will briefly be outlined.

One position encountered – more or less explicitly – is an orientation towards social realism. Here, development may be treated as a fairly practical-technical endeavour, with specific activities and support aimed at a range of measureable objectives. Donor policies and strategies, programme documents and log-frames and the numerous results-based management information tools can be seen as evidence of such a position among practitioners. Evaluation is usually considered as an area where it is meaningful to investigate 'real' change as social facts, for instance by looking at empirical indicators for impact without much consideration of the social interpretation around them (Bamberger et al. 2006). This would not necessarily preclude a view that perceptions may be important to understand the background for actions leading to change. Rather, this perspective supports the notion that evaluation in principle can treat 'reality' in a straightforward manner, by collecting, analysing and reporting on indicators for household behaviour, nutrition, schooling, livelihoods, violence or other important issues – with the understanding that this is 'real' change that can be measured accurately and correctly, also by 'outsiders'. To illustrate: in such a perspective, it would not necessarily be a main concern to consider whether different constructions and interpretations of 'reality' exist and should be considered, but to get an as objective and precise measurement and analysis of the 'slice of reality' studied as possible. Much debate on gold standards of impact evaluation can be seen to implicitly or explicitly consider knowledge in such a way.[8]

Another position is more inclined towards social constructivism. Within the fields of, for example, anthropology of development or peace and conflict studies, the notion that 'reality' may be treated as both constructed and contested is familiar. This point can be reflected in analysis of the construction of development discourse and its implications for practice (see Ferguson 1990 as an example), as well as work on the interplay between conflict and the social construction of ethnicity and nationalism (Anderson 2006), to mention a few. A constructivist perspective can be part of the arguments for use of participatory approaches, as a way of exploring different interpretations of reality. Here, the question of 'whose reality counts' is put forward to warn of the risk that views and interpretations of 'outsiders' could overlay and dominate those of the local beneficiaries or 'participants' in a harmful manner when designing, planning and assessing development efforts (Chambers 1997, 2009).

In this perspective, evaluation findings can be seen as part of the constructions of understandings or narratives 'explaining' the social context, the aims of the intervention and the significance of changes brought about. By implication, a core concern for an evaluation would not only be to consider 'whose reality counts', but to aim at a nuanced investigation of the social understanding around an intervention and its implications. Further, following this, an evaluation is arguably more likely to be seen as one particular interpretation or narrative of the social phenomenon under evaluation, among many possible. While precision in data collection and accuracy in reporting is still important, considerations of validity would also emphasise inter-subjectivity, transparency with regards to positions and interpretations, etc. In line with the above, this does not necessarily imply a 'radical' constructionist position that sees everything as social constructs, but rather an emphasis on the role of narratives, social understanding and perceptions as an important part of understanding interventions as an inherently social activity.[9] While both positions may well acknowledge that an evaluation's use will often be political, this position may to a larger degree consider the evaluation process itself as not just 'happening' in a political field, but very much being a part of the social arena of politics and will build on contested evidence and socially constructed perceptions.

It should be noted that the issue of 'the nature of learning' also ties into the rationale behind an evaluation. As such, the degree to which an evaluation explores perceptions and social understandings or aims at measuring specific tangible changes may also simply reflect whether the Terms of Reference (ToR) for the assignment focus on, for example, social processes of reconciliation between former antagonists in a conflict, or on changes in economic welfare for poor families in a conflict-affected area. Evaluations in situations of conflict and fragility may also explore issues as diverse as the number of ex-combatants to have been disarmed at what cost, and the socially constructed prejudices among specific groups and how this may influence the handling of a return of internally displaced people – to give an (constructed) example.

2.2 The use of 'theory' in evaluation

Theory-based evaluation has come to the forefront in recent years: both in the evaluation debates and in practical evaluations. It is not a new concept, however, and when discussing how an evaluation should be theory-based, and what the theory should be concerned with, a multitude of variations on understandings can be found. Here, different notions such as programme theory, theory of change, theory of action, logic model, intervention logic, implementation theory or implementation models have surfaced.[10] While there may be nuances between the different understandings and concepts, it is often pointed out that there is also an important common core. As phrased by Rogers, such concepts in relation to evaluation generally 'refer to a variety of ways of developing a causal model linking programme inputs and activities to a chain of intended or observed outcomes, and then using this model to guide evaluation' (Rogers 2008: 30).

Theory-based variations of the 'logical framework approach' as a project or programme development tool have been around for decades. It sets out what kind of impact an intervention hopes to bring about and the chain of events (in the form of different inputs, outputs and outcomes) needed to bring it about.[11] Important contextual factors may also be included in the form of so-called 'killer assumptions' – assumptions on core issues outside the realm of the intervention that may 'make or break' its achievement of results. An evaluation may then use the logic model as a basis for investigating whether the expected chain of events actually materialised, and – if not – where the chain may have broken down.

In the current debate on theory-based evaluations, this approach is often seen as overly simplistic, with too little focus on the dynamics in play in the context, the complexity of both context and interventions, and the possibility of unintended impacts.[12] If the complexity notion – that events in fragile states can evolve from self-reinforcing dynamics or tipping points, and unforeseen backlash as the multiple actors and dynamics interact – is valid, then interventions in complex systems cannot necessarily be understood by reducing them to their individual components. This can force evaluators to adopt systems approaches that 'discourage the overemphasis of either the individual or the environment and allow for the analysis of social actions within and across systems with particular emphasis on the interconnections' (Loode 2010).

In line with the change in aid modalities towards increased emphasis on sector-wide approaches, current programming of interventions will often include multiple, interlinked components and more explicitly consider changes in the context. This also includes figuring out how different factors may influence the situation in which the intervention will work, as well as the outcome. Thus, the level of details and nuance, both with regards to the intervention and the context, will vary. A common overall approach to theory-based evaluation uses the expectations of results, and assumptions on how to achieve them that lie behind an intervention (its theory of change) and assesses whether the assumptions were relevant and appropriate in the context, and whether it worked as intended. Moreover, theories can be used to help distinguish between implementation failure and design failure.

Evaluations may also set out to explore unintended consequences of an intervention. When doing so, evaluators may need a broader understanding of how an intervention may interact with the context beyond the expectations embedded in the intervention's own programme theory. This may entail looking not just at expected changes, but also at observed changes – or whether there may be other more likely assumptions with regards to how the intervention works, than those of the programmes.[13]

Theory of change thinking is, however, also found to go beyond assessing whether an intervention helped bring about the desired effects by working as intended. It is also informed by another longstanding strand of development theory and practice – 'reflective practice for empowerment and social change', also going back to the 1960s (Vogel 2012: 1). This can be seen as linked to the call for participatory approaches mentioned above, typically with a strong emphasis on ensuring that the local understanding of priorities, causalities and consequences formed the basis for development and learning, and that donors' perceptions and expectations were not just taken for granted.[14] The influence of these two strands of thinking, one seeing theory of change as almost synonymous with programme theory and as such highly focused on the assumptions behind a specific intervention, while the other sees theory of change as a more open theoretical concept that presents assumptions about how change may come about in a certain context and the causalities at play, may help explain the variation in use and understanding of the concept of 'theory'.

While Vogel (2012) identifies a range of differences and nuances in the understanding of theory of change, she also points to a shared core, in line with Rogers' point above. In her understanding, the central idea in theory of change thinking is making assumptions explicit: 'Making assumptions explicit, especially seemingly obvious ones, allows them to be checked, debated and enriched to strengthen programmes. By activating critical reflection, theory of change's real potential is seen as supporting programmes' innovation and adaptation in response to dynamic contexts' (Vogel 2012: 4).

The variation in use of theory in evaluation is, however, substantial. This can be seen to reflect both the variation in the underlying assumptions of change brought into an analysis and the understanding of the context in question. With regards to the issue of complexity it is noted that using theoretical models may also be useful, provided that assumptions on causality, impact trajectories, etc., adequately address the complex elements at hand.

A systems approach to evaluation can be seen as a highly ambitious theory-based approach that is particularly relevant for situations where a linear causal chain is seen as inadequate in capturing the interplay between intervention and context. Rather, it may consider issues of complexity, and by implication aim at encompassing interdependence and feedback loops at a systemic level, so as to be able to integrate the different influencing factors, and the way outcomes of various interventions may interact in relation to impacts. As should be clear from this book, these are issues that are highly relevant to the area of conflict and fragility. Such an approach clearly builds on establishing an evaluation framework that not just incorporates, for example, contextual prerequisites for achieving the desired outcomes and impacts, or assumptions on the specific mechanisms of the interventions, but also the dynamics between the different factors (Woodrow and Chigas 2011).[15] By implication, the requirements with regards to how sound the theory of change is and the information needed for a system level analysis are substantial.

This also ties into the point made by scholars such as Rogers and Funnell (2011) and Stern et al. (2012) that in some cases it may not be possible to have a fixed theory of change, if the change to be brought about is emergent in a way that changes if and how various mechanisms are activated. If so, rather than looking at one programme theory, issues such as adaptability, responsiveness to systems changes, etc., can be important.[16] These considerations can also have relevance when working in situations of conflict and fragility as in the cases in this book.

2.3 The use of conflict analysis – and the implications for evaluation

Moving on to the issue of understanding the context, the conflict and the change dynamics, it is presumed that assumptions about the roots of the conflict will affect the design of the intervention, and thereby the yardstick by which to evaluate the interventions' success (Ross 2004). The realisation that unless interventions are built on an adequate understanding of the context and the dynamics at play in situations of conflict and fragility then neither interventions nor evaluations of them can be expected to 'get it right', lies behind the call for use of conflict analysis.[17] The notion that interventions in settings of fragility should be based on some form of in-depth analysis is widely accepted in the field, as can be illustrated in the OECD DAC Principles for Engagement in Fragile States (OECD 2007).

The conflict analysis thus relates to the theory of change for a specific evaluation, in that it contains the understanding of the conflict and, by implication, forms the background for assessing whether the interventions are appropriate in that context.

This implies that all attempts to intervene in a conflict begin with a set of assumptions about the nature of the conflict itself. Such assumptions are clearly linked to a theory of change, as the way the nature and causes of a conflict are understood is linked to assumptions about how and why external interventions may be helpful. By implication, a conflict analysis cannot be presumed to only convey objective, undisputed facts but will also be founded on interpretations and theoretical assumptions. In this sense a conflict analysis is seldom a straightforward descriptive exercise stating undisputed facts. Instead it is a 'notoriously complex undertaking full of competing propositions about the forces that cause conflicts to emerge and the means through which these forces can be transformed' (Çuhadar-Gürkaynak et al. 2009).

It is thus important for the sake of analytical transparency and adequacy to include in the evaluation a discussion of which perspectives and theories about conflict and underlying assumptions are represented (or not) in the analysis and how these are followed through, validated, etc. However, in practice it is not always clear what underlying assumptions or 'knowledge' these conflict analyses and theories of change are based on. They might be 'embedded in skills and approaches of individual practitioners and peacebuilding organisations, their capacities and technologies, attachments to favourite methodologies and the perspectives of different stakeholders about conflict and peace' (OECD 2012: 80).

The issue of different perspectives on conflict and fragility and how it affects our view of what constitutes success has been investigated and discussed in several important studies. In a study from 2004, Ross examined the variation in practitioners' understanding of conflict and what they tried to do to mitigate it. Examples of six different approaches to ethnic conflict resolution revolved around distinct 'beliefs about the nature of social, political and psychological reality' (Ross 2004: 3). Some emphasised structural violence, some institutionalised inequalities (Galtung 1969), others preferred interest-based dynamics (Fisher and Ury 1983), while others yet focused on beliefs and narratives that conflicting parties tell about each other, while still others on the unhealed emotional wounds, trauma and victimhood.[18] Ross found that the wide range of assumptions about the presumed causes of conflict, and the resulting great variation in specific strategies of conflict resolution, and criteria of success was the case 'even among practitioners working on the same conflict'.[19]

Another attempt at mapping conflict theories at play and their underlying assumptions, although at the macro level, is made by Holmqvist (2012). Holmqvist identifies four 'grand stories' – or theories – combined with empirical evidence 'on the causes of civil war and the role played by identity and inequality', and on which much of today's international engagement in fragile states rests. The 'Collier story'[20] describes how civil war occurs when it is financially and militarily feasible, while downplaying the role of objective social grievances. The 'Stewart story'[21] points to horizontal inequalities between identity groups as being a main driver in the conflict (elections in Kenya in 2008 are mentioned as an example). The 'Zartman story'[22] describes a stylised sequencing of civil war, with different factors being decisive in different phases (with greed factors of military entrepreneurs likely to become dominant over time). The 'commitment stories' emphasise a lack of trust and failing institutions as an obstacle to agreement among conflicting parties on non-violent solutions.

These different perspectives also lead to different policy conclusions. Promoting a healthy economy and transparency of trade in extractive resources are some of the conclusions following the Collier story. Affirmative actions against horizontal inequality become a key recommendation to the Stewart story and the importance of investing in appropriate institutional frameworks and citizens' trust is a prominent policy conclusion of the commitment stories.[23] This illustrates how research influences the way development aid is conceived. The 'stories' are important because policies are designed based on them. But when Holmqvist examines the empirical findings for the different 'stories', he finds that there are several caveats within the data backing them.

An older, macro-level theory not unfamiliar to the field of peacebuilding is Grossman's (1992) theory, that aid increases conflict by increasing the rents available for capture. This had the implication that donors should give importance to conflict analysis and 'do no harm' principles. Some more recent theorists, such as Elkin (2010: 313), have noted that there is growing belief in the idea that 'peace and stability are no longer held to be prerequisites to development' and that 'one emerging idea seems to be that social, political, and economic development facilitates progress toward peace and stability, or at least will help consolidate or stabilize progressive gains'. The implication of this theory is that the impact of the individual intervention should be downplayed, and that it is the co-variation of the individual interventions, with other policy initiatives and contextual variables, that determines the societal changes.

This discussion illustrates the need for evaluations to identify implicit assumptions underpinning the theory of change and expected outcomes of interventions in fragile states, and settings of conflict, and the need for policymakers to examine the analytical basis for policy recommendations. The examples above illustrate that donors are still allocating significant amounts of resources to programmes about which purposes and causes there is a lot of uncertainty. In short, many of our actions in settings of fragility are based on untested assumptions.

In light of the different understandings of conflict and the point made that conflict analysis is seldom a straightforward descriptive exercise, it should not be surprising that different evaluations of conflict and fragility may build on different assumptions and conflict theories. It does however emphasise the point made earlier about the need to make the assumptions explicit, and to clarify and substantiate the way they inform evaluation frameworks in the form of conflict analysis and theory of change.

2.4 The impact evaluation debate

Another important set of debates in current evaluation literature and practice relates to impact assessment. A predominant critique in recent years has been that evaluations offer too little 'rigorous' evaluative knowledge with regards to the impact of the various interventions. Achieving such rigour has typically been related to 'credible counterfactual' analysis (Bamberger et al. 2006). The debate on impact evaluation in the broader field of development evaluation has suggested that assessments of impact based on 'factual' (often qualitative) analysis turned out to be inaccurate, when put to the test of a counterfactual (often quantitative) analysis. Thus, a call was made for carrying out more evaluations based on a double-difference approach with a credible counterfactual.[24] Here, randomised controlled trials (RCTs) were seen by some as the strongest evaluation approach, based on within-study comparisons of RCTs against other ways of establishing comparison groups, such as matching.[25] A relatively limited number of RCTs have been carried out in situations of conflict and fragility, but the present book includes experience from such evaluations. However, a core common point is that both the randomised experiments and the quasi-experimental approaches rely on establishing a credible counterfactual in order to be able to assess the net change in the impact indicators being investigated. As such, these approaches rely on a range of prerequisites, both in relation to the delivery of aid and whether this allows for identification of beneficiaries and non-beneficiaries as part of the establishing of the 'counterfactual'. It is however widely acknowledged that these prerequisites are not always present when dealing with development aid in general and fragile situations more specifically, and this may indeed be part of the reason why relatively few 'rigorous' impact assessments are found within this field. In addition, in the area of conflict and fragility there is often a wish to understand the impact of interventions that deal with broader change in a sector or at a societal level where, by implication, establishing a control or comparison group as basis for a counterfactual analysis is less feasible.[26]

Following on from this, literature on non-experimental evaluations of impacts in complex settings that addresses the issue of attribution of cause and effect has expanded in recent years (White and Phillips 2012; Stern et al. 2012). This part of the debate draws attention to situations where experimental or quasi-experimental approaches to impact assessment may be less relevant or feasible. In particular, it is often suggested that a quantitative double-difference approach is substituted or supplemented by a theory-based approach, looking into how the intervention worked, or it is argued that there are several different approaches where evaluations could still be looking at causality and contribution.

In the paper by White and Phillips (2012), alternative non-experimental approaches to establish cause and effect attribution are discussed. These approaches explore social phenomena, in that they examine underlying processes or mechanisms that link the intervention as a 'cause' with the impacts as the 'effect' 'beyond reasonable doubt' (White and Phillips 2012: 7). These mechanisms may comprise many parts, which individually are insufficient, but collectively are necessary for the outcomes to occur. Here it is stressed that a good mechanism-based explanation should not only ascertain whether evidence supports a theorised explanation of cause and effect, but potential alternative explanations should also be assessed.[27] An important point in this regard is that while quantitative or 'large n' analyses have widely accepted standardised models for assessing representativeness, dealing with bias and estimating accuracy, such specific models are not readily available for theory-based approaches working with a smaller n (such as case studies). Here, credibility needs to be established analytically in a non-standardised manner, depending on the situation at hand (see White and Phillips 2012 for discussions of this issue). By implication, it can be expected that greater emphasis is needed on making explicit how the various considerations have been addressed than when using well-established standards.

A recent DFID initiative also explicitly set out to explore such different 'alternative' options for looking at impact, with a particular focus on situations where the quantitative, double-difference approaches are not feasible (Stern et al. 2012). This debate has been spurred by the challenge of how to investigate impact in light of the complexity and interdependence of multiple causal strands found in much of contemporary development aid, as in the sector-wide and programme support modalities.[28] As complexity and interdependence are often found in situations of conflict and fragility, these evaluation challenges may be relevant there as well. Rather than focusing on the 'methodological war' between quantitative and qualitative approaches, current debates on how to establish the impact of aid have a marked focus on mixed methods and creative use of available information in less-than-ideal evaluative situations.[29]

3 Avoiding harm when evaluating in situations of conflict and fragility

As mentioned above, aid can become part of the dynamics of the conflict and may even prolong it even without intending to, and do harm rather than good

(Anderson 1999). This implies that donor organisations must seek to minimise the harm they may be inadvertently cause simply by being present and providing assistance or by carrying out evaluations and disseminating or using evaluation findings.[30] Here, conflict sensitivity implies efforts to mitigate such harm by systematically taking into account both the positive and negative impacts of the evaluation (OECD 2012). The assumption is that increased sensitivity to drivers of conflict and fragility can assist donors in taking unintended effects of their evaluation into account. However, as discussed above, conflict analyses are themselves subject to a set of conflict theories, which are in turn based on a set of assumptions that again might be in danger of being based on incomplete information or biased narratives.

Potential negative effects or harm caused by an evaluation include the direct and indirect effects of the evaluation outcomes, and direct and indirect effects of how, where and when an evaluation is carried out. The conflict sensitivity principle implies an ethical responsibility to mitigate threats to those involved in the evaluation process. There are many dilemmas tied to conducting activities involving vulnerable populations in a conflict, but it will always be the obligation of those responsible to give priority to the safety of all involved. With respect to mitigating the potential direct or indirect negative effects tied to the evaluation process and the way the evaluation is implemented, this implies considering who is interviewed, how and by whom, and what risks evaluators or others are exposed to as part of the conduct of the evaluation. Moreover, it relates to the need for the evaluation team to consider these issues in their planning and in the actual evaluation process. As an example, efforts must be made to avoid exposure or undue risks to local evaluators or interpreters who remain in the conflict zone when international evaluators leave the country. If there are knowledge gaps about possible consequences of hiring team members from a certain local ethnic group, or of conducting interviews with certain individuals (women, girls, clan members, ethnic groups, etc.), this information should be collected and assessed.

With respect to potential direct and indirect negative outcomes of the evaluation, this relates to taking into account how an evaluation outcome (conclusions, recommendations, etc.) might affect an already vulnerable population by increasing tensions or instigating conflict. It might have to do with local perceptions of groups that are believed to benefit from the evaluation. Collecting and analysing information about such possible scenarios is evidently challenging. Assuming that there is not one 'right way' of doing this that guarantees that harm is avoided, a minimum precaution is to systematically collect information and critically assess different sources, and the information itself, before developing assumptions about what causes or mitigates risk or harm, and then describe this in the final report.

Ideally, the evaluation team must be prepared to assess all measures taken in settings of conflict and fragility on an ongoing basis, and then monitor these actions. These concerns are at the core of most of the ethical principles guiding research and evaluations but are believed to be particularly relevant in conflict contexts, in the evaluation planning, implementation and reporting phases.[31] The ethics involved in conducting these types of activities should therefore not be underestimated, nor the challenges of putting them into practice.

4 Populating the evaluation framework: data collection and the risk of bias

By now it is hopefully clear that it is a daunting task to establish an evaluation design that will help evaluators ensure that the evaluation process and analysis are transparent, with a minimal risk of harm arising from a problematic implementation or misinterpretations or even invalid results. However, even if the hard choices about how to address the issue of causation and the theoretical ambiguities have been handled in a transparent manner, further challenges are typically encountered. Regardless of whether the evaluation framework contains an experimental or quasi-experimental approach to assessing impact; a theory-based evaluation design that looks at the interplay between context, mechanism and outcomes to assess causation and effects; or a more exploratory design, it has to get access to or collect information. Here, the issues of data collection, sampling and risks of bias are at the core. In the more 'generic' development evaluation literature, the issue of sampling and bias is discussed in greater depth than in the evaluation literature dealing specifically with conflict and fragility. Yet, it is generally – and rightly – assumed that great risks of bias are associated with data collection and sampling in potentially violent, emergent contexts where uncertainties exist about the intervention, the population and the context.

4.1 Sampling

When working with limited evaluation resources in complex contexts and/or interventions, it is not surprising that sampling is an important aspect of data collection.[32] For instance, if an evaluation is called upon to assess a broad range of donor interventions in a country characterised by conflict and fragility, or to identify the different effects of a project or programme across different population groups, decisions on how to structure data collection so as to be able to infer from the sample to the broader population that the evaluation deals with is a key issue.

Sampling is often a decision point for more than one type of data collection, and typically revolves around questions such as how many to sample in interviewing, which and how many sites to visit and events to observe, and which and how many programme documents and records to review when it is not possible to collect and study each potential datum (Bamberger et al. 2006: 327). The decisions regarding the type of sampling and the validity of the chosen strategy clearly depend on the focus and scope of the evaluation and the evaluation questions. Thus, while the overall issue of sampling is highly relevant for both quantitative approaches dealing with a 'large n', and for more case-based approaches dealing with a 'smaller n', the specific considerations will vary depending on the evaluations. Sampling strategies for small n evaluations are often labelled purposive sampling. Sampling strategies for large n evaluations often fall within what is labelled 'probability sampling' or 'random sampling' (Bamberger et al. 2006).

There are different strategies for large n probability sampling.[33] In the well-known 'gold standard' debate, the random selection of a sufficient large number of units for both the treatment group and the control group is advocated as the best strategy for ensuring that 'other things are equal'. As briefly mentioned in the section on impact evaluation above, other options exist for comparing sufficiently equal groups through matching or other approaches that lead to different sampling considerations.[34] However, for all these strategies it is clear that they are only viable if sufficient knowledge on the sampling frame is present. If doing a double-difference analysis, this entails being able to clearly identify who qualifies as 'beneficiaries', and 'comparison group', which again requires a certain geographical focus to delineate the groups, as well as conditions that allow to maintain sufficiently stable groups over time: if groups change, mix or dwindle too much, the prerequisites for a large n analysis may no longer be present.

In short, if feasible, the requirements around the use of probability sampling generally help strengthen internal validity. However, a further challenge can be the external validity. A recent analysis of evaluations and studies from Afghanistan stressed the risk of missing overarching problems and negative effects of aid, if only looking at individual interventions that may even be quite successful with regards to the immediate objectives (Grävingholt et al. 2012).[35] Thus, assessing the implications of the sampling strategy in relation to what to include in the analysis is also important for probability sampling – although the issues are different than when dealing with purposeful sampling.

Looking at sampling in evaluations based on a smaller number of units of analysis and where qualitative methods play a stronger role, a core point is to ensure that the sample matches the purpose of the evaluation by considering the fit with the scope, the analytical focus, etc.[36] Which approach is most appropriate would depend on whether the focus is on assessing results with as high coverage as possible, or to understand whether and how different conditions can influence the relevance of particular projects. Thus, the sampling questions relate to 'what' to include in addition to 'how many'.[37]

When working with smaller samples, there are several criteria for choosing an appropriate sample design and there are several sources of bias. The appropriateness of the sample is defined by the population from which the sample is selected. However, frequently the qualitative evaluator does not have access to a sampling frame (directory list, map listing all schools, households or communities to be covered by the sample) that corresponds exactly to the target population. This problem can often be encountered in settings of conflict and fragility, where national statistical figures are poor, not updated or non-existing, and especially in cases where there is a great flux of internal refugees.

This is, however, not just a matter of information on the population of possible informants. It is important to consider the information requirements stemming from the type of answers sought. In many evaluations, case studies constitute important analytical elements, often in the form of in-depth assessments of how an intervention has played out in a specific location or for a specific group. In order to assess whether and how the selected cases are 'typical' or 'atypical', information on the contextual factors that are expected to be potentially important for the functioning of the intervention would be important. This emphasises the role of theory of change and understandings of context in evaluation, where a theory-based sampling strategy will benefit from information on the different factors assumed to be of importance. However, in situations of conflict and fragility, availability of such nuanced and updated knowledge may be very limited at the time of sampling. Furthermore, security considerations or 'do no harm' principles may make it impossible to visit the areas or cases that it would be ideal to do, and the evaluators are stuck with what is often somewhat derisively labelled a 'convenience sample', although convenience does not necessarily enter the equation.[38] In those cases it must be assessed how and to what degree the sample represents the population in an analytically appropriate manner and how this might affect the validity of the conclusions (Bamberger et al. 2006). While this is clearly difficult if the problem is that too little information is available in the sampling frame in the first place, it is nevertheless important to address this issue as systematically as possible, and an iterative process, where background information is collected, different data needs are assessed, the sampling frame refined and more information is then collected etc., may be considered.

4.2 Data collection and biases

Any approach chosen must tackle the subject of data collection (in the form of sampling or not) and data analysis. All methods are subject to bias, so the issue is how evaluators can minimise the risk. Building on Kahneman and others, White and Phillips (2012) outline cognitive limitations that can affect us all. These include the risk to under- or overestimate causal relationships by seeing patterns where there are none, and the tendency to attribute changes to individuals rather than contextual factors, or to credit some persons (with whom we affiliate) with more influencing power than they have. Chambers has written at length about how both development practitioners and evaluators run the risk of such biases (Chambers 1983, 1997).[39]

If looking at beneficiaries' perceptions of the effect of an intervention in a situation of conflict and fragility, these biases are highly relevant. People see things and events from different perspectives – from their position. Thus, the combination of the sampling strategy and the actual data collection is defining the risk of bias (where the information is collected, what is collected, who gets to 'speak', etc.) – a risk that is acutely present in situations of conflict and fragility.[40] Elkin (2010: 313) notes how 'security threats dampen not only local staff recruitment and retention but significantly limit the scope for engaging a full and representative range of local stakeholders, thus affecting project results and sustainability of any impact' and how this 'alter(s) the operational environment for implementing an evaluation in the same setting'. As mentioned above, the looming risk of (subsequent) harm can cause the information obtained to be biased, incomplete and/or (voluntarily or involuntarily) censored due to, for example, the lack of possibilities to triangulate as planned or be as systematic as desirable when collecting data. And it may be that part of the battlefield is the battle of opinion, that informants and stakeholders also see an interest in using the evaluation to support a specific narrative with regards to conflict causes as well as what donors or other actors could and should do, depending on their position and perspective.

There are ways to minimise bias, or be transparent about how it is tackled. To ensure quality in qualitative research, it is important to show the audience of research studies as much as possible of the procedures that have led to a particular set of conclusions (White and Phillips 2012). Clear strategies for data collection and analysis are needed to identify risks and to counter them, and without systematic analysis evaluators might cherry-pick the cases and data which support their argument (White and Phillips 2012: 23). Similarly, stakeholder mapping and careful consideration of sampling can ensure systematic collection of views from stakeholders. Interviews should be carefully planned and targeted to explore key parts of the causal chain. They should be recorded, documented and independently carried out, be triangulated with information collected from a diverse range of individuals and settings or using a variety of methods (White and Phillips 2012: 24).[41] Further, it may be relevant to consider the fact that the evaluation process may not be perceived as 'external' or neutral, and the implications this may have for data collection and analysis. If informants may respond strategically, based on their position with regards to the conflict, this adds another dimension to the risk of bias, and the need to ensure that data allow for sufficient triangulation and validation.

At all stages, information may be scarce and compromises may be made. However, if it has been considered what types and amounts of data the analytical framework would need, where the risk of bias seems strongest, etc., there is a better chance of assessing the implications of such compromise. If for instance, it is only possible to assess a certain share of projects more in-depth, how does this affect the analytical argumentation? When real-world constraints are encountered to the degree that evaluations have to work with 'pragmatic' samples and limited data, evaluation teams should at least ensure transparency with regards to limitations, choices and assumptions. However, the way the different challenges can reinforce each other in a setting characterised by conflict and fragility is not just an additional challenge. It profoundly changes and complicates the other already significant challenges, forcing evaluators to address operational, methodological and epistemological consequences.

5 Complexity, causation and contestedness – summing up the challenges

It should be clear from the above that undertaking evaluation in situations of conflict and fragility is daunting. The methodological evaluation debates on the challenges of assessing impact and ensuring learning are all relevant, but with the added elements of uncertainty, insecurity and risk outlined above. In addition, contested theories and assumptions and the changing context and dynamics of the field make for further challenges.

The issue of complexity is at the heart of the matter. If interventions and evaluations are undertaken in complex situations, then this can have clear consequences for how evaluation may deal with the issue of causation. Analytical strategies may focus on reducing complexity by reducing the evaluation scope to a specific intervention area or a specific case, where it is possible to focus on a more clear-cut set of variables, so as to be able to analyse whether or how a specific intervention has impacted on the situation. Or it may be decided to keep the focus on higher level impacts, even if this entails dealing with interdependence between a wide range of interventions, contextual factors and actors, in a manner that will make it less feasible to address attribution and make even sound analysis of contribution highly challenging.

Some of the burning questions regarding the higher-level impact of interventions in situations of conflict and fragility thus relate to situations where a range of constraints with regards to the feasibility of impact assessment approaches may be encountered. To bring back the Utstein report, this brings forward the point that looking at the impact at the level of the specific project can be problematic as it may fall short of including important aspects of the interplay with the context and with other interventions. However, if evaluators instead aim at investigating the more overall level of international support and its impact on situations of conflict and fragility, complexity will typically enter the equation. Dealing with complexity in a situation where different theories of conflict prevail, and where interpretation of context may be contested, is analytically challenging at best. Thus, the level of analysis has marked implications for what type of questions on impact and causation can feasibly be addressed, how and under what circumstances.

The evaluations presented in this book are unique cases with different settings, tasks, methodological options and choices. They show that, even when dealing with daunting tasks, it is pivotal to aim for impartial, credible, transparent and independent conflict prevention and peacebuilding evaluations. As should be clear from the sections above, the number of challenges in relation to designing evaluation approaches that are adequate for the evaluations' objectives and questions, while both ensuring impartiality and avoiding doing harm are considerable. These are issues that all cases in this book have struggled with in different manners and with different responses to challenges encountered.

Notes

1 At the time of drafting the chapter working with Danida's evaluation department.
2 Organisation provided for identification purposes only. The opinions expressed and arguments employed herein do not necessarily reflect the official views of Norad or of the government of Norway.
3 Working at the University of Copenhagen at the time of drafting.

Evaluation approaches in situations of conflict and fragility 31

4 The distinction between the simple, the complicated, and the complex was introduced by Glouberman and Zimmerman (2002), and reiterated in Rogers (2008). A more comprehensive definition of complexity can be found in de Coning (2012).
5 This can also be related to the results agenda that came to the forefront in this period, not just in terms of peacebuilding, but in other areas of international development assistance. The evaluation community experienced a strong call, both among politicians and practitioners, for better knowledge concerning results, including requests for 'rigorous impact evaluation', building on experimental or quasi-experimental approaches, so as to better deal with the issues of biases, confounding factors, etc.
6 Upon the release of the Utstein study, a sub-committee of the OECD DAC was established to look into how peacebuilding evaluations could improve, in terms of addressing the issue of 'peace writ large' and bridging the gap between the evaluation community and the peacebuilding community. The work stream resulted in a draft guidance on Evaluating Conflict Prevention and Peacebuilding Activities (2008), which was then field tested. Final guidance was published in 2012 (OECD 2012).
7 See also Chapter 8 presenting findings from a meta-study of a range of statebuilding evaluations.
8 As an example, one may consider the USAID evaluation policy from 2011, where impact evaluation is defined as an evaluation that 'measure(s) the change in a development outcome that is attributable to a defined intervention; impact evaluations are based on models of cause and effect and require a credible and rigorously defined counterfactual to control for factors other than the intervention that might account for the observed change' (USAID 2011). Such an exercise is only feasible within a perspective where information on impact indicators can be treated as social facts, and where attribution is something that can be unambiguously estimated (i.e., by use of statistical tools), rather than being dependent on a multiverse of socially constructed interpretations. Similar understandings can be found amongst many other international donors.
9 As such, this position may be somewhat cautious about use of pre-defined categories in questionnaires, etc. (at least unless rooted in a very thorough understanding of the local context) and is likely to stress the need for participatory and qualitative approaches, aimed at getting in-depth understanding of the processes and interpretations at play.
10 For interesting and influential work on theory-based evaluation with different definitions and understandings of the concepts, and overviews of a range of the concepts commonly in use see for instance Bamberger et al. (2006), Rogers (2008) and Rogers and Funnell (2011). For on overview of different uses of theory of change, see Vogel (2012).
11 The 'logical framework approach' is often associated with the development of a design and management tool for USAID in 1969.
12 Complex is here understood as 'emergent' – that is, it is not possible to fully foresee the outcome of an intervention, or which factors that will lead to a specified outcome. The reason is that the initial changes brought about by the intervention may influence the system or context in which it takes place in a manner that may again influence the working of the intervention and the later outcomes. This way, complexity is seen as different than mere 'complicatedness' (multiple components) where it is in principle possible to chart and forecast an outcome, even though it may require management of multiple components and difficult processes.
13 This could for instance relate to looking at how the intervention is seen to play out from the perspective of the beneficiaries, the implementers or other relevant stakeholders, or looking at whether unintended but observed positive or negative impacts have been caused by the intervention. Here, theories of change would still clearly relate to the intervention in question, but the expectations about impacts, assumptions, etc., may have a different and broader rooting.

14 See for instance Chambers (1983, 1997) for influential argumentation along those lines.
15 See also Chapter 9 in this book.
16 Further, it is mentioned that there may be circumstances where donors' programme theories or theories of change are not adequate, for instance when working in situations with little prior knowledge. If so, one possible way to work with (preliminary) theories of change is suggested to focus on local understandings of change dynamics (see Stern et al. 2012). While this would clearly also entail a range of considerations on how to assess whether assumptions are relevant, etc., it would arguably at least provide a strong situational knowledge from which to work. For contributions pointing to the possible pitfalls and biases when working with local perceptions, see White and Phillips (2012).
17 See, for instance, OECD (2012) for more on the role of conflict analysis.
18 See Çuhadar-Gürkaynak et al. (2009) for a summary.
19 Ross (2004: 4).
20 Collier et al. (2008).
21 Stewart (2008).
22 Arnson and Zartman (2005).
23 See, for example, World Bank (2011).
24 Among influential works leading to an increased focus on experimental approaches, Savedoff et al. (2006) must be mentioned. Likewise, institutions such as the International Initiative for Impact Evaluation (3ie), the World Bank's DIME-initiative, work by J-PAL and others have emphasised the use of experimental and quasi-experimental approaches to impact assessment. It should, however, be noted that it is also widely acknowledged among such organisations that such approaches are not always feasible. For broader debate on whether and when a focus on experimental approaches is relevant and useful, see Rodrik (2008).
25 See, for instance, Cook et al. (2008) and Hansen et al. (2013) for discussions on the within study comparisons.
26 This ties in to the broader trend in aid, where a shift from project-based aid to sector-wide approaches is widely advocated. For projects, it will often be possible to distinguish participants from non-participants, in a manner more conducive to establishing a relevant counterfactual than for sector-wide programmes, with a broader/more diffuse area of influence. Further, in situations where the whole cannot meaningfully be reduced to the sum of its parts, it may even be misleading to look at a particular intervention in isolation, as pointed out by the Utstein report, as there could be a risk that an intervention is successful in relation to achieving its outcomes, but at the same time interacts with the wider context in a way that is detrimental to the achievement of higher-level goals.
27 Four approaches are mentioned by White and Phillips (2012) in connection to this: Realist evaluation, Shriven's General Elimination Methodology (GEM), Process Tracing and Contribution Analysis.
28 See Stern et al. (2012) for a discussion on different models of causality and evaluative approaches for assessing them, including the contributory causality and INUS conditions (insufficient but non-redundant parts of a condition which is itself unnecessary but sufficient for the occurrence of the effect).
29 See, for instance, Bamberger et al. (2006); White (2008); White and Phillips (2012); Rogers and Funnell (2011).
30 The 'do no harm' principle was an issue that first entered policy discussions in the context of humanitarian assistance and soon spread to development interventions.
31 In the Sri Lanka evaluation presented later in this book, the team experienced a great interest in who the local team members were (they represented the different identity groups in Sri Lanka), and when some of them withdrew due to fear of possible repercussions, the team decided to remove all of the local team members 1) to avoid

perceived bias, and thereby threats to the credibility of the evaluation and 2) for their own safety. Measures were taken to remove the local team members' names from all documents.
32 By sample we mean a limited number of observations rather than observations of an entire population, or universe, or persons, objects or events. The purpose is to say something about or infer to the larger group from which the sample was drawn (Knoke et al. 2002).
33 See, for example, Bamberger et al. (2006) for an introduction to different strategies for probability sampling.
34 For instance, if the target group for an intervention is decided based on the screening of a large groups of possible recipient, and selection is based on clear criteria with a specific cut-off point (such as an income threshold or similar), then this can inform a sampling strategy where groups just above and below the cut-off point are selected and compared, based on the knowledge that the difference is known and limited, so-called regression discontinuity design.
35 This also links back to the points brought forward in the Utstein report that in some situations it may be needed to focus on system level, in order to understand the fuller picture of whether and how an intervention affects situations of conflict and fragility.
36 If, for instance, the evaluation is tasked with assessing a large number of projects, it could be considered to sample based on project size to cover as large a share as possible (based on budgets, number of beneficiaries or similar), or to sample projects based on whether enabling and hindering factors were present, in order to include 'best' and 'worst' situations so as to be able to do critical case assessments (Flyvbjerg 2011).
37 Often more than one purposeful sampling strategy can be useful in an evaluation. Thus, Bamberger et al. (2006) mention several sampling strategies, including sampling strategies for interviews, which may include a 'range' sample, 'typical' sample, 'extreme case' sample, 'quota' sample, 'reputational' sample or a 'sample of sample'.
38 In some situations of conflict and fragility where sampling is very constricted by security considerations, a better label would probably be a 'pragmatic' or given sample.
39 For instance, bias may consist of preference for dry season to rainy season, urban to rural areas, rural areas with tarmac roads versus those without, sensitivity issues, consultant's bias in the form of self-censorships oriented towards not antagonising potential future commissioners, professional biases in the form of preference for certain academic/theoretical perspectives, etc., diplomatic bias in the form of 'polite responses' from informants, etc. In the recent work by White and Phillips (2012) a range of fairly parallel considerations on bias are given. Typically, more weight is given to the narratives of people, whom are met and interviewed, than 'second-hand' information and some groups are systematically underrepresented in most evaluations: traditional authorities, parliamentarians, faith-based organisations, trade unions, village chiefs, journalists and other key actors. While others – agency staff, project employees, donor headquarter staff – are more frequently interviewed. This is called 'evaluator bias' by White and Phillips (2012).
40 There are several sources of error or bias related to research. A non-sampling bias can be found in the coverage of the sampling frame and when the quality and comprehensiveness of the listing of subjects is questionable. Another type of non-sampling bias is non-response, where it should be considered that subjects who cannot be located or refuse to respond might have different characteristics than those responding. For example, respondents might be on average younger, better educated, women or higher income groups. Measurement error is another bias, where information may be wrongly recorded or systematically misreported.
41 Based on the above, White and Phillips (2012) suggest an integrated framework for small *n* causal inference. It is a five-step framework that includes the following

elements: 1) What questions are asked? 2) Setting the programme's theory of change; 3) Plan for data collection and analysis; 4) Generate avenues for alternative causal explanation; and finally 5) Examine each of these hypotheses against the facts. However, taken together with the considerations above on the challenges with regards to identifying an appropriate sample, or clarifying the characteristics of 'pragmatic' samples (not to mention the issue of lack of clarity with regards to theory on conflict and, by implication, on interventions addressing conflict), it is clear that the process of establishing an evaluation framework that is adequate for assessing the evaluation questions on cause and effects, identifying the types of information needed to populate it and actually collecting and using the data without doing harm is very far from simple.

Bibliography

Anderson, B. (2006) *Imagined Communities*, 3rd edn, London: Verso.
Anderson, M. B. (1999) *Do No harm: How Aid Can Support Peace – or War*, Boulder, CO: Lynne Reiner Publishers.
Anderson, M. B. and Olson, L. (2003) *Confronting War: Critical Lessons for Peace Practitioners*, Cambridge, MA: The Collaborative for Development Action.
Arnson, C. and Zartman, W. (eds) (2005) *Rethinking the Economics of War: The Intersection of Need, Creed and Greed*, Washington, DC: Woodrow Wilson Center Press.
Bamberger, M., Rugh, J. and Mabry, L. (2006) *Real World Evaluation: Working Under Budget, Time, Data and Political Constraints*, Thousand Oaks: Sage.
Chambers, R. (1983) *Rural Development. Putting the Last First*, Essex: Longman Scientific & Technical, Longman Group Limited.
——(1997) *Whose Reality Counts?* London: Intermediate Technology Development Group Publishing.
——(2009) 'Making the Poor Count – Using Participatory Methods for Impact Evaluation', in *Designing Impact Evaluations – Different Perspectives*, 3ie working paper 4, New Delhi: International Initiative for Impact Evaluation.
Church., C. and Shouldice, J. (2003) *Emerging Practice and Theory*, INCORE International Conflict Research, Londonderry: University of Ulster and The United Nations University.
Collier, P. and Hoeffler, A. (2002) 'Aid, Policy and Peace: Reducing the Risks of Civil Conflicts', *Defence and Peace Economics* 13(6): 435–450.
Collier, P., Hoeffler, A. and Rohner, D. (2008) *Beyond Greed and Grievance: Feasibility and Civil War*, Oxford: University of Oxford, Department of Economics.
de Coning, C. (2012) *Coherence and International Cooperation: A Complexity Theory Approach to the Coordination Dilemma in Peacebuilding Operations*, unpublished.
Cracknell, B. E. (2000) *Evaluating Development Aid: Issues, Problems, Solutions*, London: Sage.
Cook, T. D., Shadish, W. T. and Wong, V. C. (2008) 'Three Conditions Under Which Experiment and Observational Studies Produce Comparable Causal Estimates: New Findings from Within-study Comparisons', *Journal of Policy Analysis and Management* 27(4): 724–750.
Çuhadar-Gürkaynak, E., Dayton, B., and Paffenholz, T. (2009) 'Evaluation in Conflict Resolution and Peacebuilding', in D. J. D. Sandole, S. Byrne, I. Sandole-Staroste and J. Senehi (eds) *Handbook of Conflict Analysis and Resolution*, Abingdon and New York: Routlegde, pp. 286–299.

Cutillo, A. (2006) *International Assistance to Countries Emerging from Conflict: A Review of Fifteen Years of Interventions and the Future of Peacebuilding*, New York: International Peace Academy.

Davidson, E. J. (2000) 'Ascertaining Causality in Theory-Based Evaluation', *New Directions for Evaluation* 87: 17–26.

Elkin, C. (2010) 'Evaluating Development Interventions in Peace-precarious Situations', *Evaluation* 16(3): 309–321.

Fear, W. (2007) 'Programme Evaluation Theory: The Next Step Toward a Synthesis of Logic Models and Organisational Theory', *Journal of Multidisciplinary Evaluation* 47(7): 13–25.

Ferguson, J. (1990) *The Anti-Politics Machine: Development, Depoliticization and Bureaucratic Power in Lesotho*, Cambridge: Cambridge University Press.

Fisher, R. and Ury, W. L. (1983) *Getting to Yes: Negotiating an Agreement without Giving in*, New York: Penguin Books.

Flyvbjerg, B. (2011) 'Case Study', in N. K. Denzin and Y.S. Lincoln (eds) *The Sage Handbook of Qualitative Research*, Thousand Oaks: Sage.

Forss, K., Marra, M. and Schwartz, R. (eds) (2011) *Evaluating the Complex: Attribution, Contribution, and Beyond*, Comparative Policy Evaluation, Vol. 18, New Jersey: Transaction Publishers.

Galtung, J. (1969) 'Violence, Peace and Peace Research', *Journal of Peace Research* 6(3): 167–191.

Glouberman, S. and Zimmerman, B. (2002) *Complex and Complicated Systems: What Would Successful Reform of Medicare Look Like?* Discussion Paper No. 8, Commission on the Future Health Care in Canada.

Grävingholt, J., Leininger, J. and von Haldenwang, C. (2012) *Effective Statebuilding? A Review of Evaluations of International Statebuilding Support in Fragile Contexts*, Evaluation Study 2012/3, Copenhagen: Ministry of Foreign Affairs of Denmark.

Grossman, H. (1992) 'Foreign Aid and Insurrection', *Defence and Peace Economics* 3(4): 275–288.

Hansen, H., Klejnstrup, N. and Andersen, O. W. (2013) 'A Comparison of Model-based and Design-based Impact Evaluations of Interventions in Developing Countries', *American Journal of Evaluation*, forthcoming.

Holmqvist, G. (2012) *Inequality and Identity – Causes of War?* Discussion paper 72, Uppsala: Nordiska Afrikainstituttet.

Koenig, G. (2009) 'Realistic Evaluation and Case Studies: Stretching the Potential', *Evaluation* 15(1): 9–30.

Knoke, D., Bohrnstedt, G. W. and Mee, A. P. (2002) *Statistics for Social Data Analysis*, Itasca, IL: F. E. Peacock Publishers.

Loode, S. (2010) *Working in Complex Communities: What Peacebuilding Can Learn from Complex Systems Science*, paper presented at the 2010 IPRA Global Conference 'Communicating Peace', University of Sydney, Australia, 6–10 July 2010.

Mayne, J. (2011) 'Contribution analysis: Addressing Cause and Effect', in K. Forss, M. Marra and R. Schwartz (eds) *Evaluating the Complex: Attribution, Contribution, and Beyond*, Comparative Policy Evaluation, Vol. 18, New Jersey: Transaction Publishers.

Norad (2011) *Evaluation of Norwegian Development Cooperation*, Annual Report 2011, Oslo: Evaluation Department. www.norad.no/en/tools-and-publications/publications/publication?key=393706.

OECD (2001) *Helping Prevent Violent Conflict: The DAC Guidelines*, Paris: OECD Publishing.
——(2007) *Principles for Good International Engagement in Fragile States & Situations*, Paris: OECD Publishing. www.oecd.org/dac/incaf/38368714.pdf, accessed 24 May 2013.
——(2010a) *Quality Standards for Development Evaluation*, DAC Guidelines and Reference Series, Paris: OECD Publishing.
——(2010b) *Evaluation in Development Agencies*, Paris: OECD Publishing.
——(2012) *Evaluating Peacebuilding Activities in Settings of Conflict and Fragility: Improving Learning for Results*, DAC Guidelines and Reference Series, Paris: OECD Publishing. doi: 10.1787/9789264106802-en.
Paffenholz, T. (2005) *Third-generation PCIA: Introducing the Aid for Peace Approach*, Berlin: Berghof Research Center for Constructive Conflict Management. www.berghof-handbook.net, Berlin.
Paffenholz, T., Abu-Nimer, M. and McCandless, E. (2005) 'Peacebuilding and Development: Integrated Approaches to Evaluation', *Journal of Peacebuilding and Development* 2(2): 1–5.
Paffenholz, T. and Reychler, L. (2005) 'Towards Better Policy and Programme Work in Conflict Zones: Introducing the "Aid for Peace" Approach', *Journal of Peacebuilding and Development* 2(2): 6–23.
Rietjens, S., Soeters, J. and Klumper, W. (2011) 'Measuring the Immeasurable? The Effects-based Approach in Comprehensive Peace Operations', *International Journal of Public Administration* 34(5): 329–338.
Rodrik, D. (2008) *The New Development Economics: We Shall Experiment, But How Shall We Learn?* Working Paper no. RWP08-055, Cambridge, MA: Harvard Kennedy School.
Rogers, P. (2008) 'Using Programme Theory to Evaluate Complicated and Complex Aspects of Interventions', *Evaluation* 14(1): 29–48.
——(2009) 'Learning from the evidence about evidence-based policy', in Productivity Commission (ed.) *Strengthening Evidence-Based Policy in the Australian Federation*, Melbourne, pp. 195–213.
Rogers, P. and Funnell, S. (2011) *Purposeful Program Theory: Effective Use of Theories of Change and Logic Models*, San Francisco: John Wiley & Sons.
Ross, M. (2004) 'Conceptualizing Success in Conflict Resolution Interventions', *Peace and Conflict Studies* 11: 1–18.
Savedoff, W. D., Levine, R. and Birdsall, N. (2006) *When Will We Ever Learn? Improving Lives Through Impact Evaluation*, The Evaluation Gap Working Group. www.cgdev.org/files/7973_file_WillWeEverLearn.pdf, accessed May 2013.
Smith, D. (2004) *Towards a Strategic Framework for Peacebuilding: Getting Their Act Together, Overview report of the Joint Utstein Study of Peacebuilding*, Oslo: Norwegian Ministry of Foreign Affairs.
Stern, E., Stame, N., Mayne, J., Forss, K., Davies, R. and Befani, B. (2012) *Developing a Broader Range of Rigorous Designs and Methods for Impact Evaluations*, report of a study commissioned by the Department for International Development (DFID), London: Department for International Development (DFID). www.dfid.gov.uk/Documents/.../design-method-impact-eval.pdf, accessed 26 March 2013.
Stern, P. and Druckman, D. (2000) 'Evaluating Interventions in History: The Case of International Conflict Resolution', *International Studies Review*, 2(1): 33–63.
Stewart, F. (ed.) (2008) *Horizontal Inequality and Conflict*, New York: Palgrave.

USAID (2011) *USAID Evaluation Policy*, Washington, DC: USAID.
Vogel, I. (2012) *Review of the Use of 'Theory of Change' in International Development*, Review Report for Department for International Development (DFID), London: Department for International Development (DFID).
White, H. (2008) *Of Probits and Participation: The Use of Mixed Methods in Quantitative Impact Evaluation*, Nonie Working Paper no. 7, Washington, DC: Network of Networks on Impact Evaluation.
White, H. and Phillips, D. (2012) *Addressing Attribution of Cause and Effect in Small n Impact Evaluations: Towards an Integrated Framework*, Working Paper 15, New Delhi: International Initiative for Impact Evaluation.
Woodrow, P. and Chigas, D. (2011) 'Connecting the Dots: Evaluating Whether and How Programmes Address Conflict Systems', in D. Körppen, N. Ropers and H. Gießman (eds) *The Non-linearity of Peace Processes – Theory and Practice of Systemic Conflict Transformation,* Opladen/Farmington Hills: Barbara Budrich Verlag.
World Bank (2011) *World Development Report 2011: Conflict, Security, and Development*, Washington, DC: World Bank.

3 Critical reflections on the South Sudan evaluation of conflict prevention and peacebuilding activities

Chris Barnett
Itad and the Institute of Development Studies

Jon Bennett
Oxford Development Consultants

1 Introduction

While many advances have been made in clarifying the concepts and identifying key challenges of evaluating in complex conflict and peacebuilding settings (e.g., OECD 2012a), there is still little consensus over how best to conduct such evaluations. In addition to the constraints created by the conflict context itself, an obstacle to establishing an 'evaluation culture' in peacebuilding is the tendency towards self-reinforcement between funders and implementers, encouraged largely by competition over scarce resources. Evaluations often precede the next funding phase and it can be in the interest of both the funder and implementer to show positive results for the previous intervention. This has in some cases led to, 'inadvertent and unrealistic tension between funders and program implementers in making unrealistic claims' (Woodrow et al. 2008). Evaluators are aware of the challenges of rigour and attribution, but also of the highly complex non-linear processes of social change in settings of violent conflict, which cannot be captured by linear cause–effect logic. And yet the vast majority of evaluations are still characterised by a reliance on a narrow set of unsystematic qualitative methods for data collection and analysis, and relatively short visits to the field, which often do not stand up to academic scrutiny (Grävingholt et al. 2012).[1] Why is this? Is this only due to methodological inadequacies, or is there something inherent in the peacebuilding setting; something, perhaps more structural about the way in which these evaluations are commissioned and conducted, that creates this evaluation gap?

This chapter explores a 'super-sized' example of an evaluation of conflict prevention and peacebuilding activities; not only is it an ex-post evaluation undertaken in a fragile context, but it was commissioned by 15 donors, and sets out to assess the 'collective effect' of an estimated US$4.1 billion of aid and 2,189 interventions in South Sudan. Entitled *Aiding the Peace* (Bennett et al. 2010), the evaluation provided an opportunity to reflect on developments over the six-year interim period that followed the signing of the Comprehensive Peace Agreement (CPA) between North and South Sudan in January 2005; as well as to examine

Critical reflections on the South Sudan evaluation of conflict 39

how the international community as a whole upheld the promises it made at the International Donor Conference in Oslo in April 2005. In this respect, the evaluation was designed to be both backward and forward looking, with the lessons from the past few years helping to inform donor priorities as South Sudan entered a new era.

Crucially, *Aiding the Peace* looked beyond the overarching North–South Sudan conflict, asking to what extent donors were aware of, and addressing, internal lower-level conflicts that blighted the postwar landscape in South Sudan. The evaluation used the traditional OECD DAC criteria (relevance, efficiency, effectiveness, impact, sustainability). As a multi-donor (and hence multi-project) evaluation it also relied on the notion of 'cumulative impact', attempting to analyse the overall result of a plethora of activities that were planned as stand-alone interventions. One way to approach such an analysis is through using a holistic intervention logic (or theory of change) that looks at multidimensional causes and effects, and the interrelationship between many interventions. Within each individual intervention there are often underlying assumptions, practices and values that need to be unpacked. Most donors will claim that their activities contribute towards peace, but few will have explained or monitored precisely how this was done. They are even less likely to make assertions over how their specific inputs contribute towards a cohesive inter-agency approach where the sum of the impact is greater than the individual parts.

The notion that a framework for evaluations in fluid, complex environments should include a combination of conflict analysis and theories of change was introduced in the mid 2000s through, for example, the work of the Collaborative for Development Action and its Reflecting on Peace Practice project. It allows for a constantly changing context characterised by socially complex adaptive systems that are difficult to predict and may be open to risk and failure (Woodrow and Chigas 2011).[2]

This chapter considers three particular limitations of the theory-based approach. First, the challenge of embedding conflict analysis – a tool that has its origins in, and is more suited to, planning purposes – into the evaluation process.[3] Second, concerns over how to better reconcile the different – often competing – frameworks that are introduced when evaluators and peacebuilding practitioners come together. And lastly, the chapter describes some of the drawbacks to the application of theories of change to situations of conflict and fragility – particularly where there are limited theoretical foundations for vaguely stated strategic and policy options around peace and reconstruction.

The chapter concludes by arguing that the central aim of any evaluation of conflict prevention and peacebuilding should be to examine whether activities are cognisant of, or responsive to, the dynamics of conflict in the context in question. The challenge highlighted in *Aiding the Peace* was that many donors conceptualised their interventions as a 'postwar peace dividend', underplaying the fact that the end of the main war in Sudan invoked the beginning of a series of smaller, localised wars over resources and political influence that soon became major impediments to stability and security for people in South Sudan. Without a thorough understanding of the dynamics of the conflict and the political economy of low-intensity warfare in South Sudan an evaluation will miss this bigger picture. Making the connection between the underlying drivers of a conflict and how external interventions address these drivers becomes critical. And yet, in undertaking *Aiding the Peace*, the mix of multiple expectations from the different donors, the different backgrounds of evaluation and peacebuilding practitioners, and a general lack of consensus about how to undertake the evaluation, threatened to undermine this focus. The result, at least in the inception phase, was too many evaluation questions, competing frameworks that were difficult to reconcile, and a tendency to lean towards assessing interventions against a donor's *own* objectives regardless of whether these were addressing the key causes of the conflict.

2 The South Sudanese context

Six years after the peace agreement that ended the civil war with the North, the citizens of South Sudan voted for independence in the referendum of January 2011. In doing so, South Sudan became the world's newest state. The country is not only one of the poorest in the world, but also one in which violent conflict and the spread of arms are rife. In 2012, Sudan as a whole was ranked 171st out of 187 states on the Human Development Index (UNDP 2013).[4] While the past ten years has seen a remarkable growth in Sudan's economy overall, throughout its history the southern region of the country was cut off from mainstream development owing to political and physical isolation. It is only since 2005 that South Sudan, through the CPA, has received about half of the country's new-found oil wealth, amounting to approximately US$2 billion per year until 2011.[5]

After the signature of the CPA, donors began a policy of engagement with the newly created Government of South Sudan (GoSS). The prevailing paradigm was of 'postwar reconstruction' in which much of the conventional apparatus of aid, including support to service delivery, came to the fore. Despite the peace agreement however, the situation was in reality closer to a 'suspended war' – during which local conflicts frequently erupted into violence. The donors' 'post-conflict' mindset led to a serious underestimation of the residual and often complex triggers of violence. At the same time donors felt obliged not to prejudge the outcome of the referendum,[6] which made it difficult for them to focus their aid efforts in South Sudan, especially in relation to governance of the (possible) future state.

Violence in South Sudan manifests itself in different ways – for example, youth alienation and specific tensions around water and land have been exacerbated by poor progress over reintegration of demobilised soldiers and the return of large numbers of internally displaced persons (IDPs) and refugees since 2005. In the absence of fundamental reform, the legitimacy and acceptance of government institutions, especially the security apparatus (police and army), is brought into question. This is particularly the case in local government and in the ten states of South Sudan where capacities and resources are very low. The key concern of the people of South Sudan has been the security and protection of their families against various predatory forces, and the lack of adequate state mechanisms to forestall these (DFID 2008).

At the time of writing, the border between North and South Sudan has also yet to be fully defined and has recently seen an upsurge in violence between the countries. The contested area of Abyei, one of the 'Three Areas' along the North/South divide, is traditionally an area of cattle owning groups: the Dinka (from the South), and the Missiriyya (from the North). Abyei holds a vast amount of Sudan's oil and was supposed to be the litmus test for a united Sudan and for the wealth- and power-sharing arrangements set out by the CPA. The Abyei referendum, on whether Abyei should remain in Southern Kordofan State in northern Sudan or join Bahr el-Ghazal State in southern Sudan, was to take place at the same time as the southern Sudanese vote. The referendum, however, never took place.

3 The evaluation gap

Over the years there have been a large number of project evaluations and reviews assessing international assistance to South Sudan. These have mostly been commissioned by donors and other development agencies as a way of assessing specific programmes, projects and policies, as well as the different aid instruments that were in use in South Sudan – such as the Multi-Donor Trust Fund (Scanteam 2007) and the Common Humanitarian Fund (Willitts-King et al. 2007).

Many such studies were triggered by a growing perception that the failure to quickly deliver results on the ground posed a serious threat to the implementation of the CPA and the likely continuation of stability and peace. Donors lacked, however, a comprehensive view about whether the mix of interventions and funding mechanisms were delivering results, and whether different interventions were mutually reinforcing or undermining each other. In 2009, an inventory of available evaluations, evaluative studies and reviews (van Beijnum and Hemmer 2009) showed that none of these studies and reviews provided a comprehensive overview of the combined results of donor support to South Sudan since 2005. Rather, each study gave a partial assessment of the development assistance provided, and in most cases they lacked specific evidence of results on the ground. Findings tended to be relevant only to the project, programme or aid instrument being evaluated at that particular point in time.

Aiding the Peace was designed as a study to help fill this 'evaluation gap' at the strategic level. It had two parallel aims – one specific to South Sudan, the other aimed to support broader learning within the international community. The first was to carry out a results-oriented evaluation of how donor interventions in South Sudan have impacted upon peacebuilding from the signing of the CPA in 2005 to the first quarter of 2010 (MoFA 2009). And, although the evaluation attempted to look at impact, it was not an 'impact evaluation' as such since it did not address attribution through identifying a counterfactual (White 2010). Rather, the evaluation aimed to assess the totality of aid to the country using mixed methods. The main donor programmes assessed were those of the Netherlands, Belgium, Canada, Denmark, Germany, Norway, Sweden, the United Kingdom and the United States. The activities and policies of multilateral bodies such as the European Commission, World Bank and some United Nations agencies (including United Nations Mission in Sudan, or UNMIS) were reviewed, and a brief overview of assistance provided by regional and non-DAC donors – such as China, India and the Arab League – was also conducted.

Aiding the Peace was designed as a multi-donor evaluation. It was subject to all the pros and cons which define an endeavour that involves 15 donors on an evaluation steering committee – including many of the process issues that affect the dynamics and even the end-product of an evaluation (OECD 2000). South Sudan was itself a good testing ground for the principles of the Paris Declaration on Aid Effectiveness and the Accra Agenda for Action (OECD 2005 and 2008) that stress coordinated aid management between donors, and the evaluation was similarly a joint endeavour. For example, the evaluation critically examined the multi-donor funding mechanisms in the country that were meant to harmonise assistance efforts and lessen the burden on the new government. While the evaluation itself was a joint endeavour, it did not disregard bilateral programmes, nor did it suggest that jointly funded programmes were inherently more efficient or effective in addressing issues of fragility in South Sudan.[7] The crucial question was whether the collective efforts of all donors could be captured, and whether the evaluation was able to make informed judgements about their cumulative impact in respect to peacebuilding.

The second aim was of a broader nature. The evaluation was designed to improve the extent to which conflict prevention and peacebuilding activities can be evaluated, in particular by testing the applicability of the *Guidance on Evaluating Conflict Prevention and Peacebuilding Activities – Working Draft for Application Period* (OECD 2008) – hereafter referred to as the draft OECD DAC guidance. In turn, this would also inform broader thinking about engagement in fragile states, early recovery, stabilisation and other processes relating to operations in times of rapid transition.

In summary, the objectives for the evaluation were (MoFA 2009):

- To assess through the use of standard OECD DAC evaluation criteria[8] the extent of progress made by the international community in supporting conflict prevention and peacebuilding and in providing peace dividends to the South Sudanese people. This will include pointing out the factors driving success or failure, and highlighting lessons accordingly.
- To provide an input into ongoing discussions and future policies/plans on how to improve the relevance, efficiency, effectiveness and – above all – impact of the international engagement in peacebuilding processes in South Sudan in the run-up to the 2011 referendum and the post-2011 period.
- Pilot the working draft of the OECD DAC guidance (OECD 2008).

4 Key features of the evaluation methodology

4.1 Applying a conflict lens

Like many evaluations in conflict-affected regions, *Aiding the Peace* differs from the conventional approach to development evaluation. The aim is not to evaluate development activities solely in terms of their own objectives, but rather to assess them through a 'conflict lens' that asks whether these activities responded to (and addressed) the dynamics of conflict in the country. So, for example, the assessment of 'relevance' is not only about relevance of the intervention to policy priorities and people's needs (as in a classic development evaluation) but also 'the extent to which the objectives and activities of the intervention(s) respond to the needs of beneficiaries *and the peacebuilding process* – i.e. whether they address the key driving factors of conflict' (OECD 2012a: 67, emphasis added). In this way, the evaluation is less focused on the extent to which projects and programmes have met their own objectives, and more on whether the interventions have addressed underlying drivers of the conflict. In South Sudan, most donor policies have the overarching goal of contributing to peace within the CPA process. The evaluation asked whether this policy priority has translated into timely and appropriate activities on the ground, which can be said to have reduced incidents of violence or enhanced the prospects of peace between (and within) communities.

When examining the notions of 'conflict prevention' and 'peacebuilding' the interrelationship between social, economic and political programmes in South Sudan – and the wider geographic, ethnic and environmental context – have to be taken into account. Underlying causes of discontent are not purely historical nor do they pertain solely to North/South relations in Sudan. Violent conflicts are also caused by local disputes over land or other resources, the failure of political inclusiveness or the persistence of an inequitable distribution of wealth. As a result, the evaluation covered all activities that were designed to have a beneficial influence in abating the occurrence of violence and examined the extent to which they have strengthened the cultural and institutional resilience necessary for managing such conflicts without violence.[9]

4.2 An incremental approach to evaluation

Given the inherent unpredictability and frequent lack of data in conflict-affected settings, the evaluation undertook an incremental approach, which recognised that although South Sudan was classed by many as being 'post-conflict' (at the time of the evaluation) there was a need to respond to changing circumstances and security concerns. There were two main interrelated stages to this process. The first stage consisted of analytical work that synthesised the current body of evidence, while also determining the scope of the subsequent fieldwork. The second stage focused on fieldwork to assess the realities on the ground, and to triangulate preliminary findings.

In the first stage, there were four main studies.[10] First, a conflict analysis provided the principal frame of reference for the evaluation; the 'lens' through which to examine performance over the evaluation period. The conflict analysis identified the key factors relating to conflict and the linkages between them, pointing to sources and dynamics of conflict (and conflict mitigation) as well as peace (and peacebuilding). The analysis provided a starting point for assessing the extent to which an understanding of the conflict, and sensitivity to it, had been applied by donors in strategic planning and programming in South Sudan. Also, as part of the first stage, the evaluation undertook an aid portfolio and donor policy analysis that summarised the facts, figures and trends of donor support over the five-year period. These analyses were used to gain a picture of the actual support provided and to comment on the coherence of policies. In this first stage of the evaluation, donors were requested to provide quantitative and qualitative information on their portfolio over the five-year period. Then on the basis of the OECD DAC CRS[11] codes commonly used to identify substantive categories of Official Development Assistance (ODA), efforts were made to group interventions along the lines of the four categories suggested by the draft OECD DAC guidance (i.e., socioeconomic development, good governance, reform of justice and security institutions, and the culture of justice, truth and reconciliation). And lastly, an analysis of evaluation reports, project/programme completion reports and other types of source material, including academic and applied research, was undertaken.

Given the challenges of poor data and poor access (relating to security) that beset all agencies entering South Sudan, it was unlikely that a literature search would provide the required comprehensive overview of development challenges and responses. Where specific data were used to justify an intervention, there was a tendency to heavily borrow data from other agencies, data which themselves may be dubious. Moreover, it was often the case that data from one area of South Sudan was either extrapolated or simply repeated to apply to another area. In this evaluation, only in a few specific instances was it possible for the team to verify findings on the ground through observation and field methods. It would have been impossible to validate data obtained from the literature. The best recourse was to use the experience and local knowledge of the team to filter out what was either highly contentious or what was patently repeated from unconfirmed sources. There is no 'scientific' method of doing this; it is a question of judgement based on long experience. A perennial challenge in a country where staff turnover (international and national) is very high is that institutional memory is correspondingly short. In this case the team itself comprised individuals who had been consistently covering events in Sudan for more than 20 years. It is possible that a less experienced evaluation team might have accepted at face value that if three interlocutors say the same thing, it must be 'true', although the factual basis for what people are saying is actual non-existent or weak.[12] This poses an interesting question: even with the most meticulous methodology, are there important issues that might be missed simply through a lack of country experience which makes it impossible to filter out non-credible information?

Based on the conflict analysis, aid portfolio and donor policy analyses, and the analysis of evaluation reports, a Terms of Reference (TOR) was developed for the second stage of the evaluation. This summarised the preliminary findings of the desk review, set out the basis for selecting interventions and locations to visit, and outlined the methodology in more detail. The evaluation team also produced two internal documents summarising the initial hypotheses (based on the first stage literature review) and a team guide to applying conflict analysis to the field-level assessments.

For the second stage of the evaluation, the field-based assessments were carried out with the objective of conducting an in-depth evaluation of conflict prevention and peacebuilding interventions in Southern Sudan. In reality, the 'in-depth' nature of the study was qualified by financial, time and access constraints, inherent to an evaluation of this nature, but more particularly due to operational constraints in South Sudan.[13] Evidence collected in the field entailed a cross-reference of primary stakeholder views with secondary project documentation and the knowledge of individuals in the evaluation team. In every location the team found that local government officials had only limited knowledge of donor activities in their area; donor and NGO staff were often more knowledgeable. The field interviews were not, however, always able to 'look back' over five years, especially where project or government staff turnover had been high. Due to the necessity of gaining access to beneficiaries through project staff (UN and/or NGO) who hosted the teams, interviewees were generally gathered at project sites. It was not possible to have a statistically representative 'control group' (i.e., non-beneficiaries), although where interviews were held there were often individuals present who had not been directly involved in the project under review and who could, therefore, comment as non-beneficiaries. In each location, local (*payam* or county) government officials were interviewed, and in several locations senior state officials were also included in discussions. Often Sudanese project staff had the better knowledge of progress over time compared to government officials who, in many cases, had not been in office for very long.

The fieldwork in South Sudan provided an opportunity to test the assumptions arising from the literature, nuance the conflict analysis with reference to local dynamics, derive greater in-depth knowledge of specific activities funded by aid donors and evaluate these through a conflict prevention and peacebuilding 'lens'. Importantly, the evaluation was not dependent on these field-level interviews and discussion groups – which might be seen as partial or biased – but rather these were used to triangulate the more substantial evidence and preliminary findings emerging from the first stage literature review and analysis. Furthermore, the sample of activities was not representative in a statistical sense, but was a purposive and indicative selection of activities from which broader lessons could be drawn. Central to the approach was the use of 'working hypotheses' around which to cluster the evidence and select interventions and locations for the field-level assessments to then test these hypotheses.

4.3 A purposive sample of projects

As mentioned, the evaluation did not intend to cover any single programme or project, or any single donor's inputs, but rather to assess the collective impact of international assistance over the period 2005 to 2010. Meanwhile, there was an imperative for the evaluation to contribute to overcoming the 'lack of information on the actual results of the assistance in the field' (van Beijnum and Hemmer 2009: 20). In short, there was an inherent tension between being strategically-orientated (i.e., assessing the collective impact of international assistance) while also retaining some elements of a project-focus to consider actual results in the field. The figures highlight the stark reality of the challenge faced by the evaluation team: in 2009 alone there were 436 interventions in operation across South Sudan (GoSS 2010) and, over the five-year period of the evaluation, the Aid Portfolio analysis recorded a total of 2,189 interventions.

The budgeted allocation to South Sudan amounted to about US$4.1 billion. About half of this went towards humanitarian activities (including to the 'Three Areas' along the borders that are not all within the borders of South Sudan – Blue Nile, Abyei and Southern Kordofan). Together with the estimated contributions assigned to UNMIS in the same period (averaging about US$1 billion per year including contributions from non-DAC donors), this would bring the total to upwards of US$8 billion. About 85 per cent of this total assistance was from the donors involved in the evaluation – and there were clear choices to be made between focusing on donor priorities (particularly around pooled funds, even though these were only 20 per cent of total funding), focusing on donor spending (with most aid going to basic service delivery), and focusing on core evaluation priorities identified in the conflict analysis (such as security sector reform).

The rationale for selection among the more than 2,000 interventions was deliberately based on fulfilling the overarching evaluation questions, while also 'ground-truthing' and testing assumptions that emerged from the first stage findings. Such an approach did not attempt to cover all types of programmes or geographic areas, but rather the projects and locations that can best provide evidence to answer a set of evaluation questions, based on the conflict analysis, accompanied by the analysis of the aid portfolio, donor policies and past evaluations. This purposive sampling meant that findings from the field assessments could be strategically located within a wider body of evidence (drawn from past evaluations, grey literature, research studies and statistics). It also meant that that there was less reliance on the primary data collected during relatively short field visits – that can be unpredictable and changeable as a result of security concerns (and therefore partial and potentially biased). While this type of purposive sampling had disadvantages (i.e., it could not by itself provide robust, primary data of results and impact), it did at least provide the advantage of keeping the evaluation focused on a fewer, more strategic[14] issues (as drawn from the working hypotheses). This contrasts with other similar evaluations, where the requirement to conduct a large number of project evaluations is said to have diverted efforts too much towards individual project-level results (which then became challenging to aggregate).

In practical terms, the purposive sampling was based upon a list of preliminary findings and hypotheses that were drawn from the first stage analysis, and related to key conflict factors.[15] Other variables were then taken into account by the evaluation team, including: (i) the interplay and overlap of conflict prevention and peacebuilding categories; (ii) geographical variance in Southern Sudan (the importance of context, place and time); (iii) the 'clustering' of activities and the extent to which they were interrelated; and lastly (iv) other variables such as access and logistics, and whether the programmes were still 'active'.

Although the evaluation team covered most of the subcategories in the so-called Utstein palette,[16] the choice of these was not determined by the proportion of donor support to each. Some 80 per cent of funding had gone into 'socioeconomic development' (the first main category), but some smaller programmes aimed at directly conflict-related stakeholders – security sector reform and governance programmes for example – may have had greater impact on conflict prevention. It was also important to examine other issues not covered by the Utstein palette, such as the channels of donor support (bilateral, multilateral and through pooled funds) to determine how effective such choices have been.

Conflict analysis in South Sudan suggested certain flashpoints that required more attention. These may be due to ethnic mix in an area, its proximity to valuable resources, tensions over land use, etc. Donors were in some cases aware of these flashpoints, and directed their resources accordingly. The evaluation included these flashpoints in the selection of cases that were studied in greater depth. For example, there has been a recent concentration of resources in conflict-prone areas such as Jonglei and Upper Nile. At the same time, patterns of migration and return have, to some extent, determined where and when a greater percentage of social service resources are allocated, such as Northern Bahr el Ghazal, as aid followed population movements.[17] The major infrastructure programmes – notably roads and related demining – were initially concentrated in the Equatoria States where access to Uganda and Kenya were vital to opening trade routes and where there were large numbers of internally displaced people returning to hitherto 'closed' areas of the country.

Other examples of the working hypotheses included the lack of a strategic joint diplomatic and developmental approach between donors, and even a disjuncture between the two. This division between politics and aid derives from the traditional separation of the two areas within ministry structures but also from the difficulty of merging and harmonising donor countries' political relationships with Sudan. The point was highlighted in an evaluation of the Joint Donor Team in Juba that found a 'lack of joint diplomatic and developmental approaches and JDT's disconnection with embassies in Khartoum…[and] the intended separation of aid and diplomacy by donors resulted in poor lines of communication between the two, despite the obvious link between aid and political developments in the South' (Bennett et al. 2009). In South Sudan, this split between aid and diplomacy means that there has been a failure to engage with fundamental political issues, particularly at local levels, and to design aid programmes that help mitigate rather than exacerbate conflict. This applies particularly to conflicts related to land and

48 *Chris Barnett and Jon Bennett*

natural resources. Experience in other putatively 'post-conflict' contexts suggests that lack of political cohesion among leaders and their political factions can lead to renewed conflict, although power-sharing is hardly sufficient for a sustainable peace. There is a notable absence of an overall framework to deal with such problems. In South Sudan the evaluation was able to identify areas of intervention where there had been somewhat ad hoc approaches or a lack of donor coordination; for instance in SPLA reform and in environmental governance.

The country also suffers from the combined effects of two sets of crises that are closely interrelated: a crisis of governance and a livelihoods crisis. The complexity of South Sudan should have led planning processes and assistance organisations to incorporate conflict-sensitive approaches regardless of whether they are directly addressing conflict issues in their work. This seems not generally to have been the case so far, and part of the field assessments sought to review the activities of socioeconomic programmes in outlying areas.

5 Critical reflections

5.1 Disconnects between conflict analysis and the evaluation

While the working hypotheses from the first stage helped to incorporate the conflict analysis into the scoping of the fieldwork, retaining a conflict lens proved more challenging in practice. First, there are a number of different ways in which a conflict analysis can be used as part of an evaluation. It may simply inform the evaluation team, providing the context and ensuring that the evaluation is conducted in a conflict-sensitive manner. It can also be used to shape the evaluation questions and guide the approach of the evaluation, setting such evaluations apart from conventional forms of development evaluation. To this end, the OECD DAC guidance proposes that evaluators should test whether donors have based their actions on such a conflict analysis. For example, under the 'relevance' criterion, they should ask: 'Is the intervention based on a valid analysis of the situation of conflict and fragility? Has the intervention been flexibly adapted to updated analyses over time?' The guidance also states that: 'A thorough and up-to-date understanding of the conflict is the first step for a conflict sensitive evaluation process' (OECD 2012a: 36).

In *Aiding the Peace*, an attempt was made to take this further, and ensure that the conflict analysis was integral to the evaluation. Two conflict analyses were conducted using the Strategic Conflict Assessment (SCA) method (Goodhand et al. 2002). The first of these aimed to capture what well-informed donors could or should have understood in 2005 (reflecting to a large extent the findings of the Joint Assessment Mission (JAM), which became a key framework for aid planning). The JAM did not itself contain a conflict analysis as such, but rather a contextual overview. There was, however, considerable convergence in the literature about the factors underlying conflict in South Sudan. For instance, Johnson's comprehensive *The Root Causes of Sudan's Civil Wars* (Johnson 2003) informed many subsequent analyses. The evaluation's first conflict analysis relied solely on evidence readily available at the time, and to a large extent written into key background documents used by donors. As such, there was reasonable consensus (both at the time and now) about the material from which the first conflict analysis was drawn. It should be pointed out however, that greater weight ultimately was put on the second (contemporary) conflict analysis because it incorporated an understanding of conflict dynamics that emerged particularly since 2008 and have had a profound effect on the operational environment since then.

The second conflict analysis focused on an updated (2010) understanding of conflict factors in relation to South Sudan and the extent to which donors had adapted to the changing situation over time. It was based on a summary of the literature (including Vaux et al. 2008; Thomas 2009; DESTIN 2010; UN Security Council 2010) that was corroborated through a workshop of leading experts on conflict in South Sudan. This was used to help address one of the key problems of evaluations, as noted in the draft OECD DAC guidance, that donors cannot be expected to have the full benefit of hindsight. One could not simply apply a 2010 analysis to programmes planned in 2005. On the other hand, donors could be reasonably expected to adapt and change their programmes on the basis of regular (or continuous) analysis. This was rarely done; several of the larger integrated programmes were of three to five years' duration, with little evidence of updating analysis or adapting to new realities on the ground.

Where it worked best, the evaluation's conflict analyses informed both the selection of the 'working hypotheses' for testing in the field, and led to findings that would not necessarily have emerged when evaluating an intervention within its own terms (and objectives). For instance, the conflict analysis highlighted that violence was exacerbated by the frustration of few postwar employment opportunities. The civil war had a profound impact, especially on young men. Their lives have been disrupted by warfare and now, when they may want to get married, the bride price (in cattle) has increased. Plus, at least locally, their traditional means of acquiring cattle, mainly through relatives, had declined (with so many relatives killed and so much cattle lost). This tended to propel young men towards criminal activity, including cattle raiding, especially with the availability of small arms. In this way, the conflict analysis helped to inform the evaluation of donor interventions, and focus attention on the extent to which alternative livelihood programmes for young men were aligned to the disarmament process. Through our focus group discussions in the field, we found that the short-term settlement 'package' given under the Disarmament, Demobilisation and Reintegration programme was inconsistently followed up with viable employment opportunities for young men. This may not have surfaced so readily in a more orthodox approach to evaluation that would have posited underemployment as a 'perennial problem' rather than an urgent factor contributing towards conflict.

Another conclusion emanating from the conflict analysis relates to the importance of identifying the individual political motivations of the 'spoilers' of peace, and separating these from the underlying root causes (economic deprivation, historically rooted ethnic mistrust). South Sudan demonstrates the disproportionate influence exerted by certain 'strong men' who aim to disrupt the peacebuilding process because of local allegiances or personal interests. It is in the interests of these men to provoke conflict so as to maintain prestige and influence in their area. A conflict analysis should identify such 'individual' issues, especially at local levels, because a broad-brush socioeconomic analysis may miss these dynamics.

In other areas of the evaluation process however, there was a tendency for evaluators to revert back to questions derived directly from the DAC evaluation criteria (relevance, effectiveness, etc.), without sufficient regard to the underlying drivers that were unearthed by the conflict analysis – a disconnect that seems to occur when evaluators are caught between assessing performance against the achievement of objectives (objective-based evaluation), rather than against the underlying driver or cause of the conflict.

For example, the assessment of capacity-building focused primarily on the Capacity Building Trust Fund (CBTF), which was created in 2004 to support the Sudan Peoples' Liberation Movement (SPLM) transition to government through capacity-building measures, as well as to support to SPLM operating expenses and private sector development projects. While this analysis was intended to be illustrative of how capacity-building was understood and being addressed since the signing of the CPA – and how it supported key GoSS staff and functions – in reality the evaluation team focused more on assessing the CBTF within its own terms. This included a focus on the CBTF in terms of its impact, effectiveness and efficiency – showing some evidence that the CBTF was appreciated for its flexibility and ability to quickly fund projects and activities, but with little evidence of capacity enhancement and impact (in part due to a lack of specified objectives and indicators to assess performance). There were other capacity-building programmes, interventions and activities operating in South Sudan,[18] and the evaluation missed the more strategic questions around whether the landscape of donor capacity support had focused too much on the central institutions of GoSS and not enough on building up democracy in states (and perhaps counties) and how this might have contributed to or otherwise affected to conflict prevention and peacebuilding.

5.2 Categories of peacebuilding: organising or analytical framework?

The challenge of retaining a conflict lens throughout the evaluation – and by all evaluators – raises further questions about what constitutes an appropriate framework for such a complex topic as the prevention of violent conflict or peace efforts. Conflict prevention and peacebuilding do not exist as distinct sectors of activities or even as recognised policy goals, but rather represent the influence of various types of interventions. The draft OECD DAC guidance (OECD 2008), drawing on the so-called Utstein palette, provided a list of four interrelated categories of conflict prevention and peacebuilding activities. These categories provide a sense of the wide range of activities that might be considered in a peacebuilding and conflict prevention evaluation even though they are not explicitly labelled as such in their objectives. In *Aiding the Peace*, these categories were used to identify the range of activities that donors thought could contribute to conflict prevention and peace. If the evaluation had only concentrated on those interventions that hold the prevention of conflict or the rebuilding of peace as their main (and explicit) aim, the evaluation would have missed most of the international effort. Thus the Utstein palette proved invaluable in the early stages of the evaluation as a generic 'checklist' of areas of intervention to look at beyond socioeconomic and mediation activities.

In terms of analysing donor or GoSS strategies however, the Utstein palette proved more problematic. Hardly surprisingly, nowhere in these strategies was there explicit reference to an organising principle of peacebuilding support. There was no jointly agreed pursuit of conflict prevention and peacebuilding by donors and/or GoSS – only individual programmes that addressed some of the subcategories described in the draft OECD DAC guidance. Moreover, there was never any explicit joint goal with respect to working 'on conflict'. Broadly speaking, the consensus among donors (wrongly, as it turned out) was that South Sudan was 'post-conflict', and therefore relatively few programmes intentionally tried to impact upon conflict or peace in a direct sense. For this reason (in part at least), the Utstein palette did not provide a useful analytical framework in the latter stages of the evaluation.[19] Indeed, the palette itself has no such utility as there is no underlying conceptual basis to link categories and pillars, and which can be used to determine sequencing and prioritisation. At best it is a non-exclusive checklist of key sectors.

In short, the palette is not an analytical framework as such, but provides a descriptive means that can be used to define the scope of the conflict prevention and peacebuilding activities being evaluated. Indeed, in almost all contexts (including South Sudan) several new categories could be added to the palette that would render it inoperable as a comparative tool with other countries. Evaluative judgement is better served by the analysis of the conflict, and the identification of those elements that would help donors and agencies have an influence on its course. *Aiding the Peace* thus adopted a 'conflict lens' through which to explore the extent to which programmes have been conflict sensitive, and how different categories of assistance combine to contribute to an overall effect.

5.3 Hidden theories of change

The concept of 'theories of change' has had a meteoric rise in recent years, although it clearly draws on much earlier work on the use of programme theory in evaluations (Weiss 1972; Rogers et al. 2000). There is little consensus in the literature about what constitutes a theory of change (Stern et al. 2012), with some seeing it as another form of logic model, and others taking the view that it is more a 'way of thinking' and something that should not be too prescriptive (Vogel 2012). For the purposes of the evaluation, a programme theory was viewed as an explicit theory or model of how a programme is intended to produce stated outcomes and impacts, and the factors affecting or determining its success (Bamberger et al. 2006). The OECD DAC guidance on evaluating peacebuilding argues that, 'Developing a sound, clear, evidence-based theory of change is one potentially useful way to improve design. Theory of change thinking is an approach that encourages critical thinking throughout the programme cycle' (OECD 2012a: 29). The guidance argues that when conducting an evaluation, the evaluator should ascertain the theories of change of the peacebuilding intervention in question:

> A theory of change can take different forms at different levels. Theories of change at the country and conflict levels may be quite general – for example, strengthening the capacity of the government will help improve governance and therefore reduce conflict and violence…Evaluations of specific projects or programme would be likely to formulate more directly causal theories of change which link specific inputs and activities to desired micro-level outcomes and to broader peace dynamics.
>
> (OECD 2012a: 59)

In *Aiding the Peace*, the evaluation found that rarely did donor activities articulate a clear theory of change in relation to conflict prevention or peacebuilding objectives. For the most part this was implicit only: the intervention was 'a contribution towards establishing the peace' or a 'peace dividend'. Missing from such assertions was a baseline analysis or a set of indicators predicated on the notion that the intervention would move us from conflict to post-conflict in a measurable way. This was especially true at the policy or strategy level, where documents were often vague or deliberately left open to broad interpretation (sometimes due to political sensitivities), and was further compounded by the strategic nature of the evaluation; it was assessing the combined effect of more than 2,000 interventions over a five-year period, rather than conducting a project evaluation of a single intervention. At the end of the first evaluation stage, the 'working hypotheses' approach proved to be a useful way to address this issue, by combining findings from the conflict analysis, portfolio review, etc., with a more theoretical understanding of the underlying assumptions of aid in South Sudan. This led to a more strategic set of hypotheses, which avoided becoming overly focused on any one intervention in isolation.

One such example is the dominant paradigm that a lack of development and services translates into a major cause of conflict – and without the 'peace dividend', conflict would flare up. While local conflict arises from disputes over access to resources, these tend to escalate because of either historical factors or political manipulation. Lack of development in South Sudan might, at most, be a cause of disaffection that contributes to tensions in some cases, but it cannot be cited as either a sole or significant cause of conflict. In our fieldwork in Jonglei State, for instance, we mapped the (increasing) number of reported violent incidents over a two-year period. We further noted that Jonglei had, in that same period, received increasing amounts of aid (greater than in neighbouring states) and an increase in the number of NGOs on the ground delivering assistance. By contrast, the relatively aid-neglected neighbouring states were subject to fewer violent incidents. There are many different reasons for the occurrence of violence in one area as opposed to another, but it does underline a salient feature of the conflict/aid nexus in South Sudan: there appears to have been no correlation between the quantity of services delivered and the incidence and intensity of violence.

There is nothing particularly revelatory about this conclusion, but it does highlight how easily donors slip into the 'comfort zone' of assuming that all interventions are necessarily a contribution to peace, therefore removing the urgency to prioritise and sequence their interventions. All subsequent events in South Sudan confirm one of the conclusions of the evaluation – that the reform of the security sector and disarmament of renegade groups was a prerequisite to any degree of stability that would make social service interventions viable. Yet many donors continued the 'business as usual' model underpinned by a loosely applied discourse around post-conflict, rehabilitation or recovery, often without any specific contextual or conflict analysis.

The evaluation also demonstrated the difficulties of measuring results from a group of rather elusive theories of change. In particular there are difficulties when donor strategies and policies are deliberately vague (for institutional and political reasons) about underlying assumptions and theories, and the very objective of peacebuilding support is not clearly acknowledged in the programming processes. While the evaluator can attempt to reconstruct the underlying theory behind such documents, it can, in some cases, expose the evaluator to making assumptions which cannot be verified – because the strategy was essentially a document of compromise or consensus, or because key individuals driving the process have since moved on. We should, however, acknowledge that applying a retroactive and generic theory of change can still be useful as an evaluative tool, for it provides a putative framework and logic against which to judge performance beyond just immediate outcomes.

5.4 The evaluation process

The Steering Committee for *Aiding the Peace* comprised representatives of 15 key donors to South Sudan. Some were from their respective evaluation departments, others from programme departments. The committee met on four occasions, with open email contact with the evaluators in between. The formal process of comments – on the inception report, first phase report and final report – was mediated through a core group of four agencies chaired by the evaluation department of the Ministry of Foreign Affairs in the Netherlands.

Despite there being comprehensive Terms of Reference and a concept paper prepared in advance, there was a lack of consensus within the Steering Committee over the approach, particularly in the early stage of the evaluation. Different views were expressed over whether a 'conflict lens' should be rigorously applied retrospectively, or whether projects should be assessed against their own objectives. The debate was perhaps not helped by the lack of clarity over whether the evaluation should be assessing the impact of the totality of interventions on 'peace writ large' or purely in terms of the peacebuilding merits of individual donor programmes. The former approach would have accepted 'conventional' programmes on their own merit whereas the latter would have unpacked individual donor intentions and programmes and reviewed them through a conflict lens.

These differences persisted throughout the 12 months of the evaluation with the formalised process allowing limited space for methodological refinement and a rather open-ended discussion that allowed certain issues to dominate in meetings even though they may not have been the most important ones. The process was chaired very fairly and diligently, but the evaluation team was left having to defend their chosen approach (outlined above) in the absence of a clear consensus. In the latter phases of the evaluation, newly arrived representatives argued, without reference to the interim discussions, for a return to the original Terms of Reference and (in one instance) a wholly different approach that used the Utstein palette as an analytical framework and prism through which all findings should be viewed.

The lengthy 'tail end' of the process involved commenting and revision based on hundreds of unfiltered comments from the Steering Committee. The evaluation team, now reduced to just two to three members (since much of the team had moved on to other assignments), found that much of this refinement process was a continuing dialogue with donor representatives. To the credit of Netherlands MFA, the independence of the evaluation team was defended and a coherent document was produced. Nevertheless, about six months of the 12-month evaluation timeline was spent in dialogue with the Steering Committee rather than with the original full team or with South Sudan interlocutors.

The important lesson here is that the process of finalising a report can itself influence findings, yet methodologically this final commentary and advisory process is rarely taken into account. Most of the current debate in evaluation focuses on methods of the evaluation alone (Picciotto 2012; Stern et al. 2012), rather than the process surrounding the evaluation research. In this case, however, we found that the final stage of the evaluation was equally important; it was in the final negotiations with the steering group that the nuanced language and general tenor of the report emerged.

6 Concluding remarks

This chapter demonstrates a number of strengths behind the methodological approach taken in the *Aiding the Peace* evaluation. First, the iterative, two-stage approach to the evaluation provided a strong evidence-base upon which to select the locations and interventions to be reviewed in the field assessments – something that also reduced the dependency of the evaluation on primary data collection that could be disrupted due to the very real security and logistical constraints of operating in South Sudan. In particular, the focus on published and unpublished literature and other evidence gave a logical sequence to the assessment: the *conflict analysis* (assessing the 'problem' in terms of the drivers of the conflict), the *analysis of donor strategies* (assessing donor response to the conflict, or problem), the *aid portfolio analysis* (donor interventions in response to strategic priorities), and the *evaluation review* (synthesising the results and impacts of these interventions).

Secondly, this evidence base enabled the development of a number of working hypotheses – a useful tool for bringing together the conflict analysis and other studies around themes where there are gaps in knowledge, or areas where field assessments could be used to provide depth or corroborate findings. It also provided a means to retain the essentially strategic focus of the evaluation (by using higher level hypotheses that went across several interventions or sectors).

Third, the field visits, individual projects, programmes or instruments mainly selected using criteria of how best they could help ground-truth these hypotheses. This helped to provide a framework for synthesising the field-level assessments, by avoiding ending up with lots of individual project evaluations that are difficult to aggregate – especially since any sample would have been so small that it would not have been possible to undertake a more mechanistic meta-evaluation approach. The process of selection was, nevertheless, problematic since it relied on three key variables – the 'flashpoints' of conflict (mentioned above), access and the availability of project staff and recipients. Thus, many older projects could not be sampled, and the use of a 'control' group (non-recipient) was, under challenging access constraints, only occasionally possible. The sample of projects was, then, purposive and not necessarily representative. This is precisely why the triangulation and confirmation of findings through extensive consultation in Juba was so important. It should also be borne in mind that with an evaluation team of 15 persons on the ground, any 'singularity' finding was likely to be countered from within the team by other stakeholders.

Nevertheless, without a thorough understanding of the dynamics of conflict and the political economy of low-intensity warfare (which continues to this day in South Sudan), any evaluation will miss the big picture. One answer is to incorporate conflict analysis as the analytical tool into the evaluation itself. In some respects this would be a dialectic process: the Terms of Reference presented by the client on 'big questions' would be refined and narrowed by a conflict analysis. The hypotheses emerging from the conflict analysis would then give direction to, and a set of priority questions for, the evaluation.

Arguably, the three strengths of the evaluation cited above could also be weaknesses, for they depend upon a level of contextual knowledge not always available to external evaluation teams. Evaluation is not only about obtaining inviolable 'evidence' – rarely found in a fluid conflict-ridden environment. It also depends heavily on informed judgement about that evidence. On more than one occasion the evaluation team were accused of elaborating evidence with 'expert analysis'; but the expert knowledge counterbalanced some evidence presented by agency staff who only very recently had arrived in the country and had an even weaker factual base to support their positions.

Since the conflict analysis is actually part of the evaluation, the findings cannot be predicted or pre-empted when writing the original Terms of Reference. When the conflict analysis however becomes part of an extended inception phase, evidence from the analysis can be used to reach agreement on the scope of the evaluation. The implications are that both client and evaluator accept a fairly open-ended Terms of Reference at the outset, subject to refinement backed by a clearly argued rationale drawn from the conflict analysis.

Too often, evaluators tend to revert back to the familiar OECD DAC evaluation criteria, rather than focusing on how to assess relevance, effectiveness, and impact against the drivers of the conflict. The risk is that evaluators overly focus on the achievement of the objectives of an intervention, rather than the ability of the intervention to address drivers of the conflict (the underlying problem). A crucial element of a conflict analysis is the emerging hypotheses: if the situation is 'X', and the way to address it is 'Y', then to what extent is the intervention cognisant of, and designed to address, this? The difficulty – and one that emerged in the evaluation under consideration here – is that one is judging the actor (donor) against a set of criteria developed by a conflict analysis in which the donor did not participate.

Finally, we highlight how the consultation process over the final document (in this case with a large number of interested donor parties) can itself influence the evaluation findings. Defending the independence of the evaluators and ensuring that the panel of donor commentators is clear about the boundaries of their influence over the final product is critical to ensuring a credible evaluation process. Another important dimension is addressing the extent to which consultants – especially those who have worked extensively in the country concerned – might themselves have biased views. Crucially, evaluation literature to date has given relatively little attention to the tail-end of the process when findings are refined, consolidated and prioritised into recommendations. It is our belief that this final phase of the evaluation is of utmost importance and merits further analysis.

To conclude, *Aiding the Peace* was an evaluation conducted in the midst of an evolving conflict environment. It challenged donors to accept that there are certain sectors – security, policing and rule of law – where international support may have been of greater priority than basic services. This was not only because of the importance of these functions in the formation of a legitimate state, but also for the reason (often stated by government and community respondents) that the effectiveness and sustainability of basic services were compromised by insecurity. In dynamic conflict settings, an analysis of the political economy of the transition from war to peace must be continuously revised. The evaluation was imperfect, reflecting the difficulty of choosing an evaluation design where there are many contending interests at stake. However, methodologically it raised important questions over the assumed causal link between delivering services and abating violence. If, as in the case of South Sudan, this link was not apparent, the evaluation at least contributed towards developing an alternative paradigm.

Notes

1 See also Chapter 8 in this book.
2 An introduction to some of these concepts is contained in Chapters 2 and 9 in this book.

Critical reflections on the South Sudan evaluation of conflict   57

3 A conflict analysis can be defined as 'the systematic study of the profile, causes, actors, and dynamics of conflict' (APFO et al. 2004). There is a diverse set of tools for undertaking a conflict analysis, with six highlighted by the OECD (2012a).
4 Figures for the UNDP human development index exist for Sudan, but not yet for South Sudan.
5 The oil wells were shut down from January 2012 as a result of disputes between Sudan and South Sudan over pipeline fees.
6 The point was frequently made to the evaluation team by donors based in Khartoum.
7 Interestingly, some of the more effective programmes were bilateral, pointing to important factors such as presence of international staff on the ground for extended periods (who were able to adapt more quickly to a changing context).
8 These were relevance, effectiveness, impact, sustainability, efficiency and the additional criteria of coherence, coordination, linkages and coverage (OECD 2008).
9 A fully comprehensive review of progress in supporting conflict prevention and peacebuilding should also examine the adequacy, or otherwise, of diplomatic initiatives in relation to Khartoum and the Government of South Sudan (GoSS). This was however outside the remit of the evaluation, although the evaluation does comment on the link between political and aid efforts of the Joint Donor Team (JDT), and in relation to Khartoum-based initiatives with respect to the Three Areas and to the political economy of oil.
10 These were mostly literature reviews of published and unpublished papers, statistical datasets and the internal documents from various aid agencies – with some aspects corroborated through stakeholder interviews.
11 Creditor Reporting System (aid activity database).
12 The focus here is on the process of gathering evidence, rather than other potential biases introduced by 'expert judgement' during the interpretation and presentation of findings. In this way, it is not argued that the experience of the evaluation team is inherently more important than the views of various interlocutors, but rather that their longer-term experience and expert knowledge of a country provides another source of triangulation. So for example, whereas an inexperienced team may have triangulated the views of several short-term UN, NGO or government staff to reproduce a 'received wisdom', a more experienced team member is able to probe more deeply; to uncover the premise of an individual's views and knowledge base (such as whether it is based on a specific research, a generally held agency view or a factual inaccuracy).
13 Financial, time and travel constraints meant that, for instance, the team was bound to UN flight times and days. The choice could have been made to have a smaller team for a longer period in fewer locations, but in the end seven of ten states were visited, even if not 'covered' extensively.
14 While it is difficult to judge how strategically relevant the evaluation was, informal feedback suggests that many of the findings of the evaluation had greater resonance with the policy departments and programmes of major donors – rather than the evaluation departments.
15 This was an internal document entitled, *Hypotheses from Stage 1 (Extracts from Stage 1 Report)*, 2010.
16 The palette was modified and agreed to by members of the DAC Networks at a workshop in Oslo in 2006, and is based on the 'Utstein palette' in Smith (2004).
17 This is the strong perception among both government officials and local people interviewed. We note, however, that it has not been an overall trend. Lakes State, for example, saw a relative decline in assistance when the capital moved from Rumbek to Juba.
18 Other programmes that specifically targeted capacity building include: MDTF's Capacity Building, Institutional and HR Development (CABIHRD) programme, SEADGOSS, Capacity Building for GoSS, the CBTF, Skills for Sudan, UNDP's Local Government Recovery Programme financed from the Strategic Partnership Fund (SPA), and UNDP's States Support Programme.

19 This is despite pressure from some members of the evaluation's steering group to use the palette in this way.

Bibliography

APFO et al. (2004) *Conflict-sensitive Approaches to Development, Humanitarian Assistance and Peacebuilding: A Resource Pack*, APFO, CECORE, CHA, FEWER, International Alert, and Saferworld. www.conflictsensitivity.org/publications/conflict-sensitive-approaches-development-humanitarian-assistance-and-peacebuilding-res, accessed 24 May 2013.

Bamberger, M., Rugh, J. and Mabry, L. (2006) *Real World Evaluation: Working Under Budget, Time, Data and Political Constraints*, 1st edn, Thousand Oaks: Sage Publications.

Bennett, J., Kluyskens, J., Morton, J. and Poate, D. (2009) *Mid-Term Evaluation of the Joint Donor Team in Juba, Sudan*, conducted by ITAD, Oslo: Norad Evaluation Report.

Bennett, J., Pantuliano, S., Fenton, W., Vaux, A., Barnett, C. and Brusset, E. (2010) *Aiding the Peace: A Multi-Donor Evaluation of Support to Conflict Prevention and Peacebuilding Activities in Southern Sudan 2005–2010*, Hove: ITAD Ltd.

DESTIN (2010) *Southern Sudan at Odds with Itself: Dynamics of Conflict and Predicaments of Peace*, London: London School of Economics/DESTIN.

DFID (2008) *Justice and Police Development Programme, 2008/9–2012/13, Project Memorandum, 15 October 2008*, Khartoum: Department for International Development (DFID).

Gamble, J. A. A. (2008) *A Developmental Evaluation Primer*, Victoria, BC: The J.W. McConnell Family Foundation.

Goodhand, J., Vaux, T. and Walker, R. (2002) *Conducting Conflict Assessments – Guidance Notes*, London: Department for International Development (DFID).

GoSS (2010) *Donor Book 2010*, Juba: Ministry of Finance and Economic Planning, Government of Southern Sudan.

Grävingholt, J., Leininger, J. and von Haldenwang, C. (2012) *Effective Statebuilding? A Review of Evaluations of International Statebuilding Support in Fragile Contexts*, Evaluation Study, June 2012, Copenhagen: Danida, Ministry of Foreign Affairs.

Johnson, D. H. (2003) *The Root Causes of the Sudan's Civil Wars*, Oxford, Bloomington and Kampala: International African Institute.

MoFA (2009) *Terms of Reference: Multi-Donor Evaluation of Support to Conflict Prevention and Peacebuilding Activities in Southern Sudan, 2005–2009*, The Hague: Policy and Operations Evaluation Department of the Netherlands Ministry of Foreign Affairs (MoFA).

OECD (2000) *Effective Practices in Conducting a Multi-Donor Evaluation*, Evaluation and Aid Effectiveness Paper 4, Paris: OECD DAC Working Party on Aid Evaluation.

——(2005 and 2008) *The Paris Declaration on Aid Effectiveness and the Accra Agenda for Action*, Paris: OECD Development Assistance Committee. www.oecd.org/dac/effectiveness/34428351.pdf, accessed 13 May 2013.

——(2008) *Guidance On Evaluating Conflict Prevention and Peacebuilding Activities – Working Draft For Application Period*. Paris: OECD. www.oecd.org/dac/evaluation/dcdndep/39774573.pdf, accessed 3 March 2013.

——(2012a) *Evaluating Peacebuilding Activities in Settings of Conflict and Fragility: Improving Learning for Results*, DAC Guidelines and Reference Series, Paris: OECD Publishing, doi: 10.1787/9789264106802-en

—— (2012b) *Fragile States 2013: Resource Flows and Trends in a Shifting World*, International Network on Conflict and Fragility. Paris: OECD Publishing. www.oecd.org/dac/incaf/FragileStates2013.pdf, accessed 23 May 2013.

Paffenholz, T. (2011) *Peacebuilding Evaluation: Assessing the Relevance and Effectiveness of Peacebuilding Initiatives: Lessons Learned from Testing New Approaches and Methodologies*, paper presented for the Annual Convention of the International Studies Association, Montreal, 16 March.

Patton, M. Q. (2010) *Developmental Evaluation: Applying Complexity Concepts to Enhance Innovation and Use*, New York: Guildford Publications.

Picciotto, R. (2012) 'Experimentalism and Development Evaluation: Will the Bubble Burst?', *Evaluation* 18(2): 213–229.

Rogers, P., Petrosino, A., Huebner, T. and Hacsi, T. (2000) 'Program Theory Evaluation: Practice, Promise, and Problems', *New Directions for Evaluation* 87: 5–13.

Scanteam (2007) *Review of Post-Crisis Country Multi Donor Trust Funds*, Final Report and Annexes, commissioned by World Bank, Norwegian Ministry of Foreign Affairs, and Norad in cooperation with CIDA, Netherlands Ministry of Foreign Affairs and DFID, Oslo: Scanteam.

Smith, D. (2004) *Towards a Strategic Framework for Peacebuilding: Getting their Act Together. Overview Report of the Joint Utstein Study of Peacebuilding*, Oslo: Royal Norwegian Ministry of Foreign Affairs.

Stern, E., Stame, N., Mayne, J., Forss, K., Davies, R. and Befani, B. (2012) *Developing a Broader Range of Rigorous Designs and Methods for Impact Evaluations*, report of a study commissioned by the Department for International Development (DFID), London: Department for International Development. www.dfid.gov.uk/Documents/.../design-method-impact-eval.pdf, accessed 26 March 2013.

Thomas, E. (2009) *Against the Gathering Storm – Securing Sudan's Comprehensive Peace Agreement*, London: Chatham House.

UNDP (2013) *Human Development Report 2013 – The Rise of the South: Human Progress in a Diverse World*, New York: United Nations Development Programme.

UN Security Council (2010) *Report of the Secretary-General on the United Nations Mission in Sudan*, New York: Security Council S/2010/168, April 2010.

van Beijnum, M. and Hemmer, J. (2009) *Approach Paper for a Multi-donor Evaluation of Conflict Prevention and Peacebuilding Activities in Southern Sudan, 2005–2008*, The Hague: Policy and Operations Evaluation Department of the Netherlands Ministry of Foreign Affairs

Vaux, T., Pantuliano, S. and Srinivasan, S. (2008) *Stability and Development in the Three Areas*, Report for the Steering Group (Draft), London: Department for International Development.

Vogel, I. (2012) *Review of the Use of 'Theory of Change' in International Development*, Review Report, April 2012, London: Department for International Development.

Weiss, C. H. (1972) *Evaluation Research: Methods of Assessing Program Effectiveness*, Englewood Cliffs, NJ: Prentice Hall.

White, H. (2010) 'A Contribution to Current Debates in Impact Evaluation', *Evaluation* 16(2): 153–164.

Willitts-King, B., Mowjee, T. and Barham, J. (2007) *Evaluation of Common/Pooled Humanitarian Funds (CHF) in DRC and Sudan*, December 2007, New York and Geneva: OCHA ESS.

Woodrow, P. and Chigas, D. (2011) 'Connecting the Dots: Evaluating Whether and How Programmes Address Conflict Systems', in D. Körppen et al. (eds) *The Non-Linearity of Peace Processes – Theory and Practice of Systemic Conflict Transformation*, pp. 205–28. www.berghof-peacesupport.org/books/sct_book_2011_Woodrow.pdf, accessed March 2013.

Woodrow, P., Moore, C. W., Reinhard, I. and Aeberhard, P. (2008) *The Berghof Foundation in Sri Lanka: Resource Network for Conflict Transformation: Lessons Learned Evaluation Report*, Berlin: The Berghof Foundation.

4 Battlefields of method

Evaluating Norwegian peace efforts in Sri Lanka

Jonathan Goodhand
SOAS

Bart Klem
Zürich University

Gunnar M. Sørbø
Chr. Michelsen Institute

1 Introduction

From 1999 to 2009, Norway was involved as 'sole facilitator' of the Sri Lankan peace process. Negotiations ultimately broke down, leading to a return to full-scale war which ended with the military victory by the Sri Lankan army over the Liberation Tigers of Tamil Eelam (LTTE) in May 2009. An evaluation was commissioned by the Evaluation Department of the Norwegian Agency for Development Co-operation (Norad) in 2010 to tell the story of Norway's engagement, assess the effects and identify broader implications and lessons. This was the first Norwegian evaluation to be commissioned in the area of peace diplomacy, which has become one of the most distinctive aspects of Norwegian foreign policy.

Somewhat provocatively, our evaluation report, published in November 2011, was entitled *Pawns of Peace* (Goodhand et al. 2011a). We borrowed and adapted the title of Harriet Martin's book on peace making, *Kings of Peace, Pawns of War* (2006) in order to make the point that peace mediators are often minor players in a much larger game.

Analysts who evaluate peace efforts, it might be added, are also part of 'the game'; just as mediators enter into intensely politicised and contested environments, so do evaluators. Evaluating attempts to resolve conflict involves grappling with competing and partial interpretations of complex processes. As with all forms of historical assessments that call for explicit evaluation of events and policies, there is clearly a need for a systematic and robust methodology, but peace evaluation can never be reduced to a technical exercise. Evaluators inevitably get sucked into the politics surrounding conflict and intervention, and run the risk of becoming 'pawns', just like peace mediators. In this chapter we aim to explore both the methodological and political challenges associated with the evaluation of peace efforts in Sri Lanka, and we will argue that the two sets of challenges are inseparable.

Unlike most other chapters in this book, the primary focus is not on development cooperation in support of peacebuilding. Rather, our evaluation encompassed a wider range of international interventions, including diplomacy, ceasefire monitoring as well as aid. Although aid provision – which included high-profile donor pledging conferences and efforts to bring about collaboration through joint aid mechanisms – was an important part of the international strategy to support the peace process, development cooperation was not at the centre of our evaluation. The peace process, and the Norwegian role within it, was largely determined by politics and not by the provision or withholding of aid.[1] This explains the analytical focus of the evaluation and also of this chapter.

The chapter starts with a discussion of the research literature on peace processes and its relevance to the design and practice of evaluating such efforts. We then provide a brief overview of Norway's peace efforts in Sri Lanka, followed by an exploration of the methodological challenges and how we attempted to deal with them. We then tell the story of how our evaluation evolved in practice, dividing its implementation into three chronological phases. The concluding section draws on our experience in Sri Lanka to suggest some broader implications.

2 The challenge of evaluating peace efforts

2.1 Social science challenges: structure, agency and uncertainty

The quantitative literature on mediation provides a rather mixed picture on the efficacy of external mediation (Sarkees 2000; Dixon 2009; Licklider 2009). Historically, most wars ended through military victory rather than through a mediated settlement, and one body of research has found that conflicts terminated through a negotiated settlement had a higher level of recidivism (cf. Stedman 1997; Licklider 2009). Another, growing body of quantitative research finds that peace settlements are becoming more 'sticky', identifying a positive correlation between external intervention and sustainable peace (Doyle and Sambanis 2006; Human Security Centre 2005, 2010; Fortna 2004). This literature does not provide a clear explanatory account about what works or does not work in relation to peace processes, but it does have value in pointing to some of the key structural variables that shape civil war termination, while also giving the evaluator (and peace mediator) a useful reminder that peace processes frequently fail.

One has to turn to the more qualitative literature, including case studies, in order to gain insights about peace mediation in practice and capture the specificity and contingency of individual contexts and interventions. This literature explores the 'how to' of mediation. Much of this work is concerned with extracting lessons from analyses of particular peace processes. The analytical focus tends to be on the design of peace negotiations, the question of timing and 'ripe' moments, the necessary inclusion and sequencing of key conflict issues, dealing with information asymmetries and security dilemmas, the role of incentives and disincentives, and spoiler management strategies (Stedman 1997; Regan 2002; Zartman 2000, 2009). Much of this literature is informed by rational choice models that assume that individual agents make rational calculations and choices and that the decision-making of elite actors is a key determinant of 'success' or 'failure'. Mediation, in this sense, is about negotiating a complex 'prisoners' dilemma'. Protagonists can 'choose' peace over war, if mediators deploy the right combination of (dis)incentives. Therefore a significant role is ascribed to individual agents, including peace mediators.

One of the implications of this perspective is that the failure of peace negotiations can be traced back to flawed decision-making processes, the incorrect deployment of carrots and sticks, the failure to grasp opportunities and so forth. Also this approach is based upon a teleological understanding of war to peace transitions – events, processes and actors are judged in relation to the desired outcome (a negotiated settlement), leading to assessments about whether they are for or against peace and more broadly whether the peace process is moving 'forwards' or 'backwards' (Klem 2012). While, like the quantitative research, this literature yields some important insights, it has some major weaknesses. First the rational-actor model is largely blind to non-material, symbolic and collective factors that influence and shape individual decision-making in peace processes. Second, by ascribing such an important role to agency, the significance of wider structural factors is downplayed. This leads to unrealistic expectations about what mediators can be expected to achieve and be held accountable for. Just because a peace process fails, for instance, does not necessarily mean that mediators made the 'wrong' decisions or failed to deploy their resources optimally.

The rational-actor perspective is particularly questionable in the case of non-coercive mediators such as Norway, with only limited means to persuade protagonists to change their course of action. The stakes and interests vested in protracted warfare often outweigh the instruments of international actors, who of course have their own sets of interests. Therefore, although one should not deny the role of agency, particularly during peace processes when institutions may be in a state of flux, the wider structures place considerable constraints on both mediators and protagonists. Many after-the-event accounts of peace processes tend to 'write agency back in'. Yet unless done in a balanced and critical way, this may obscure the complex, messy reality of peace processes in which actors are always partially sighted; they are responding to events rather than shaping them – in other words making it up as they go along – and they are often severely constrained by wider power structures.

Therefore, while the research literature on peace processes and peace settlements provides useful insights to the evaluator, there are also limitations that need to be borne in mind. There is no definitive theory in this field to guide action. Existing theory at best provides general guidance, rather than clear prescriptions, for both practitioners and evaluators (Stern and Druckman 2000). The most obvious yet important point, therefore, is to take contextual diversity seriously. Peace processes take place in particular contexts at particular moments in history and universal prescriptions and approaches have limited value. For the evaluator, this means that the foundation for any credible assessment must start with a robust political economy analysis of the context.

2.2 Political challenges: contested narratives, expressions of power

Like any other policy-oriented research, research on peace efforts is not detached from the field it claims to study. While it may be conventional wisdom that sound policies must be 'evidence-based', it is also true that the relationship between research and policy may run in the opposite direction, in the sense that policy priorities can shape the kinds of evidence and findings generated by research. Evidence may be drawn upon selectively or manipulated to support a particular policy narrative, a phenomenon that Cramer and Goodhand (2011) call 'policy based evidence'. Policy priorities shape the kind of research that is done and determine what questions are considered relevant. Policymakers may also be under pressure to make selective use of scholarly literature to legitimise or de-politicise certain policies. This phenomenon is reinforced when research findings are heterogeneous or contradictory, as is often the case.

This is particularly true for evaluations, whether of peace efforts or other activities, which are commissioned by intervening institutions. Of course, the formal rationale for evaluations is to provide a critical, independent view. Evaluators are expected to serve a watchdog role, assessing policy outcomes and questioning policy dogmas. However, evaluations are shaped by the mandate set by the commissioning agency. In order to be relevant, evaluators need to adapt themselves to the policy logics and institutional practices they are studying. Evaluations are to some extent political instruments that serve to legitimise policies and their impacts by packaging and presenting them in particular ways. They capture messy realities in a 'scientifically' endorsed narrative. They make sense of institutions and interventions, even if they criticise them. Evaluations are thus not simply instruments of empirical verification, they 'do political work', and as such are expressions of power.

This point is elaborated and developed in a much wider (broadly Foucauldian) literature on development, state rule and neo-liberal assemblages (cf. Duffield 2007). For example, James Ferguson's (1990) seminal work on the 'anti-politics machine' argues that development interventions tend to obfuscate the deeply political interests that they promote, by breaking things down into bureaucratic units, projects, and categories. They render technical what is in fact very political (Li 2007). Evaluations of peace or development interventions may be seen in a similar light. They provide coherent narratives of policy and practice, thus reducing messy realities to manageable proportions, and lend themselves to political usage; to legitimise or de-legitimise particular courses of action. This does not mean that evaluations necessarily become 'scientific' smokescreens for political actions – after all, technical narratives often invoke counter-narratives – but it recognises that evaluations operate in political force fields that affect their methodological approaches and outcomes. This applies to all varieties of policy research,[2] yet peace evaluations are likely to be particularly vulnerable to such pressures because it may be more difficult (although not impossible) to 'render peace technical', given the fact that it so obviously touches upon critical political issues related to security and sovereignty.

Evaluators of peace interventions thus unavoidably have to navigate a political arena throughout their assignment: from the discussion of Terms of Reference to the tug of war over contentious findings and last-minute rephrasing of the executive summary. Arguments about methodology and evidence-base are usually at the heart of these struggles, but the underlying reasons these issues are contentious often have more to do with vested political interests, public perceptions and bureaucratic fears of possible political fall-out. When the stakes are high, pressures are likely to increase. In this context, evaluators use similar arguments to protect their product (and the voices and convictions manifest in it) as well as their reputation, while also preserving their relations with possible future clients. Evaluation politics permeate the entire evaluation process.

Interventions in war-torn areas generate their own information economies. Information is a valuable resource, which is hoarded, manipulated and disseminated, and can literally be the difference between life and death. And the brokers operating in these information economies have to navigate numerous issues to do with the nexus of power and knowledge. Who gets to say what? Which voices are heard or suppressed? What data count as valid? What findings are considered policy-relevant? Whose truth prevails in the echelons of power? If we are to study peacebuilding evaluations as an empirical phenomenon, an acknowledgement of these forces and interests is warranted.

3 Our object of study

According to the Terms of Reference, the main purpose of our evaluation was to learn from the unique Norwegian experience as a facilitator in the peace process in Sri Lanka. More specifically, evaluation questions required us to: 1) map the Norwegian peace engagement in Sri Lanka from 1997 until 2009; 2) assess the role as facilitator between the parties on the one hand, and the relationship to the international community on the other; 3) assess the Norwegian facilitator role and the relationship to local parties and stakeholders; 4) assess the ceasefire agreement and how the parties observed it; 5) assess Norway's efforts in the last phase of the war (January–May 2009); 6) assess results achieved through the Norwegian facilitation of the peace process; and 7) draw lessons from the Norwegian engagement in the Sri Lankan peace process.

These questions did not explicitly engage with the history, roots and dynamics of armed conflict in Sri Lanka. However, given the importance of context, noted above, and to avoid an overly teleological approach that places interventions at the heart of the analysis, we decided the evaluation should not treat the rise and fall of Sri Lanka's peace process as simply a derivative of Norwegian intervention. Rather, the ambition was to review the turbulent 15 years of Sri Lankan history, and then place Norway's efforts in that historical process, to identify results and draw lessons.

Conceptually and methodologically, this is difficult. Incorporating a much wider set of issues and factors into the evaluation makes it very difficult to demarcate the scope of the study. If an understanding of Norwegian peace efforts in Sri

Lanka requires a fine-grained analysis of the evolution of the island's 'conflict system' over 15 years, including the involvement of the Norwegian mediators and other international actors, there is clearly a risk that it all becomes too much to handle, particularly within the time constraints of an evaluation. In our case this was indeed a major challenge, even if the team could draw upon prior knowledge and research.

For readers who are unfamiliar with Sri Lanka, we provide below a nutshell summary of the conflict's historical background and the past 15 years of the war in particular.

Sri Lanka's minority question has long historical roots, but became particularly pronounced in the post-colonial era (from 1948 onwards). In our understanding, the clash between Sinhala nationalism and Tamil separatism is rooted in the nature of the Sri Lankan state and the way its democratic politics played out in a multi-ethnic environment. The contention between the Sinhala (73 per cent) majority and the Tamil minority (18 per cent of which at least one quarter are so-called 'Indian Tamils') has always been most salient, but other groups – such as the Muslims (9 per cent) – have not escaped these dynamics (Moore 1985; Coomaraswamy 2003; De Silva 2005; Spencer 2008; Uyangoda 2011).[3] After several agreements on minority rights and regional autonomy were not implemented, anti-state armed violence began in the early 1980s. The LTTE subsequently emerged as the dominant Tamil faction fighting for an independent Tamil homeland in the northeast of the island. India's diplomatic and military intervention in the late 1980s resulted in renewed warfare and a further entrenchment of positions (Bullion 1995; Loganathan 1996).

It was in the wake of Indian withdrawal, in 1991, that the possibilities of a Norwegian role were first explored. But Norway was only formally invited as a 'facilitator' in 1999, from among several other candidates who had offered to play this role. Initial backchannel negotiations proved unsuccessful and it was only with the election of a new Sri Lankan government in late 2001 that a first major breakthrough was reached: the February 2002 ceasefire agreement between the government and the LTTE. The agreement was subsequently monitored by an unarmed Nordic mission. Direct talks, backed by Sri Lanka's aid donors (most prominently Japan, the European Union and the United States), soon entered an impasse. The subsequent 'no-war-no-peace' phase was characterised by a fragmented political landscape, continued violence and eroding popular support for the peace process, despite an apparent window of opportunity after the December 2004 tsunami. Finally, full-scale military offensives resumed in 2006. Sri Lanka's replenished armed forces gradually pushed back the LTTE and defeated the insurgents in May 2009, killing its entire leadership. This military victory came at the cost of an estimated 30,000 to 40,000 civilian deaths and bolstered a reform resistant government with little inclination to address the underlying ethno-political issues of the war.

A basic starting point for our analysis was to define the war in Sri Lanka as a manifestation of a deeper state crisis. This led us to analyse the changing nature of the Sri Lankan state within its global, regional and domestic settings, and to examine shifts in state–society relations over time and the role of inter- and intra-elite competition in shaping political bargains, coalitions and settlements. The rivalry between the United National Party (UNP) and the Sri Lankan Freedom Party (SLFP) concerns issues and interests that are different from the country's ethno-political crisis, but have often complicated the conflict and impeded the search for its peaceful resolution (Venugopal 2009; Uyangoda 2011). Such dynamics help explain both the continuities and shifts in Sri Lanka's political economy during the course of peace negotiations. And they help place international intervention, and specifically the role of Norway, in perspective. A political economy analysis of the Sri Lankan peace process shows the relative autonomy of domestic political elite decision-making, which limited the options for international actors. This is particularly the case where international backers are divided and when the legitimacy of, and domestic constituency for, such changes are limited (Goodhand et al. 2011b).

It is important to note that a conflict analysis also involves looking at the changing external environment before and during the course of Norway's engagement. Sri Lanka's political elite have had to balance and mediate different, sometimes competing external pressures. Other domestic actors, including the LTTE, have likewise adapted to changes in the international arena to generate political capital, gain access to resources and build their legitimacy. It is important to avoid a narrowly internal understanding of the civil war and to recognise the inter-connectedness of domestic and external dimensions.

This was the analytical starting point for the evaluation. Our analysis placed Norway's peace efforts in Sri Lanka in a broad historical perspective and showed the magnitude of the challenges the mediators faced. Drawing on this conflict analysis, we posited that a durable peace settlement would require the following elements: 1) constitutional reform; 2) some level of support for these reforms from the three largest ethnic communities (Sinhalese, Tamils, Muslims); 3) a fundamental transformation of the LTTE into an organisation able to operate in a context of democratic power-sharing; 4) addressing the rivalry between the two largest Sinhala-dominated political parties (UNP and SLFP); and 5) ensuring that the settlement would be acceptable to India. In parallel to these core political issues, there was an imperative to address immediate humanitarian issues and preserve a level of respect for human rights, both for moral reasons and to ensure the legitimacy of the settlement.

4 Methodological challenges and approach

Having provided an overview of our evaluative approach, we now turn to the core topic of this book: the methodological challenges associated with evaluating peacebuilding efforts in conflict settings. As discussed in this book, and elsewhere, these challenges are numerous (cf. Stern and Druckman 2000; OECD 2012).

First, there is the very basic question of what is the measure of 'success' or 'failure'? Because the Sri Lankan peace process broke down, does this mean that Norwegian efforts were a failure, or should other accomplishments still be valued?

Second, there is the challenge of dealing with uncertainty. Uncertainty plays a bigger role in questions of armed conflict (and peace) than is typically acknowledged by policymakers and researchers. Attempts at constructing measurable, predictive models in particular tend to inadequately approach conflict and peace processes as 'closed systems'. Conversely if one understands peace processes, like other domains of social relations, as an 'open system' this means that the same causes can have different outcomes and similar outcomes can have different causes. Furthermore, mediators in conflict settings are at a disadvantage compared to evaluators in the sense that they cannot 'postdict' (Stern and Druckman, 2000: 53) i.e., evaluators are able to make 'after the fact' assessments based upon a knowledge of outcomes. Mediators are operating with incomplete knowledge – and often information is deliberately withheld or massaged by the conflicting parties – which makes planning and prediction extremely difficult. In such a situation of uncertainty, a strategy that seemed logical at the start of a process may prove to be erroneous or lead to fatal mistakes further down the line. And yet, the fact that a particular decision had undesirable effects does not mean that this was inevitable. While evaluations usually have the benefit of hindsight,[4] they still have to grapple with the challenge of open systems and uncertainty – for example they often take place too early to judge the long-term effects of the intervention studied. With regard to Sri Lanka, the historical significance of the collapsed peace process and the subsequent military victory depends to a large extent on political developments in the years to come.

Third, and related to the problem of uncertainty, is the problem of attribution: the challenge of trying to separate out the effects of Norwegian interventions from the impacts of wider international and domestic interventions. Impact on larger scale processes can normally just be inferred rather than confirmed. Related to the attribution problem is the conceptual problem of counterfactual history. Whether a different Norwegian strategy would have resulted in different outcomes is impossible to prove. Whether the final war and military defeat of the LTTE would have occurred without the peace process is similarly difficult to judge.

Fourth, there are questions of access and secrecy. Peace efforts often require confidentiality and actors may have information which they cannot or will not reveal. Key informants may be dead, imprisoned or otherwise hard to reach.

Finally, as in all reconstructions of historical events, there is the challenge of dealing with conflicting or unreliable accounts and discourses. The narratives of key protagonists are in a sense 'scripted' and aimed at particular audiences. Actors may inflate their own roles, present a greater level of coherence and logic to decision making than was actually the case, and smooth over the frequent gaps between declared intentions and actual behaviour. Furthermore these narratives often clash with one another, reflecting the highly contested nature of war to peace transitions.

We identified these difficulties at the very start of the evaluation and tried to develop strategies for addressing them, while also being conscious of the fact that some of them are intractable. Perhaps the most important strategy for dealing with several of these challenges is that of triangulation – drawing upon different qualitative data sources (archival study, historical analysis, individual interviews and focus group discussions) and different levels of analysis (macro, meso and micro) – to reduce possible biases and provide as firm an empirical foundation as possible.

In order to place Norwegian intervention in perspective, we combined an 'inside-out' approach (a detailed account of Norway's involvement in the peace process) and an 'outside-in' approach (analysis of the broader structural context, conflict and peace-making dynamics) and then sought to link the two. A careful 'inside-out' analysis of Norwegian involvement provides an actor-oriented perspective that recognises the spaces and opportunities for individual agents to influence conflict dynamics and outcomes. This is not restricted to Norwegian actors, but also explicitly recognises the political agency of domestic elites. The background to the Sri Lankan conflict provides an 'outside-in' perspective, giving an analytical baseline of key trends and conflict dynamics, placing Norwegian interventions within a wider structural context. This combination of approaches aims to capture the complex dynamics and chains of causality that link individuals, institutions and structures in peace processes.

In order to connect the outside-in and inside-out perspective in a larger historical plot, we identified key turning points ('critical junctures') in the period studied. It is at these moments of change, we posited, that the outlook or composition of the LTTE and the government changes or shifts take place in the political space and military options available to them. Therefore, these events also had a profound – restraining or enabling – impact on Norway's room for manoeuvre as peace facilitator. Some of these turning points resulted from political-military calculation – for example the LTTE withdrawing from the peace talks in 2003. Others may be seen as manifestations of structural political trends (the election of Rajapaksa as president in 2005) and others yet were entirely contingent (the tsunami in 2004). We used these turning points to scrutinise Norwegian responses in relation to the knowledge and opportunities that were available at the time. This close analysis of turning points seemed to be the best way of dealing with problems of causation and attribution, structure and agency. It enabled us to reconstruct critical events and engage in careful 'process tracing' to explore causal mechanisms and the linkages between individual decision making and wider institutions and structures.

In sum, we adopted a historical, political economy approach, where inside-out and outside-in perspectives were linked through the use of key turning points. This approach aspires to balance and connect structure and agency. It recognises long histories, the centrality of the state and the structural constraints in which key actors operate, thus acknowledging a level of path dependency. Mediators, like all other actors in a conflict, never have complete context freedom – they inherit a particular situation, which places constraints on their choices and actions. But on the other hand, our approach acknowledges that key actors have some room for manoeuvre, and it does not dispense with contingency and uncertainty. We thus explicitly attempted to 'write key individuals back into the story' without adopting a radically contingent, actor-centred perspective. After all, the world does not follow Newtonian rules and principles – it is more chaotic, random and uncertain, and individuals make a difference, even though they do not act in contexts of their own choosing.[5]

5 Evaluation methodology and politics in practice

The sections below review the evaluation process in chronological order, including the methodological challenges and strategies that came up at different points in time.

5.1 Overtures: contracting and designing the evaluation

The word overture has a double meaning: on the one hand it can mean a (musical) introduction; on the other it can mean a performance of subtle self-promotion in order to establish rapport (making overtures). The second meaning of this term resonates with the process through which evaluators secure a contract. Prospective evaluators need to submit a proposal that fulfils two basic requirements: it needs to be good (in order for the assignment to be carried out successfully) and it needs to look good to the commissioning agent (in order to get the contract). Often, of course, the two align, but they are not the same thing. For example, reputed senior researchers may add gravity to a bid, even when their actual involvement in the research may be minimal; tight time frames may look efficient, but may be hard to enforce once a bidder gets into the assignment; limiting staff time may help make the budget competitive, but will create the risk of massive unpaid overtime.

Team selection is one of the most crucial parts of the evaluation exercise. This particularly applies to highly sensitive evaluations in the field of peace and conflict. To what extent are the evaluators known and trusted in terms of the quality of their analysis? Do they have a track record in this field? Is there a good combination of established and emerging talent in the team? Do they have the necessary thematic, methodological and area-based expertise? Is there any conflict of interest? To what extent is there a balance between 'international' and 'local' researchers? Is there an adequate gender balance? These were all important considerations for us when putting together our evaluation team, which was composed of a core team of international and Sri Lankan researchers, in addition to an advisory group of senior academics and analysts.

Even after having won the Norad Evaluation Department bid (22 July 2010), the question of team composition remained a contentious issue and raised a number of ethnical challenges. The timing of the evaluation coincided with a number of developments in relation to Sri Lanka, which heightened its sensitivity and politicisation. After a brutal military victory in the northeast in 2009, the Sri Lankan government had come under growing international pressure to account for alleged war crimes. Therefore the regime, already suspicious of anything that had to do with Norway and what it regarded as a flawed peace process, was especially sensitive to any initiatives that attempted to look at the past. In parts of the Sri Lankan media, the evaluation was lumped together with wider international efforts pushing for accountability in relation to war crimes. As a result of tense political climate and the increasing visibility of the evaluation, some of the Sri Lankan members of the team felt that they had to withdraw from the endeavour. Because selective withdrawal would have upset the balanced ethnic background of the team, it was eventually decided that none of the Sri Lankan researchers would be included in the team. This suggests that the principles of independence and transparency, considered to be essential pillars of 'good practice' in evaluation, may be very difficult to abide by in highly politicised and conflict environments.

The initial phase of the research focused on interviews with key Norwegian actors and the perusal of the archives of the Norwegian Ministry of Foreign Affairs (MFA) in Oslo. Archival research led to the production of several lengthy annotated summaries, detailing Norwegian efforts, perceptions and internal discussions throughout the study period. However, we were aware that the archives did not provide us with a comprehensive database of historical facts. One of the key Norwegian actors explained to us that the whole process had been relatively informal. While the key decisions and statements were well-documented, many of the preceding discussions, disagreements and considerations had only been discussed through SMS communication or in private conversations. For example, it remained unclear how exactly the 2002 ceasefire agreement had been negotiated. This made it very difficult to judge Norway's mediator role, especially whether or not some of the alleged flaws in the truce (exclusion of the president, weak monitoring mission, unclear arrangements at sea) could have been avoided.

Archival research yielded further deliberation about the identification and significance of various turning points. We tried to deal with these key moments in their historical context. In other words, rather than assessing decisions and actions with the benefit of hindsight, we tried to construct a historical plot that faithfully captured the uncertainty that characterised Norwegian involvement in Sri Lanka. It was also clear, however, that our selection of turning points was nonetheless informed by knowledge of outcomes, something that the Norwegian mediators did not have at the time. To evaluate the effectiveness of the Norwegian efforts, the team needed to distinguish between processes and consequences that were clear at the time, and might have been anticipated (and for which people could thus be held accountable), and dynamics that could not have been anticipated (for example, the tsunami) and only became clear afterwards.

Alongside the archival research and the initiation of our interviews with key actors, we commissioned a number of sub-studies and data-gathering efforts to inform our analysis. This included: 1) a review of the literature on mediation and peacebuilding; 2) a study of prevalent perspectives among Sri Lankan Tamil diaspora on the peace process; and 3) a (tri-lingual) review of Sri Lankan media coverage of the peace process, and of our turning points in particular.

5.2 'Fieldwork': navigating an arena of conflicting and missing narratives

Partly overlapping with the previous phase, the main part of the evaluation comprised 'fieldwork', that is interviews with key informants, along with the review of written sources. The crucial part of 'the field' however proved off-limits to us when Sri Lankan government officials made it known to the Norwegian embassy in Colombo that it would be better not to pursue our visa applications. Losing access to the country was a major setback. However, this problem was partly mitigated by interviewing key people on Skype or by telephone. The impossibility of visiting Sri Lanka forced the team to focus our resources on accessing key informants internationally: interviews in Norway (and Sweden), other European countries (including Brussels, Geneva), the US (Washington, DC, New York), India (Delhi, Chennai) and – somewhat coincidentally – Singapore (where a significant Sri Lankan government official happened to reside). Arguably this enhanced the complementary value of the evaluation in relation to the existing scholarship on the Sri Lankan peace process, which is often not as thorough when it comes to empirical research on Norway and other international actors. Nevertheless, the team was concerned that its inability to visit Sri Lanka would undercut the legitimacy of the exercise, particularly because our visa application had not officially been rejected. Fortunately, this did not prove to be a problem when the evaluation was published.

Among the key conflict protagonists, the main group missing from our list of interviewees was the LTTE. The insurgents were clearly a vital player through the rise and fall of the peace process and the dramatic end of the war, but the movement is much less well understood than the political elite in the capital Colombo. Rather opaque and speculative interpretations about the leadership and factions within the movement in the press or elsewhere tend to obfuscate as much as they elucidate. Both written and verbal accounts of the LTTE tend to reinforce, rather than debunk, the movement's somewhat mythical self-image.[6] We had met with some of the key LTTE figures in the past, including S. P. Tamilselvan (former leader of the political wing) and Pulidevan (former head of the LTTE peace secretariat). We had access to people who could provide credible accounts for other key cadres such as Karuna (the break-away eastern commander) and Anton Balasingham (the former LTTE negotiator). The latter moreover wrote rather extensive memoirs (Balasingham 2004). But we never had access to the key military figures (e.g., Pottu Amman, Soosai and the LTTE leader Prabhakaran), who were dead when our evaluation started, and there was little reliable information that gave an insight into their thinking and decision-making.

Crucial aspects of the evaluation were thus difficult to substantiate. What were the objectives of the LTTE when they signed a ceasefire and started talks in 2002? Were the stated reasons the real grounds for walking away in 2003 and what was their longer-term plan B? What was the cause of the Karuna split? Why did they provoke the government into resuming hostilities in late 2005 and mid 2006? Why did they not resort to guerrilla style warfare when they could not sustain a state-like posture in late 2008 and 2009? We tried to address all these questions by working our way through the various theories and speculations by perusing the LTTE's own statements, accounts in public media and interviews with people who are well-positioned to reflect on the LTTE. We discarded accounts that were clearly conspiratorial or lacked any evidence. Beyond that, the evaluation report could only spell out plausible interpretations but had no means to verify these conclusions.

Among the Colombo elite, the challenge was different. Most of the key people were still accessible (either abroad or on the phone), most of them were quite willing to share their perspectives and many of their actions and statements are well documented. However, many of them were politicians, with a strong vested interest in presenting their actions in a positive light. The same, it might be noted, can be said about interviews with international policymakers and (mainly Norwegian) politicians – many interviewees were prone to a level of revisionism, and reframing of events with the benefit of hindsight. Many of them had strong views on counterfactuals – if only the others had let them do things this way… – but these could not be verified. Former President Chandrika Kumaratunga for example was very angry about the fact that she had been left out of the ceasefire negotiations, because the newly elected Prime Minister Wickremesinghe saw her as his primary rival. This, she correctly argued, was unconstitutional, because the president is the commander-in-chief, but it was impossible to say what would have happened if she had actually been consulted. Would she not have blocked or delayed the process so much that it would have scuttled the deal altogether? Would the LTTE have accepted her involvement in the process after her 'war for peace' a few years earlier? It was hard to get a credible account of whether Kumaratunga's involvement would have strengthened or disabled the ceasefire agreement, which was probably Norway's most significant accomplishment in Sri Lanka. In our analysis, we acknowledged that these were indeed difficult judgements, but also underlined that it was 'problematic' to exclude an actor with 'a legitimate stake in the conflict' and 'sufficient political power and support to destabilise the peace process' (Goodhand et al. 2011a: 88).

On the Norwegian side, the evaluation had excellent access. The Norwegian government provided full support to the evaluation, allowed unrestricted access to the archives and we were able to do interviews with the key actors, such as government minister and former peace envoy Erik Solheim, his successor as envoy Jon Hanssen-Bauer, former state secretary Vidar Helgesen, ambassadors (to Colombo) Jon Westborg, Hans Brattskar and Tore Hattrem, successive heads of mission of the ceasefire monitoring mission,[7] and other current and former Norwegian ministers. As was the case with the Colombo elite, however, some of these respondents had staked significant political and professional capital on the Sri Lankan peace process. Although they supported the evaluative exercise and were open to critical reflection, it did of course matter to them which version of the story would prevail in our report; or – to be more precise – in the public perception of the report. We return to this below.

With regard to contextual knowledge, there was a widespread conviction among many of our Indian and Sri Lankan respondents that the Norwegians were insufficiently savvy when it came to the Sri Lankan polity, its layered rivalries and competing dynasties, the symbolic meaning of its actions, its use of the vernacular media and its relation to Buddhist leaders and other prominent figures in society. We found some of this criticism credible, particularly because the architects of Norway's involvement had eschewed the creation of larger institutional structures (often called 'track 2 and 3') and the involvement of specialised academics in support of peace efforts in Sri Lanka. However, it is rather difficult to provide evidence for the lack of contextual awareness, although there were a few quotes indicating that this was the case. It is hard to provide specific examples of how some people had misunderstood something that happened several years ago.

Interviews with key Norwegian respondents were particularly important to construct what we have called an inside-out perspective. The more structural outside-in perspective also drew on interviews, but was largely based on the existing literature on Sri Lanka's recent history and available statistics (including opinion polls, electoral results and economic growth figures). This approach shifted the focus away from the minutia of day-to-day Sri Lankan politics to the longer-term structural changes that took place in our study period. This included shifts in the international context, most saliently the changing attitudes towards insurgent movements after 9/11 and the rising power of Asian states, including India and China. Other examples were the increasing importance of diaspora networks, and the significance of globalised circulation of politically vocal streams, which assumed significance within Sri Lankan Buddhism. Some of these structural changes were themselves influenced by the peace process. The split in the LTTE in 2004, for example, may have been influenced by several contingent events, but it also reflected the difficulties for a rebel movement to preserve unity and discipline under ceasefire conditions. On the Sinhala side of the political spectrum, the peace process opened up major political space for ethno-nationalist, anti-elitist forces.

The way our evaluation dealt with these unintended side effects of the peace process caused some debate, both among our Norwegian interlocutors and more widely. Paradoxically, we found that the political dynamics around Norway's involvement in the peace process became centrally important in Sri Lanka, while Norway's ability to influence these dynamics was in fact very limited. The outside-in perspective brought into focus the powerful forces that constrained Norwegian peace efforts. The inside-out perspective revealed that although some of these structural forces were not immune to the effects of the internationalised peace process, Norway did not have the power to steer these forces in intended directions.

5.3   Coda: contested conclusions

If we understand evaluations as attempts to understand and justify policy choices to particular audiences, the last phase of writing, re-writing, deleting and rephrasing is clearly an interesting one. Frequently the submission of a draft report provokes a 'tug of war' between evaluators and the commissioners that ordered the evaluation. Though this is sometimes driven by concerns over reputation or political fall-out, the legitimate way of criticising draft reports is to take issue with methodological rigour and the reliability of evidence. Given that peace evaluations are not a 'hard science', it can be quite challenging to reach consensus on these matters. Moreover, the actors concerned know that once the report is made public, it is not just the nuanced treatment of evidence that wins out: most readers will only read the title and the executive summary. Different users may interpret (or frame) the main findings of the report quite differently, irrespective of the evidence and analysis in the report.

In brief, our report argued that Norwegian peace efforts were heavily constrained by the structural forces of Sri Lanka's political economy. The demise of the peace process eventually culminating in the government's military victory was as much a story of the government winning and the LTTE losing as it was a story of Norway failing. In addition to this general conclusion, we highlighted seven broader implications about international peace mediation in a changing global context. Some of these points met with agreement; others were (sometimes quite fiercely) contested. Our draft report underwent two cycles of elaborate feedback. Apart from a long list of minor comments and corrections, the main issues of debate can be summarised under three points.

First, some of the people involved felt that we had subjected Norwegian efforts to a 'negative framing'. The criticism was that we 'downplayed' the positive results of Norwegian intervention (such as the signing of the ceasefire), while painting a negative gloss to the overall narrative. Also, some commentators felt we were providing a platform for politicians (such as former President Chandrika Kumaratunga) who had an interest in disqualifying key parts of Norway's efforts while downplaying their own responsibility. Particular phrases were considered to be problematic, specifically the title of the report (*Pawns of Peace*) and parts of the executive summary. The draft summary stated that the 'Norwegian involvement in Sri Lanka is a story of failure', that Norway's accomplishments were ephemeral, and that the 'structural dimensions of the conflict' had not been addressed.

These conclusions were considered too strong in view of the more nuanced narrative in the report. In the view of our strongest critic: 'The executive summary should be completely revised.' We did rephrase parts of the summary, but the gist of it remained unchanged. Rhetorical softening would undercut the strength of the report and the legitimacy of the whole exercise particularly among non-Norwegian audiences, who might interpret our efforts as part of a Norwegian whitewash campaign if we adopted overly diplomatic phrasing.

The second point of discussion was analytically more fundamental. Some commentators argued that the report suffered from structural determinism; others took a more nuanced position and said it was inconsistent in its positioning on structure and agency. In short, both groups felt the analysis over-emphasised structural factors and longer-term trends, leaving little analytical space for the way Norwegian decisions and efforts impacted (or could have impacted) on these processes. While we firmly rejected the allegation of being determinists, the more moderate critique of mixing structural perspectives with agency was not altogether unfounded. As mentioned above, there was an apparent paradox in our analysis, which argued on the one hand that Sri Lanka's plight was driven by an entrenched conflict system in which Norwegian peacemakers were only pawns, while on the other hand reviewing turning points, which were subject to contingency and political decisions. Moreover, how could we criticise Norwegian efforts if the conflict was path dependent anyway? One of the comments read: 'You cannot at the same time argue that outcomes were predetermined in the way the conflict worked and at the same time attribute so much responsibility for failure (only) to Norway.' We were convinced of the need to acknowledge structural factors as well as agency and contingency, but to do so in a coherent and robust way is difficult. There are ample examples of both: the significance of Sri Lanka's post-colonial state institutions and the entrenched rivalries in domestic politics are monumental; and yet there are clear moments of contingency (the tsunami) and political choice (signing the ceasefire, the LTTE walking away from the peace talks in 2003, the LTTE split in 2004, the government not signing the joint government–LTTE aid mechanism in 2005, the LTTE boycotting the 2005 elections resulting in the victory of the more hard-line candidate Rajapaksa). Our approach of inside-out and outside-in perspectives woven together on the basis of key turning points was designed to provide a measured (in our view) balance between structural and agency-based perspectives, but it does not provide a waterproof defence against this sort of criticism.

The third set of criticism took issue with the adverse effects of Norwegian involvement in Sri Lanka that we had identified. We argued that Norway's involvement was not only the victim of Sinhala ultra-nationalist forces gaining strength, but contributed to it as well. The internationalised peace process fuelled well-established Sinhala anxieties about foreign infringements on Sri Lankan sovereignty and left a lot of political space for the forces rallying against Norwegian peace efforts. We also argued that Norway's continued involvement after the resumption of large-scale territorial offensives in 2006 posed an ethical problem: there was no feasible space to work on peace talks of any sort, and the continued involvement of Norwegian diplomats and Nordic ceasefire monitors lent itself to abuse by the parties. Neither of the parties requested a Norwegian departure; the fiction of a ceasefire plausibly provided tactical military advantages and served to limit the diplomatic fall-out of resuming a war that resulted in large numbers of civilian casualties. We were critical of Norway's role during this phase of the conflict and argued for a consequentialist ethic (there comes a point where you must withdraw when your involvement lends itself to such abuse), rather than the duty-based ethic that some of our Norwegian respondents advocated (peace is a noble endeavour that must always be tried).

This line of argument was met with strong criticism from some of our Norwegian counterparts, who felt these were 'unacceptable' and 'unsubstantiated allegations'. The continuation of Norwegian involvement after the resumption of war in 2006 had been intended to limit the humanitarian damage, but our report questioned this rationale. We argued that unintended and unforeseen consequences are not exceptional; they feature in virtually every such intervention. War-making and peace-making are not neatly distinguishable categories; they influence each other and they may overlap. Norwegian-supported peace efforts were not a marginal political process in Sri Lanka; they were at the centre of the island's political dynamics. They were very controversial and played a dominant role in media debates and successive elections. Though Norway's room for manoeuvre and its ability to effect change was very limited, its involvement produced a number of unintended effects, in part because its efforts fuelled counter-forces or lent itself to strategic manipulation by domestic actors. Although it was clearly impossible to prove the counterfactual, the fragmentation of the LTTE (the split in 2004, which fundamentally shifted the military balance) would not likely have happened without the peace process. And the internationalised peace process opened up a large political space for more radical Sinhala nationalist politics to enter the political mainstream. Not only were the Norwegians attacked by these forces; the very notion of peace through political negotiations lost its legitimacy. We thus defended these observations about unintended negative effects, while also making clear that Norway was not solely responsible for these dynamics.

5.4 Public reception: divergent interpretations

Our argument was sustained with a detailed historical narrative, but this was not sufficient to pre-empt or deflect the political forces that came into play when the final report was publicly disseminated. Providing transparency and contributing to public debate were explicit objectives of the evaluation and for that reason Norad's Evaluation Department and the Ministry of Foreign Affairs organised a high profile dissemination event. During the event, Erik Solheim, who had been the most visible Norwegian player in the Sri Lankan peace process and was now Minister of Environment and International Development, reacted to the report and then it was discussed by a panel. His ministry had selected a small group of panellists who were considered close to the minister. Solheim highlighted some challenges they had faced on the way, reiterated some of the positive accomplishments, welcomed the criticism and lessons learnt (without discussing them in much detail) and argued that the report suffered from a structural determinist perspective and made criticisms that could only be made with the benefit of hindsight.[8]

In parallel to the launch in Oslo, the report was published online on some of Sri Lanka's primary political debate platforms (Groundviews, Transcurrents). It was important for us to make sure 'our version' of the story and the entire report were directly accessible, because we were concerned that some of Sri Lankan media reporting on the evaluation would be skewed and politicised. *The Island* in particular, had been a source of rather speculative, even conspiratorial coverage of our evaluation efforts. At the beginning of the evaluation, the paper underlined that CMI (the lead evaluation agency) had long been 'a major recipient of Norwegian funds' (*The Island*, 19 December 2011), while also suggesting we would investigate some of the assassinations and shed light on what happened at the end of the war (the allegations of war crimes). It explicitly connected the evaluation to other ongoing international efforts: the inquiry by the UN into allegations of war crimes (the Secretary General's Panel of Experts), the Lessons Learnt and Reconciliation Committee (LLRC, the domestic response to international pressure to investigate) and the rather inflammatory documentary of the UK TV station Channel 4 (*Sri Lanka's Killing Fields*). Particularly the UN panel and the Channel 4 film became symbols of what was perceived as foreign infringement on Sri Lankan sovereignty driven by supposedly pro-Tamil and/or neo-colonial international actors. Our evaluation had neither the explicit mandate nor the means to investigate war crimes or gather forensic evidence on killings; its aim was to reflect on Norway's role over a 12-year period. But, *The Island* presented the evaluation as part of a larger international effort to undermine the government's victory over the LTTE and whitewash Norway's errors (if not malign intentions). For instance, when the release of our report was delayed, *The Island* wrote:

> Norway seems to be reluctant to make public a costly evaluation of its unsuccessful peace efforts in Sri Lanka. Although Norway initially planned to unveil the final report in the first week of April 2011, ahead of UNSG Ban Ki-Moon's unsubstantiated 'war crimes' report, an influential section in the Norwegian government is concerned about the outcome. Sources told *The Island* that in view of a spate of revelations made by Wikileaks with regard to the Norwegian-led peace process since February 2002 the interested parties would not be able to manipulate the Norwegian evaluation.
>
> (*The Island*, 27 July 2011)

Coverage of the release of the report followed suit:

> There is an unmistakable tendency to apologize on behalf of and whitewash the Norwegian effort – not surprising considering that this is a Norwegian government commissioned study and the evaluation team would not have got the job if they were not going to write something to absolve their paymasters of blame.
>
> (*The Island*, 12 November 2011)

Meanwhile the Ministry of Defence selectively highlighted a quote in the report to commend Defence Secretary Gotabhaya Rajapaksa (who is also the president's brother) as the only person with the foresight to predict the LTTE could be defeated militarily.

An article in the internet newspaper *Asian Tribune* (12 November 2011), by contrast, observed that through our report, Norway 'finally admitted' that its peace efforts were a 'political disaster, despite the carefully-calculated spin applied over the catalogue of significant failures'. The author acknowledged our point about unintended and unforeseen consequences of peace efforts, but underlined that 'rubbishing the sentiments of the majority community as irrelevant, belongs to neither' and closed with the argument that the report ought to have 'apologized for using 20 million inhabitants of Sri Lanka as guinea pigs for the botched geopolitical experiment' (*Asian Tribune*, 12 November 2011).

A more astute, pro-Sri Lankan government response came from political scientist and journalist Dayan Jayatilleka, who was the ambassador representing Sri Lanka in the UN Human Rights Council at the end of the war. He complimented the report as 'useful and good', but 'empty at its very core', because it failed to confront the question, 'how does one make peace with a non-state (therefore unconstrained) actor that is fanatical, politico-ideologically fundamentalist and totalitarian?'. In other words, we should have accepted that the insurgents were not amenable to a negotiated settlement. From a realist perspective, he argued, the LTTE's track record of violence and recalcitrant positions made a 'final war' the only feasible option. The Norwegian effort 'was foredoomed' and 'the war had to be fought to win'.

On the opposite side of the political spectrum, the criticism was quite different, but no less fierce. *Tamilnet* – an established Eelamist website, associated with what used to be the LTTE – underlined that our report 'subconsciously sees "victory" in the war', while failing to acknowledge that international peace efforts had 'abetted genocide'. In sum: 'Norway washes its hand of its responsibilities to victims' (*Tamilnet*, 11 November 2011).

We discuss these reviews at some length because they illustrate the political arena into which the evaluation entered. The political work of the evaluation was not simply the drawing of lessons on the basis of scientific findings. Instead, the evaluation had to create as firm a methodological ground as possible to navigate divergent political pressures and withstand critical attacks from various quarters. We produced a text that explicated underlying assumptions, conceptual foundations, contradictory interpretations and their varied evidence bases and sought a reasonable middle ground between competing versions of the story, attempting to preserve nuances and tensions in a productive way. But this nuanced openness made the report more vulnerable to knowledge brokers from across the political landscape drawing out simplistic – and diametrically opposed – punch lines to serve their own agendas.

This section has highlighted the range of opinionated responses to our report. This provides insights into the polarised political landscape in which our efforts were set, but it may wrongly create the impression that the evaluation created an enormous reaction. That was not the case. Some media – including much of the Norwegian media – in fact had rather minimal coverage of the report. And the heated debate that did take place on some platforms died away within a matter of days or weeks. The launch of our report provided an occasion to contest and confirm established positions; it did not necessarily influence those positions. This sobering fact also became clear from the follow-up to our report in Oslo. Norad's Evaluation Department received written comments from the Ministry of Foreign Affairs which repeated some of Solheim's main points, but also recognised that the report 'largely reflects main challenges and, partly, constraints that Norway faced in Sri Lanka', including the difficulties of trying to combine different roles (facilitator, monitor and aid donor) and the importance for mediators to have a strategy towards media (Norad 2012). There was, however, no willingness to discuss whether the Norwegian decision to continue as mediator rather than pull out in 2006 might have been morally questionable, and most of the general lessons that we tried to draw from Norway's engagement in Sri Lanka were ignored in the official response to the evaluation.

6 Conclusions and broader implications

The methodological, analytical and political insights from this evaluation cannot simply be carried over to other contexts. Norwegian peace efforts in Sri Lanka involved a lot of 'high politics'. Our evaluation assessed the performance of relatively powerful and politically savvy actors, and there was a significant amount of media attention to both the Norwegian involvement and our evaluation. Given that this was the first comprehensive evaluation of Norwegian peace efforts and that a government minister (Erik Solheim) had played a major role, it meant that the stakes were high on the Norwegian side. That is not always the case for such evaluations. The experience of other evaluators, particularly in terms of the political reactions to the release, is likely to be somewhat different. And yet the argument of this chapter has purchase beyond Sri Lanka. Other high profile evaluations have clearly been subject to similar dynamics (cf. Waage 2008) and we believe lessons from our evaluation can be useful to others.

First, such evaluations are ineluctably political exercises. While there are strong pressures to present them as technical, scientific and dispassionate analyses, this is never an accurate representation of reality. As we have highlighted here, good evaluation is partly about improved methodology, but also (and perhaps more so) about the ability to navigate and engage with politics. To some extent this is the case with all forms of evaluation. However, evaluation in conflict-affected environments tends to bring out in much sharper relief the political stakes of the evaluated interventions. We can understand peace processes as charismatic moments in politics when the stakes are extremely high and the protagonists have a strong interest in selling particular narratives and versions of events and limiting what can and cannot be said and what is considered legitimate and illegitimate. Much in line with Ferguson's (1990) and Li's (2007) work on development, peace interventions and evaluations may be prone to 'rendering' technical. People's careers and even their lives may in fact depend upon which version of events prevails.

Some very practical and concrete implications for evaluators and those who commission evaluations flow from this analysis. For example, it is clear that evaluation teams should be composed primarily of individuals who have had a long engagement with the context(s) in question and who can navigate the politics and interpret and decode the information economy. This suggests that those funding conflict-related evaluations should think very carefully about the balance between such context knowledge and general 'technical' knowledge on conflict/peacebuilding or evaluation methods. There has been a trend in recent years for knowledge on conflict issues to be commoditised and universalised – with the growth of conflict advisors and strategic conflict assessment experts who have general knowledge of the field outside of particular conflict settings. We feel that there should be a stronger commitment to context-based expertise and robust political economy analysis.

Another implication of acknowledging the politics of evaluation is to recognise that evaluators do not simply look down objectively from the commanding heights and pass neutral judgements on the messy reality below them. They are part of the 'mess' they are evaluating, and this needs to be explicitly acknowledged to avoid doing harm, i.e., not making the 'mess' even worse for those who have to live with it on a daily basis. Therefore, just as there has been some significant work done in recent years on the ethical and methodological challenges of doing research in areas of conflict (Nordstrom and Robben 1995; Finnström 2001; Smith and Robinson 2001; Gould 2010), there is a need to develop ethical guidelines for evaluators operating in conflict settings, which set out clearly how they should endeavour to 'do no harm'.

Second, the chapter has discussed the methodological challenges and our way of dealing with them in the evaluation of Norwegian peace efforts in Sri Lanka. Our approach involved 'systematic eclecticism', using mixed methods in a systematic way. We were transparent about underlying assumptions, causal inferences and associated methods, to enable readers to make their own judgements about the accuracy and validity of our findings and conclusions. Whilst conflict and peacebuilding can never be reduced to universal laws and dictums, comparative and quantitative research on peace processes can certainly add insight. Evaluators should aim for more systematic and innovative mixes of quantitative and qualitative methods. Our contribution to that end has been on the qualitative end of the spectrum with an exploration of a historical political economy approach combining an inside-out perspective with an outside-in perspective and using turning points to deal with the perennial problems of uncertainty, attribution, conflicting accounts and the balance between structure and agency.

The overarching argument of this chapter has been that the political arena of peace evaluations and the methodological challenges they face are related. It is clearly important to improve the rigour and transparency of the methodologies used in evaluating peace efforts, but these scholarly advances will never provide a watertight, 'neutral' scientific vantage point for evaluating deeply political interventions. In fact, evaluations that claim to have neutralised or circumvented the political content of the interventions they study may in fact be missing critical aspects of these interventions. Our chapter has sought to ask some uncomfortable questions about the links between the worlds of research and policy. The evaluator often sits in a twilight zone bridging these two worlds, acting as a broker and translator between them. In the development world, critical evaluation is presented as a learning tool, leading to smarter and more effective policies. Yet, it is also clear that evaluation, often the result of crises of legitimacy or political attacks on development policies or projects, has the effect of re-legitimising the world of development (e.g., Ferguson 1990; Duffield 2007). In this context, commissioning evaluations shows openness to learning, without forcing significant structural changes. The findings of research projects are used selectively by policymakers to provide ammunition for existing policies or new policy departures that have already been decided. While there has been a remarkable professionalisation of evaluative practice over recent years, there remains a significant rift between the elevated aspirations of scrutinising and improving policy practice and the political work that evaluations actually do.

Notes

1 International aid to Sri Lanka, and the politics around it, is a relatively well-studied area (Goodhand et al. 2005; Bastian 2007; Goodhand and Walton 2009; Orjuela 2011; Rainford and Satkunanathan 2011).
2 The controversies around the fourth assessment of the Intergovernmental Panel on Climate Change (IPCC) in February 2010 reminds us that the supposedly less politicised natural sciences may fall prey to such dynamics as well.
3 Ethnic statistics are clearly sensitive in Sri Lanka and there has not been a country-wide census since 1981 because of the war. The figures mentioned are a composite of the national census (2001), which did not cover the war-torn northeast, and district-level data (2007) and thus provide a general indication only.
4 One exception to this is 'real time' evaluation, which is carried out while an intervention is ongoing. Likewise ex-ante or mid-term evaluations may not have the same benefits of hindsight.
5 This approach bears some semblance to what Paul Richards has called causal process tracing in a stimulating recent article (2011). For earlier discussion on process tracing, see, for example, George and McKeown (1985).
6 There are a number of publications that claim authority in this regard, including journalistic accounts such as *Tigers of Lanka* (Swamy 1995) and *Inside an Elusive Mind* (Swamy 2006) the latter referring to LTTE leader Prabhakaran. These provide interesting insights, but provide only a somewhat speculative basis for making rigorous assessments with regard to some of the key considerations and decisions within the insurgent movement. See also the rather hard-nosed scholarly confrontation between Stokke (2006) and Sarvananthan (2007).
7 Except the first one, who was no longer alive.
8 A full video of the launch is available at www.regjeringen.no/nb/dep/ud/lyd_bilde/nett-tv-2/fred_srilanka.html?id=662709.

Bibliography

Balasingham, A. (2004) *War and Peace: Armed Struggle and Peace Efforts of the Liberation Tigers*, Mitcham: Fairmax Publishing.

Bastian, S. (2007) *The Politics of Foreign Aid in Sri Lanka: Promoting and Supporting Peace*, Colombo: ICES.

Bullion, A. (1995) *India, Sri Lanka and the Tamil Crisis, 1976–1994: An International Perspective*, London and New York: Pinter.

Coomaraswamy, R. (2003) 'The Politics of Institutional Design: An Overview of the Case of Sri Lanka,' in S. Bastian and R. Luckham (eds) *Can Democracy be Designed? The Politics of Institutional Choice in Conflict-torn Societies*, London: Zed Books, pp. 145–169.

Cramer, C. and Goodhand, J. (2011) 'Hard Science or Waffly Crap? Evidence-based Policy Versus Policy-based Evidence in the Field of Violent Conflict' in K. Baylss, B. Fine and

E. Waeyenberge (eds) *The Political Economy of Development. The World Bank, Neo-Liberalism and Development Research*, London: Pluto Press, pp. 215–238.
De Silva, K. (2005) *A History of Sri Lanka*, Colombo: Vijitha Yapa Publications.
Dixon, J. (2009) 'Emerging Consensus: Results from the Second Wave of Statistical Studies on Civil War Termination', *Civil Wars* 11(2): 121–136.
Doyle, M. and Sambanis, N. (2006) *Making War and Building Peace*, Princeton: Princeton University Press.
Duffield, M. (2007) *Development, Security and Unending War: Governing the World of Peoples*, Cambridge and Malden: Polity Press.
Ferguson, J. (1990) *The Anti-Politics Machine: Development, Depoliticization, and Bureaucratic Power in Lesotho*, Cambridge: Cambridge University Press.
Finnström, S. (2001) 'In and Out of Culture: Fieldwork in War-torn Uganda', *Critique of Anthropology* 21(3): 247–258.
Fortna, P. (2004) 'Does Peacekeeping Keep Peace? International Intervention and the Duration of Peace After Civil War', *International Studies Quarterly* 48(2): 269–292.
George, A. and McKeown, T. (1985) 'Case Studies and Theories of Organizational Decision Making', *Advances in Information Processing in Organizations* 2: 21–58.
Goodhand, J. and Klem, B., with Fonseka, S. I., Keethaponcalan, D. and Sardesai, S. (2005) *Conflict, Aid and Peacebuilding in Sri Lanka, 2000–2005*, Washington, DC: The Asia Foundation.
Goodhand, J. and Walton, O. (2009) 'The Limits of Liberal Peacebuilding: International Engagement in the Sri Lankan Peace Process', *Journal of Intervention and Statebuilding* 3(3): 303–323.
Goodhand, J., Klem, B. and Sørbø, G. (2011a) *Pawns of Peace: Evaluation of Norwegian Peace Efforts in Sri Lanka, 1997–2009*, Oslo: Norad evaluation 5/2011.
Goodhand, J., Rampton, D., Venugopal R. and de Mel, N. (2011b) *Strategic Policy Assessment*, London: Department for International Development (DFID).
Gould, K. (2010) 'Anxiety, Epistemology, and Policy Research "behind enemy lines"', *Geoforum* 41: 15–18.
Human Security Centre (2005) *Human Security Report 2005: War and Peace in the 21st Century*, Vancouver: University of British Columbia.
——(2010) *Human Security Report 2009/2010: The Causes of Peace and the Shrinking Costs of War*, Vancouver: Simon Fraser University.
Klem, B. (2012) *In the Wake of War: The Political Geography of Transition in Eastern Sri Lanka*, PhD dissertation, Zurich: University of Zurich.
Li, T. (2007) *The Will to Improve: Governmentality, Development, and the Practice of Politics*, Durham: Duke University Press.
Licklider, R. (2009) 'Civil War Outcomes,' *Saltzman Working Paper*, No. 11, November 2009. www.siwps.com/programs/SWP.attachment/no-11-/No%2011%20-%20Licklider.pdf, accessed 10 January, 2011.
Loganathan, K. (1996) *Sri Lanka, Lost Opportunities: Past Attempts at Resolving Ethnic Conflict*, Colombo: University of Colombo.
Martin, H. (2006) *Kings of Peace, Pawns of War: The Untold Story of Peace-making*, London: Centre for Humanitarian Dialogue, Continuum.
Moore, M. (1985) *The State and Peasant Politics in Sri Lanka*, Cambridge: Cambridge University Press.
Norad (2012) *Evaluering av norsk fredsinnsats på Sri Lanka, 1997–2009*, Oslo: Norad.
Nordstrom, C. and Robben, A. (1995) (eds) *Fieldwork Under Fire: Contemporary Studies of Violence and Survival*, Berkeley: University of California Press.

OECD (2012) *Evaluating Peacebuilding Activities in Settings of Conflict and Fragility: Improving Learning for Results*, DAC Guidelines and Reference Series, Paris: OECD Publishing. doi: 10.1787/9789264106802-en.
Orjuela, C. (2011) 'Buying Peace? Politics of Reconstruction and the Peace Dividend Argument,' in K. Stokke and J. Uyangoda (eds) *Liberal Peace in Question: Politics of State and Market Reform in Sri Lanka*, London: Anthem Press, pp. 121–140.
Rainford, C. and Satkunanathan, A. (2011) 'From SIHRN to Post-War North and East: The Limits of the "Peace through Development" Paradigm in Sri Lanka', in K. Stokke and J. Uyangoda (eds) *Liberal Peace in Question – Politics of State and Market Reform in Sri Lanka*, London: Anthem Press, pp. 121–141.
Regan, P. (2002) 'Third Party Interventions and the Duration of Intra-State Conflicts', *Journal of Conflict Resolution* 46(1): 55–73.
Richards, P. (2011) 'A Systematic Approach to Cultural Explanations of War: Tracing Causal Processes in Two West African Insurgencies', *World Development* 39(2): 212–220.
Sarkees, M. (2000) 'The Correlates of War Data on War: An Update to 1997', *Conflict Management and Peace Science* 18(1): 123–144.
Sarvananthan, M. (2007) 'In Pursuit of a Mythical State of Tamil Eelam: A Rejoinder to Kristian Stokke', *Third World Quarterly* 28(6): 1185–1195.
Smith, M. and Robinson, G. (eds) (2001) *Researching Violently Divided Societies: Ethical and Methodological Issues*, London: Pluto.
Spencer, J. (2008) 'A Nationalism without Politics? The Illiberal Consequences of Liberal Institutions in Sri Lanka', *Third World Quarterly* 29(3): 611–629.
Stedman, S. (1997) 'Spoiler Problems in Peace Processes', *International Security* 22(2): 5–53.
Stern, P. and Druckman, D. (2000) 'Evaluating Interventions in History: The Case of International Conflict Resolution', *International Studies Review* 2(1): 33–63.
Stokke, K. (2006) 'Building the Tamil Eelam State: Emerging State Institutions and Forms of Governance in LTTE-Controlled Areas in Sri Lanka', *Third World Quarterly* 27(6): 1021–1040.
Swamy, N. (1995) *Tigers of Lanka: From Boys to Guerrillas*, Colombo: Vijitha Yapa.
——(2006) *Inside an Elusive Mind*, Colombo: Vijitha Yapa.
Uyangoda, J. (2011) 'Travails of State reform in the Context of Protracted Civil War in Sri Lanka,' in K. Stokke and J. Uyangoda (eds) *Liberal Peace in Question: Politics of State and Market Reform in Sri Lanka*, London: Anthem Press, pp. 46–75.
Venugopal, R. (2009) *Cosmopolitan Capitalism and Sectarian Socialism: Conflict, Development, and the Liberal Peace in Sri Lanka*, PhD dissertation, Oxford: University of Oxford.
Waage, H. H. (2008) 'Postscript to Oslo: The Mystery of Norway's Missing Files', *Journal of Palestine Studies* 38(1): 54–65.
Zartman, W. (2000) 'Ripeness: The Hurting Stalemate and Beyond,' in P. Stern and D. Druckman (eds) *International Conflict Resolution after the Cold War*, Washington, DC: National Academy Press, pp. 225–250.
——(2009) 'Interest, Leverage and Public Opinion in Mediation', *International Negotiation* 14: 1–5.

5 The case of Congo
An evaluation approach focusing on context

Emery Brusset
Channel Research

Ivo Hooghe
FPS Foreign Affairs, Foreign Trade and Development
Cooperation of Belgium

1 Introduction

As stated by a recent paper on impact evaluations, 'Evaluators are at their best when links between "interventions" and policy goal are relatively direct and short term; and when policy interventions are relatively self-contained. Parallel and overlapping interventions make it difficult to disentangle causes from effects' (Stern et al. 2012). This ideal situation is quite the opposite of contexts of conflict, where one finds a highly complex relationship between various policies and between policies, actual execution and results.

The commissioning and conduct of evaluations in these settings also has to relate to actors and populations directly involved in the conflict. This includes warring tribes, militia and government structures – often entangled and overlapping. These groups pursue strategies that change over time. While the evaluation seeks to define the value of an intervention, this is tied up with the appreciation of the conflict on the part of these people. Engaging in a conflict-sensitive way implies maintaining a degree of distance from the conflict while remaining participatory. It also needs to be balanced with the need for participatory approaches, and even simply with the requirements of maintaining optimal access to information as well as the mobility and integrity of the team.

The present chapter describes how a large joint evaluation on conflict prevention and peacebuilding (carried out in 2010–2011) in the Democratic Republic of Congo (DRC) dealt with these complexities. It considers the implications of the methodological choices made. The chapter is written by the principal evaluation manager from the commissioning donors and the team leader of the evaluation team.

The evaluation was commissioned by a group of 11 bilateral donors and multilateral agencies to assess the relevance, results and the effects of their conflict prevention and peacebuilding policies and interventions.[1] The aim was to evaluate the efforts as a whole – not to assess each donor or agency separately, let alone to compare them. The evaluation was to inform decision-makers' efforts to achieve a more strategic, coherent and coordinated set of policy interventions. The findings were to serve a wide range of stakeholders, for example by covering the diplomatic and security dimensions, and assisting the Congolese authorities in their cooperation with foreign agencies.

The evaluation questions were based on the five OECD DAC criteria for the evaluation of development assistance, namely relevance, effectiveness, efficiency, sustainability and impact. Furthermore, the evaluation paid attention to the additional criterion of coordination among donors and among implementing organisations. The evaluation was executed in a classical approach comprising four phases: an inception phase, a desk study phase (with a separate report), a field phase and the synthesis of all findings leading to the drafting of the final report.

Given the complexity of both the conflict context itself and of the interventions under evaluation, the evaluation team adopted an approach that combined participatory conflict analysis, desk/policy review and case studies to provide credible overall findings on the main evaluation questions. The approach focused on analysing the links between observed intervention outcomes at the local level and the drivers of conflict identified by a conflict analysis and had three key dimensions:

- The evaluation used the conflict as the main frame of reference to evaluate the interventions under review. This ensured that the impact of the interventions was not examined only in terms of intended peace-related objectives – either stated or reconstructed by the evaluators – but rather in terms of the actual outcomes as related to key conflict drivers. The recourse to conflict analysis, and more particularly to participatory methods to elicit from the local population their own key events and trends, was the main evaluation referent.
- Case studies were used to examine the results of donor interventions in each of five thematic areas.[2] A large sample, aiming to be representative for the donor aid portfolio, was selected for desk study. Considerable resources went into researching a small number of individual projects. This two-pronged approach of combining a large sample with an in-depth study of a small number of interventions was designed to allow a generalisation of findings without having to handle excessive amounts of information.
- The third dimension was the application of an impact assessment method imported from impact assessments used for large industrial projects, for example environmental impact assessment. This method was translated for peacebuilding evaluations and evaluates the relevance, extent and duration of the influence of the intervention outcomes on a delimited number of aspects, identified to be the most critical conflict drivers in the eastern DRC. This enables the analysts to handle extremely complex causal chains and to avoid the laborious reconstruction of theories of change in a complex conflict setting.

2 The conflict in the DRC

The Congolese wars (1996–1997, 1998–2003) constitute one of the most severe humanitarian disasters since World War II.[3] Some observers claim that up to

5.4 million people have died since August 1998, when the second Congo War began (International Rescue Committee 2008).[4] After the December 2002 peace accord that formally ended hostilities, 1.5 million people died from the ongoing consequences of war such as food insecurity, dysfunctional health services, dilapidated infrastructure and widespread displacement.[5]

From 1994 onwards, with the inflow of 1 million Rwandan Hutu refugees, eastern Congo has been the scene of a complex cross-border war, a proliferation of local militias, large refugee flows, unsuccessful peace processes and failing military operations. Even the deployment of the largest UN peace-keeping mission in the world (MONUC) could not stop the protracted conflict that affects the Eastern Provinces of the DRC in waves. The surges in the conflict also make it difficult to implement activities and plan an evaluation as one can never foresee when it will be safe to go into the field (this will be further discussed below).

The origins of the wars are to be found amongst the conditions that operate at the local and national levels, and also within the broader Great Lakes region, in particular in relation to Uganda and Rwanda. The literature on the conflict in DRC shows considerable diversity of views on the main sources and dynamics of the conflict, but the dominant, recurring causes can be summarised as follows:

- ethnic grievances and clashing identities.[6]
- the effects of state collapse and inter-elite power struggles (Stearns 2011).
- conflicts over resources, including land and natural resources (Mathieu and Willame 1999; Van Acker 1999).
- a regionalised war context, and particularly the impact on the DRC of the neighbouring conflicts and political strategies.[7]

Faced with the complexity of the war, the international community tried to facilitate various peace processes between the different warring parties, which resulted in 2002, after the assassination of President Laurent-Désiré Kabila, in the signing of a number of regional and national agreements. In July 2002, the Sun City Peace Agreement was signed between the DRC and Rwandan governments, leading to the withdrawal of Rwandan troops. This agreement marks the beginning of the evaluation period.

In December 2002, the parties of the Inter-Congolese Dialogue signed a 'Global and Inclusive' peace accord. After the approval of the final act of this peace agreement in 2003, a transitional government was put in place to create a new legal and institutional framework, prepare general elections and reform the security sector. Along with the International Monetary Fund and the World Bank, the European Union and several of its member states significantly increased their diplomatic and financial support for the government's transitional reform. International aid increased from a few hundred million in 2002 to US$1.5 billion to $2 billion each year by the end of the decade (OECD 2011).[8]

3 The evaluation and its scope

The complexity of conflict called for careful management of the evaluation. In this section we outline the manner in which the exercise was implemented, and how stakeholders were engaged in the process. The sensitivity of the subject and the considerable challenges posed to interventions in a conflict environment made this evaluation a high-risk exercise, in particular the permanent threat of resurging violence and difficult access to the intervention sites.

3.1 Designing the evaluation to minimise risk

In 2008 the first public tendering process for the evaluation was launched, but was cancelled, after a number of proposals had been received by the evaluation steering committee, when one of the main rebel groups, the CNDP, started an offensive in eastern Congo. The evaluation commissioners judged the security of the evaluators could not be guaranteed and that this surge of violence made it impossible to do the fieldwork, which was considered indispensable to the evaluation.

In 2009 a second tendering attempt was completed, and the design of the evaluation was made more risk-resistant by splitting the evaluation analysis into two phases. The objective of the first policy phase was to evaluate the donor policies based on an analysis of documentation, an analysis of the conflict, a portfolio review, telephone and face-to-face in-depth interviews. The latter took place in Brussels, Goma, Bukavu and Kinshasa. The result of this first phase was a full analytical report on the relevance of the donor policies, donor coordination and policy coherence. The objective of the next phase was to evaluate the actual conflict prevention and peacebuilding results of the interventions in the eastern part of the country, assessing their relevance, effectiveness, efficiency, sustainability and impact. In case of new violence, the field phase could have been adjusted, postponed or cancelled. At the end, the reports of both phases would come together in a synthesis report.

In retrospect, this precaution of having two distinct phases proved not to be necessary. The evaluation team gained full access to the conflict zone due to a temporary halt in the violence. However, even during a rather calm period in the conflict, the access to project sites outside the provincial capitals of Goma, Bukavu and Ituri, presented a high risk. Outside of these urban centres it was quite difficult to reach local populations because of bad roads, unreliable flights and a high degree of insecurity, caused by the endemic violence.

3.2 Involvement of Congolese stakeholders

The evaluation approach was also designed to ensure lateral and downward accountability to the authorities and local population groups. In addition to the Steering Committee of international donors and organisations, four Reference Groups were created. These groups were chaired by the government of DRC, both at the national level (Kinshasa) and the provincial level (Ituri, North and

South Kivu). Meetings were organised periodically throughout the evaluation, and were designed to provide an independent view on the gradual evolution of the evaluation.

3.3 A conflict-sensitive evaluation

Because of the conflict situation and the manifold risks present in Congo, the Steering Group requested that the evaluators be conflict-sensitive, in particular that they be aware of the possible unintended effects of the evaluation on the conflict and on the persons met. The evaluation process had to demonstrate sensitivity to the gender, beliefs, manners and customs of all stakeholders. The rights and wellbeing of participants in the evaluation had to be protected as well as the anonymity and confidentiality of individual informants. During the field mission, the evaluators had to avoid unnecessary risks to the safety of all aid personnel, partners and beneficiaries, as well as to themselves.

Openness and discretion were considered essential in this regard. While the team shared full information on the evaluation process (in fact seeking Congolese stakeholder participation in the selection of the case studies), there was complete anonymity in the use of the information. The team had been briefed on the importance of suspending judgement, and being conscious of the risk of creating false expectations.

An important aspect was the deployment of experts with a balance of different backgrounds – not just in terms of knowledge (in particular country expertise), but also in terms of nationality, and even ethnicity, for the Congolese members. The evaluation team, fifteen persons in total, was made up of eight nationalities, and included individuals from many groups from the Great Lakes region (including DRC as well as Burundi). This contributed to an understanding of the findings by the local interlocutors during public presentations and to the interpretation of cultural knowledge by the team.

3.4 Defining the scope of the evaluation

The analysis covered North Kivu, South Kivu and the Ituri District, all situated against the borders of Burundi, Rwanda and Uganda. The period covered by the evaluation ran from the signature of the Sun City Agreement in December 2002, when Rwanda and Uganda claimed full withdrawal from the DRC, to the revision of the mandate of the peace keeping mission MONUC in July 2010.

The commissioning donors provided the evaluators with a combined portfolio of 350 conflict prevention and peacebuilding-related interventions, representing around US$650 million. Most funding went to disarmament, demobilisation and reintegration of former combatants and to humanitarian aid, with respectively US$124 and $102 million. Other sectors receiving significant amounts of funding were peace education, elections, civil society development, the repatriation/reintegration of refugees, security sector reform (SSR) and sexual and gender-based violence (SGBV). The Terms of Reference stated that the evaluators had to propose 3 to 5 relevant themes and a sample of 50 to 60 interventions of various sizes within these themes. The identification of these themes will be explained in Section 4.4 below.

The geographic focus on the three provinces was chosen for reasons of feasibility. The donors considered covering the full regional conflict unrealistic. The three provinces were selected because they suffered the most from the conflict. This evaluation's geographic focus de-emphasised significant national or international issues, such as the centre-periphery tensions between the national government and the governments of the provinces, and the critical role of Rwanda in the internal strife.

However, even though these dynamics went beyond the spatial scope of the evaluation, to get a complete picture of the conflict these dimensions were included in the conflict analysis. The broader dynamics did feature in aspects such as the chronic weakening of the state, and the high levels of criminal activity around mineral exploitation.

The time frame of the evaluation also required a balance between projects that started in 2002 and those that were running in 2010. While justified in terms of overall strategies, this time frame was shown to be over ambitious, in particular when considering the limited evidence available at the project level. As a consequence, the field visits concentrated on the more recent interventions. Only the projects of the later years could be studied in the field and this inhibited broader generalisation.

However while the portfolio of 350 interventions demarcated rather well the borders of the evaluation scope, it posed a challenge in terms of what was covered under the concept of conflict prevention. There was no guiding definition as to what a conflict prevention or peacebuilding intervention exactly was, and every donor and agency introduced their own understanding into the database of 350 projects.

This wide range of meanings presented a risk of considerable inconsistency. This was illustrated for example by a discussion within the steering group as to whether humanitarian aid should be part of the scope of the evaluation, with humanitarian projects representing 40 per cent of the volume of funding in the database. Is it fair to judge humanitarian aid through a conflict prevention lens, if humanitarian aid is supposed to deliver aid in a neutral and impartial way? Should, for instance, a humanitarian programme supporting refugees coming back to eastern Congo be considered as a pure humanitarian intervention even though it can have an effect on land issues, which is an important conflict driver?

In the end the Steering Committee decided to include humanitarian action, which was seen as relevant from a conflict sensitivity angle, as part of the scope of the evaluation. Accepting that it is not a main objective of humanitarian aid to contribute to peace, it was important to recognise that humanitarian aid can still have a positive or negative influence on peace or conflict. This notion of conflict sensitivity (related as it was to conflict drivers, as we shall see below) broadened the scope of the evaluation to most forms of assistance provided to the eastern provinces of DRC.

4 Methodological choices

4.1 Difficulties in using the theory of change approach

The Terms of Reference emphasised policy analysis and identified donor strategies as the most appropriate frame of reference for assessing interventions. This was reflected in the structure of the evaluation, which was divided into two separate parts: an analysis of policy and programming and an analysis of implementation and impact. The use of theories of change was advised in the Terms of Reference.[9]

From the first phase of the evaluation the evaluators were confronted with major difficulties in obtaining or reconstructing clear theories of change. The complexities of the conflict compounded the difficulty of tracing the programme theories and their respective theories of change for a large number of projects. It was then difficult to assess whether the intended outcomes were achieved. This problem arose not just because aid agencies had not been clear on their programme theory, but because of some deeper structural factors.

Specifically the major challenges to a theory-based model for this evaluation encountered from the first review of documentation and visits to the country were the following:

- The objectives of the project interventions were frequently blurry and could not serve as a stable point of reference, either because they quickly dissolved with the passage of events, or because they remained too general, ambiguous or informal. This informality is partly due to the fact that many interventions were only very indirectly related to the conflict. The interventions of the UN peace-keeping in the human rights field, for example, were related clearly to the legal mandate, rather than to objectives of conflict prevention and peace-building. Moreover, they evolved considerably over the years, depending on which structure within the UN dealt with this aspect of human rights.
- The forces external to the evaluated interventions were often strong and difficult to deal with. Tumultuous changes took place in the context and conditions varied per province. As a result, assumptions and risks became more important than the theories to which they were supposed to apply.
- There were many barriers to coordination between actors and a high degree of compartmentalisation both within and between different institutions. The contrast between different delivery channels (military versus civilian, humanitarian versus political, for example), the multiple sub-contracting of implementation from two to six levels between the central funding to the actual field execution, and in some cases the competition between organisations, prevented the team from identifying a unifying theory of change.

As a consequence, the policy analysis stage made it clear to the evaluation team that using a traditional theories of change approach would pose a challenge. The challenges listed above had methodological consequences that require some explanation.

The first is that tracing consistent theories of cause and effect would require considerable resources. This was confirmed more particularly during the field phase when the team observed what could be described as an evaporation of peace-related objectives or project goals. Only a handful of projects could concretely claim to have followed, or dynamically maintained, their implicit or explicit theory of change in a way that connected them in a cogent way to building peace (these included in particular those dealing with the mining industry, and other such recent and limited interventions).

The second consequence was the considerable discrepancy between intervention design and what actually happened during implementation. Some evaluation methods propose a design based on reconstruction, or even interpretation, of the chains of inputs leading to outcomes and to higher level impact.[10] However in the case of the EU military cooperation mission for example, the mandate was revealed to be a logic model that expressed the intentions of programming staff at the design stage, ignoring the actions and intentions of other stakeholders. The actual activities undertaken were frequently revised to take account of changed circumstances and, although they fit well within the mandate, were in substance based on the pragmatic judgement of the expatriate personnel.

These methodological challenges are further illustrated by the following two cases. In the case of one donor country there were indeed strategies and a careful documentation of programming decisions which could have offered a good basis to analyse the strategy. A closer look revealed, however, that funding rhythms tended to coincide with ministerial visits, while the strategies only served to provide a very broad framework which the succession of ambassadors could use to frame relatively personalised approaches to the conflict.

This is also illustrated in the case of another bilateral cooperation where the team found carefully designed programmes and project interventions, often set against a conflict analysis. These programme theories however tended not to aggregate toward an overall strategy, but were really aligned with institutional configurations. Different ministries' funding activities in Congo had developed separate strategies. Furthermore, programmes handled out of the donor capital sometimes contrasted with those of the embassy in Kinshasa, which in turn tended to ignore the objectives of some of the agencies in the provinces targeted by large scale multi-year programmes. More importantly, however, the evaluation was asked to concentrate on the projects funded by the Ministry of Cooperation, leaving aside those of the more political, and arguably more important, Ministry of Foreign Affairs.

4.2 Adopting conflict analysis to address complexity

By far the most significant challenge to the evaluation stemmed from the point at which there is probably most difference between development evaluations and conflict evaluations: while the first have a higher degree of linearity between causes and effects, and the quality of information is higher, in the case of conflict interventions, complexity and unavailable data predominate. The evaluation of conflict interventions thus requires a methodology that preserves rather than suppresses this complexity.

Complexity thinking is premised on the importance of non-reductionist social science, precisely to acknowledge such particular conditions, and lead to the appropriate methodological adaptation. Cilliers writes:

> We have seen that there is no accurate (or rather, perfect) representation of the system which is simpler than the system itself. In building representations of open systems, we are forced to leave things out, and since the effects of these omissions are nonlinear, we cannot predict their magnitude.[11]
>
> (Cilliers 2005: 13)

In a follow-up publication Richardson (2009) notes that just because a complex system is incompressible (in other words it refuses to be reduced to a few linear cause and effect relations) does not mean that incomplete representations of the system are not useful, arguing that knowing something and knowing where it is wrong is as far as knowledge can go. A complex system is sometimes described as a system that has more than two non-overlapping, potentially contradictory descriptions (de Coning 2012). It tolerates simultaneous rival theories which still help to arrive at a deeper understanding. This was particularly useful in understanding the nature of the conflict in eastern DRC.

As remarked by de Coning in the area of peace interventions:

> The common-sense understanding of complexity usually refers to two frequently cited factors. The first is the large number of international and local agents involved, and the second is the wide-ranging scope of activities undertaken by these agents. The scale of the interactions among the agents and the interconnectedness and the diverse range of activities they undertake make it impossible to meaningfully track the overall system.
>
> (de Coning 2012)

There is a growing recognition, among both the research and practitioner communities, that peace and stabilisation interventions are intervening in systems that are too large and interconnected to allow for models of linearity between cause and effect (Körppen et al. 2011). This recognition is still gaining ground in the evaluation community, where, as reflected in the Terms of Reference, more linear approaches still predominate (Blamey et al. 2002). This shift towards a more complex understanding is generally visible in the emphasis given to multi-causal theories of change, or understanding the assumptions and risks within programme theory, as the primary focus of the evaluative analysis.[12]

By the middle of the policy analysis phase, the team gradually came to understand that the key challenge for the evaluation was the adoption of a multi-narrative model combining possibly conflicting views of both the interventions and the conflict. At the same time it was imperative to preserve the case study approach for purposes of some generalisation, and to enable analysis specific to project results. The choice was therefore made to put the conflict analysis at the centre of the methodological approach and to build the model around the influence of the observed outcomes of aid programmes on the drivers of conflict.

The evaluation team pursued an approach built on two pillars:

1. A desk review and participatory analysis to identify key conflict or peace drivers. This analysis of the conflict was based primarily on expert judgement captured through a review of the academic literature and use of the existing analytical reports by aid agencies and UN bodies. It was balanced with a participatory mapping of events and trends, as seen from the perspective of specific stakeholder groups in villages and organisations scattered across eastern DRC.
2. An impact assessment based on a generalisation from case studies drawn from individual aid outcomes, and grounded in a contribution model gauging the influence of specific intervention outcomes on the identified key drivers of peace. This model was inspired by the methods used for impact assessments for large infrastructure projects, for example for mining and oil companies, which analyse the influence of key project aspects on important social and environmental issues.

In the case of humanitarian assistance for instance, the intended humanitarian outcome could be the consumption of food aid within a particular family structure, where the different members could systematically receive smaller or greater amounts than their health required due to the local perception of fair entitlements, in spite of aid policies of inclusive targeting. An outcome related to the conflict was the presence of a large humanitarian aid organisation in a remote area, recruiting trained cadres to manage the distribution. This, if not well handled, could lead to a brain drain of educated civil service staff, weakening the functions of the state. This last aspect was retained as the core element in the case studies (to which we return in Section 4.4) used to assess effects on peacebuilding, rather than the objectives of the programme itself (feeding people).

This concentration on the observed project outcomes of interventions on certain key aspects of the conflict, rather than on the stated objectives of the projects themselves, also made it feasible to evaluate the conflict sensitivity of interventions.

4.3 A two-stage conflict analysis

The conflict analysis was carried out in two stages. The first stage comprised a desk study of the existing literature on the conflict in the DRC by an expert. This review identified the key drivers of conflict and peace as presented in current research. The analysis was based on the narrative synthesis of existing literature, plus some original research carried out by members of the evaluation team.

The second stage used participatory methods and consisted of localised conflict analyses based on perceptions of local populations in intervention areas.[13] The evaluation team was trained and tasked to carry out seven participatory sessions of events and trends mapping, which were organised in different locations in eastern DRC, involving stakeholders from a variety of backgrounds. This was a participatory method, using qualitative capture of pluralist views and a quantitative comparative scoring.

The participants to these sessions were invited to tell the story to two facilitators, who then visually portrayed these stories as an input for discussion. In this focus group, participants were asked to spell out key trends and events over a given time period on a wall-sized sheet of paper (usually relying on coloured sticker notes). Subsequently, these trends and events were connected with arrows, which contributed to the identification of other events or trends. Specific nodes emerged, which were then highlighted as being central: those events and trends on which there was a higher convergence of arrows demonstrated a high level of intensity. These were identified as tipping points, or drivers, in the conflict situation.

The key challenge is to capture a multi-narrative understanding, rather than falling into the trap of projecting the evaluation team's thinking onto the workshop. The selection of the participants in these mapping sessions was based on their proximity to specific projects, in other words on the nature of the case studies selected in the first two stages of the evaluation (this is described in the next section of this chapter). These were identified projects with recognisable stakeholders and beneficiaries. Specific participants were selected because of their particular views or expertise, and even because of their contradictory positions.

The stakeholders were diplomatic and aid officials in the capital, government administration personnel and journalists in the provinces, as well as village populations in very isolated areas and diverse forms of civil society. The groups were not always literate, but could be guided to rely on visual patterns to best express their cumulative knowledge.

The identification of key events or trends is particularly useful to complement the desk-based conflict analysis with a local layer – a form of reality check. The events and trends maps can confirm the conflict and peace drivers identified in the academic literature and add or refine other drivers. They can also give weight to certain conflict drivers or causes. This was the case with 'weakness of the state' that came out very strongly from the conflict mappings in the DRC. It can also allow geographic differentiation: drivers perceived as very relevant in one province can be of lesser importance in another.

However, it was important for the evaluation team to take into account the possible pitfalls of participatory conflict mapping. The main danger is an unbalanced composition of the participants of the workshop, which could skew conclusions about the conflict. Participants look at the conflict from their own perspective and project staff may come up with conflict drivers relevant to the project they work in. For example, project staff of a justice intervention may stress that impunity is an important conflict driver.

Therefore the participants at the workshop need to be carefully selected. One way to reduce potential biases was to organise multiple workshops. The workshops also called for a skilled facilitator to control dominant personalities, in addition to another facilitator who transcribes the statements as faithfully as possible. Participants can become very passionate narrators during discussions on a conflict, but by focusing on descriptive elements and the linkages in the mapping, rather than a weighting given to more or less significant events and trends, it was possible to bring together conflicting perspectives in a manageable group dynamic.

The outcomes of both processes of conflict analyses conducted by the team were combined and led to the identification of the following conflict drivers:

- Weak state capacity in the rural areas, as demonstrated by absence of services, irregular salary payments and dilapidated infrastructure.
- Frequent land conflicts, linked to customary and modern interpretations of law, the frequent population movements as a result of war and the unregulated exploitation of natural resources (forests and minerals in particular).
- Economic and political opportunities captured by elite to mobilise armed groups.
- Emergence of extraction and trade chains for minerals, often controlled by armed groups, and criminal networks.

In line with the notion of 'incompressible complexity' (Richardson 2009), the analysis did not seek to rank drivers according to some external interpretation of what would be a root cause or a secondary cause. Instead, the conflict analysis aimed to identify factors that were considered influential.

The results of both the desk study analysis and the participatory analyses converged on similar findings, although the country workshops led to very locally defined conflict drivers (for example the interference of a specific warlord in a particular mine), which in the literature were linked to more theoretically formulated causes (such as the interference of militias in mineral production more generally).

In hindsight, the evaluation was weakened by the fact that the participatory events and trends analysis workshops were carried out in parallel with the analysis of the projects. The organisation and facilitation of the workshops required considerable resources, and the drivers provided by the participants emerged at the same time as the evaluation findings. Instead they could have served to provide a template from which to select particular interventions, on the basis of their apparent relation to the particular drivers.

This simultaneous merging of two streams of analysis (local elicitation of drivers and assessment of the projects) complicated the drafting of the final assessment, as part of the project analysis was already finished when the results of the conflict analyses were still coming in. The analysis could still be done retrospectively, ascribing an influence of an outcome on a driver, but the quality of the evidence was not as good as it would have been had it been done in proper sequences.

In the lessons learned session carried out by the evaluation team at the end of the process, it was concluded that the participatory events and trends mapping process should have taken place in the inception stage, even before the sample of case studies had been selected. The sequencing could have included adjustments to the conflict analyses in the course of subsequent field visits. This would have had budgetary implications (it would have meant an extra field visit during the inception phase), but it would have ensured a more efficient analytical process and a more in-depth account of the context.

4.4 Using case studies

From the very start, the evaluation design ruled out methods aimed at identifying net-change (using a baseline, control groups and before/after contrast). This was decided because the team did not succeed in identifying valid baselines and reliable sets of indicators necessary for such an analysis. It turned out that, for the most part, the information on the conditions prevailing at the start of the interventions could not inform subsequent monitoring – either because it was insufficiently detailed for specific aspects, or because conditions had changed so dramatically to make before/after or with/without comparisons meaningless.

The case study approach was used as a means to identify critical outcomes rapidly while minimising the management of large bodies of information. Case studies were also used to enable the team to study projects in-depth, interpreting them in their sociopolitical context. The team felt that case studies enabled the bringing together of multiple perspectives and the exploration of contested viewpoints, and were therefore an ideal means of producing a frame of reference against which interventions could be assessed.[14]

The sampling strategy was partly determined before the launch of the actual evaluation. The Terms of Reference stated that the evaluators had to propose 3 to 5 themes and a sample of 50 to 60 interventions of various sizes within these themes. During the main mission 20 to 25 interventions had to be visited, from which 5 to 6 interventions would undergo an in-depth evaluation. Suggesting this approach, it was the commissioners' intention to combine a large scope with an in-depth analysis, to facilitate both insight and generalisation of findings. These requirements were accommodated in the case study approach.

The idea behind such a large sample was to cover the wide range of interventions that were part of the evaluation scope, but it resulted in a laborious process of data collection. The poor quality of data, plus transportation costs, meant that in the final analysis a large part of the evaluation work was dedicated to the collection of information on the large number of individual cases.

The selection of the sample started with the identification of certain crucial themes for peacebuilding in eastern Congo, leading then to the case studies. These themes were generated on the basis of previous policy analysis, the desk-based conflict analysis, donor portfolio analysis, interviews and discussions within the Steering Group. They were then tested through a consultation process through the creation of the four Reference Groups, composed of interested stakeholders (one in Kinshasa, three in the main cities in the east). These themes then structured the evaluation field.

These themes were:

1. Humanitarian aid and the fight against sexual and gender-based violence (SGBV): these sectors were taken together given the highly specialised focus of their activities, but equally due to their large proportion of projects within the overall database – something that was considered an indication of their importance in the DRC. It was also an illustrative theme for the question of compartmentalisation of aid efforts in terms of differing procedures, specialisations and mandates.
2. Justice: justice is at the core of donor and UN agency policy for the DRC. It clearly illustrates the constant tension between, on the one hand, the risk of justice's effectiveness being undermined by the state, and on the other hand, the creation of sovereign, independent judicial powers and the popular confidence that should envelop justice initiatives.
3. Security Sector Reform (SSR) and Disarmament, Demobilisation and Reintegration (DDR): the efforts in these sectors underline the contrast between the technical quality of the projects and the complex environment in which they operate, where local interests and dynamics often usurp these processes and use them for political benefit.
4. Mineral exploitation: mining activities were also identified as one area in which local predatory interests come forward. The theme is also closely linked to regional cooperation (trade, smuggling and international efforts at certification), the governance of natural resources and overall economic growth.
5. Capacity-building: from the outset, the evaluators saw capacity-building as a key theme. Following the team's successive visits to the DRC, the evaluators became increasingly aware of the problems related to the weakness – perhaps even the complete absence – of the state in the conflict zones. This problem was raised strongly during local interviews.

These themes were used to narrow down the number of projects. The projects were then assessed in terms of their effect on conflict drivers (situated in relation to these themes).

This facilitated the selection by the evaluation team of a number of projects which best represented the contrasts and similarities within these themes, predominantly because of physical location, types of agencies and donors. In the latter case, this was to ensure that the members of the Steering Committee recognised the projects from their portfolio in the evaluation. At the end of this process, drawing on the database, the team selected 51 projects as a sample for review, out of a total of 353 proposed. As requested in the Terms of Reference, out of the 51 projects, 8 were the subject of field visits, while stakeholders of another 21 participated in face-to-face interviews. The others were evaluated via individual interviews with stakeholders or based on available documents.

The approach was based on an emergent design (Simons 2009), with the potential to shift focus in response to a growing understanding of the case, and the engagement of participants, even during the data-collection phase. In some instances it proved necessary to alter the selection of cases due to the poor quality of evidence, or to new information, which had not been available initially.

This approach of gradually defining the scope during the evaluation was different from the approach used in the first attempt (2008) to start up the evaluation. At that time, the donors had decided which sectors should be part of the scope, based on what they thought to be the important sectors. The chosen sectors in the first attempt were sexual and gender-based violence, mining and child soldiers; three issues that were very present in the debate around the conflict in eastern DRC at that time. However, only mining was an important driver of the conflict, the other two were focused on consequences, and the evaluation would have missed some important contributions aimed at the heart of the issues at stake. In the first approach, the important justice sector, linked to an equally very important driver of conflict – tensions around the ownership and use of land – had been overlooked.

Finally, the data-gathering process in a situation of conflict has its particularities, which lends itself well to a case study approach. Access and logistics in particular tend to play a primary role in the site visits. The team had to use the resources at hand to visit the project sites, such as helicopters deployed by the UN peacekeepers, local airlines or local car rentals.

5 Tracking contribution

5.1 *The translation of an industrial impact assessment tool to peacebuilding evaluation*

The case studies made statements about the contribution of particular interventions to different dimensions of peace. The method that enabled the case studies to do this was derived from the social and environmental impact assessment methods used in relation to extractive industries (as defined in professional bodies such as the International Association of Impact Assessments).

In their original form, these impact assessments are usually done as part of a permitting process to launch a large industrial project. When presented as prospective analysis, in effect a risk assessment, they do not make assumptions of causality, but rather describe models of influence which are assessed in terms of the severity of the influence (for example the acidity of a chemical or the loss that trucking accidents can cause), the extent of the influence (are leaks affecting large areas, are haulage roads crossing many inhabited areas) and the duration of the influence (is the leaking repetitive or brief, are the trucks going to be using the haulage roads for two days or many years). This type of analysis can also be done in a retrospective manner.

It should be pointed out that this method was originally designed to deal with the mass of technical detail and information generated by engineering projects to analyse the effect of a particular aspect of an industrial project on a valued component in its environment. However, we found that the underlying framework was a useful model to trace the interaction of an outcome on a conflict driver.

The use of the method is based on the assumption that conflict prevention and peacebuilding interventions can convincingly contribute to peace when they are targeted at the most significant contextualised drivers of conflict, rather than to long causal chains. As mentioned earlier, a part of the evaluation was to identify certain critical drivers. Once the conflict drivers were identified, the evaluators could use them as a reference point to review the policies and activities of the participating donors and agencies. The evaluation question was: do policies and interventions address the most relevant drivers of peace/conflict, and if so how?

This 'contribution model' used for the analysis of the impact revolves around the strength of the influence of a specific type of outcome on specific drivers. The evaluation had to then carry out two steps:

1. The identification of the observed outputs and outcomes achieved by the projects in the case studies (as opposed to the intended outcomes).
2. The analysis of the influence of these outcomes on key drivers in the local context, as informed by the desk-based conflict analysis and the events and trends maps.

The core of this analysis is to define the contribution in terms that reflect the effect of the outcomes on the broader conflict, through the conflict drivers. Each case study (the project) then defines a set of principal outcomes, and explores their relation to the drivers that operate in the region where the project takes place. This relation is defined along three dimensions:

1. Was the influence of the outcome on the driver relevant (was it well targeted, did the nature of the outcome truly align with the decisive conditions for the driver)?
2. Was the influence of the outcome on the driver extensive (did it cover the populations which were affected by or were affecting the driver, in geography and in numbers)?
3. Was the influence of the outcome on the driver durable (was it timely, repetitive, long-lasting, sustainable)?

The key element of the evaluation is to identify the influence of the outcomes on the drivers. This influence is of a causal nature, but this causality is not defined as a simple 'if X then Y' relation. Rather, it is a probabilistic analysis: is the influence severe (or relevant)? Is it extensive? What is its duration, is it timely, does it repeat itself over time, and is it sustainable?

The evaluation thus used conflict drivers to replace so-called valued social and environmental components, which are often used in impact assessment in this field. Through the case studies, a different type of observation could be made about aid performance. For example, aid may be highly effective in ensuring access to legal services for populations most in need, but it may not deal with land ownership, which is a crucial driver of conflict.

It was this assessment that resulted in the aforementioned observation that aid donors had wrongly neglected two important drivers of conflict when they first initiated this evaluation: the land-ownership conflicts and mineral exploitation.

Finally, the perceptions of aid among populations in outlying areas are heavily guided by their interaction with humanitarian agencies. Humanitarian aid is the most visible outreach of international organisations, as those interventions are the ones that tend to go furthest. Not to capture the symbolic, as well as economic and decision-making effects of these programmes would have meant ignoring an important effect of international aid. Many donors also label humanitarian aid as peacebuilding in their programmes, as they estimate that it has a beneficial effect. Not to review this theme would have been detrimental to the evaluation.

5.2 Revisiting 'contribution'

The debate on assessing the contribution of interventions through evaluations has expanded very quickly in recent years, in the search for more precise causal models.

We argue that in some situations of active civil war taking place over many years, the complexity becomes predominant and affects the legibility of diagrams of effects, or theories of change, even the most convoluted ones. The erosion of clarity occurs not only in the field, but also within the institutions that manage the aid programmes, where there can be feedback loops between outcomes and outputs. Biases become too predominant, and feedback loops too frequent, to be analytically manageable.

These concerns are echoed by other researchers. White and Phillips (2012) argue that there is considerable scope for cognitive biases in tracking contribution: in the way respondents report causal relationships, and the way in which evaluators collect and analyse data. They call for a significant increase in the level of effort in qualitative data collection in 'small n' evaluations, which, as we have explained above, is the prevailing type of conflict evaluation. While their paper focuses on development type initiatives, these challenges are amplified for interventions in conflict settings.

The option taken in this evaluation was to avoid drawing ambitious causal links between inputs and impact, and instead focusing on causalities of a much more proximate type: between outcome and driver, at the level of project implementation on the ground. To understand this one should see 'the ground' not so much as one dimension of the reality of aid work, but where change is experienced, and the outcomes of aid are observed.

While the events and trends maps do represent some form of causality and a theory of change, it is not the simplified form of change which is usually understood in the cascades that underpin programme theory. They are rather a combination of multiple loops, moving forward and backward, describing what happened, where no meta-narrative is present. Specific causal inferences could not be found in such a challenging and complex context, and so a more dynamic understanding of constructed or lived relationships was used, as these relationships are understood by the people inhabiting Congo.

6 Conclusion

This chapter describes the challenges encountered in the context of a multi-donor evaluation of peace interventions in the DRC. These challenges can also be found in other environments, but are clearly exacerbated in an assessment with such characteristics: conflict-based, multi-agency, over long periods.

The foremost challenge encountered was in tracking the logic of the interventions, over time, across organisations, and in different sectors and regions. The evaluators concluded that although it would have been possible to engage in a theory-based causal analysis, a more practical alternative existed in focusing on drivers and on the influence of specific aid outcomes, based on a case study design. It was possible, in other words, to avoid long linear models of attribution, with a high risk of bias, and replace them with proximate and highly localised causalities, identified on the basis of participatory and deductive methods.

Two aspects were crucial in the approach: the importance of the conflict analysis and the focus on observed outcomes instead of intended outcomes.

The conflict analysis was vital in the identification of themes and as such for the delineation of the most appropriate scope for this large joint evaluation in a wide and volatile conflict area. In a similar vein, the conflict analysis was indispensable for the identification of conflict (and peace) drivers which were used to measure the relevance (did donors target the most crucial drivers?) and the contribution to peace (did the observed outcomes have an influence on these important drivers?).

The focus on observed outcomes helped to get around the laborious reconstruction of the theories of change leading to the intended outcomes. This approach was particularly helpful to evaluate the conflict sensitivity of interventions without intended outcomes targeting the conflict.

This approach made it possible to envisage and complete an evaluation even in conditions where the lack of historical evidence, the absence of clearly articulated strategies, plus the partly unknowable nature of the causes of conflict, seemed overwhelming. The focus on identified outcomes and drivers is highly contextualised, while generalisation is possible to a certain extent thanks to the use of a case study approach.

Notes

1 Agencies involved were: the Belgian Federal Public Service Foreign Affairs, the Canadian International Development Agency (CIDA), the German Federal Ministry for Economic Cooperation and Development (BMZ), the Japanese Ministry of Foreign Affairs, the Netherlands Ministry of Foreign Affairs, the United Kingdom Department for International Development (DFID), the Office of the High Commissioner for Human Rights (OHCHR) attached to the UN peace-keeping mission MONUC, *Mission des Nations Unies au Congo*, the United Nations Development Programme (UNDP), UNICEF, UNIFEM and UNFPA.

2 The five thematic areas were: 1) humanitarian aid and sexual and gender-based violence; 2) justice; 3) security sector reform and disarmament, demobilisation and reintegration; 4) mineral exploitation; and 5) capacity-building.
3 Overviews of the DRC wars include: Turner (2007); Lemarchand (2008); Prunier (2009); Reyntjens (2009).
4 Death rates from the DRC conflict have been subject to debate. A Human Security Report (2009) argues that the IRC estimate is based on an inappropriately low baseline mortality rate. With a more appropriate baseline rate, the death toll would be one-third of IRC's estimate, or 500,000 people (Human Security Report Project 2009). The 2007 population of the DRC was estimated at 62 million (www.rescue.org/special-reports/special-report-congo-y).
5 www.rescue.org/special-reports/special-report-congo-y.
6 On the position of the Banyamulenge and Banyarwanda, see Willame (1997).
7 A good overview of regional stakes in the DRC war is Clark (2002).
8 The funding for the MONUC, US$1.3 billion in 2010 (www.oecd.org/dac/stats/COD.gif), is additional to these aid figures as it considered as security related and as such not ODA eligible.
9 See Pawson and Tilley (1997). And, for a more methodological interpretation, Funnell and Rogers (2011).
10 One example of this is a DFID-funded study CARE (2012). The most developed form is that adopted by the European Commission external relations evaluations, which include highly detailed logic of intervention graphs. Evaluating EU activity: (http://ec.europa.eu/dgs/secretariat_general/evaluation/docs/eval_activities_en.pdf).
11 See also Cilliers (2007).
12 See for example OECD (2012).
13 Thus, the approach of the evaluation followed a long tradition of using participatory methods within development (see, for example, Chambers 1983, 2009).
14 A debt is acknowledged here to Simons (2009: ch. 1, on the political dimensions of case studies).

Bibliography

Blamey, A., Judge, K. and Mackenzie, M. (2002) *Theory-based Evaluation of Complex Community-based Health Initiatives*, Glasgow: University of Glasgow.
CARE (2012) *Peacebuilding with Impact: Defining Theories of Change*, London: CARE.
Chambers, R. (1983) *Rural Development: Putting the Last First*, London: Longman.
——(2009) 'Making the Poor Count – Using Participatory Methods for Impact Evaluation', *Designing Impact Evaluations – Different Perspectives*, 3ie working paper 4, New Delhi: International Initiative for Impact Evaluation.
Cilliers, P. (2005) 'Knowing Complex Systems' in K. A. Richardson (ed.) *Managing Organizational Complexity: Philosophy, Theory, and Application*, Charlotte: Information Age Publishing, pp. 7–19.
——(ed.) (2007) *Thinking Complexity – Complexity and Philosophy Volume 1*, Mansfield: ISCE Publishing.
Clark, J. (2002) *The African Stakes in the Congo War*, New York: Palgrave McMillan.
de Coning, C. (2012) *Coherence and International Cooperation: A Complexity Theory Approach to the Coordination Dilemma in Peacebuilding Operations*, unpublished.
Funnell, S. and Rogers, P. (2011) *Purposeful Program Theory: Effective Use of Theories of Change and Logic Models*, San Francisco: Jossey-Bass.

International Association for Impact Appraisal (2012) 'Impact Assessment and Project Appraisal', *Journal of Impact Appraisal* 30(1). www.tandfonline.com/toc/tiap20/30/1, accessed May 2013.

Körppen, D., Ropers, N. and Giessmann, H. J. (eds) (2011) *The Non-linearity of Peace Processes: Theory and Practice of Systemic Conflict Transformation*, Opladen/ Farmington Hills: Barbara Budrich Verlag.

Lemarchand, R. (2008) *The Dynamics of Violence in Central Africa*, Philadelphia: University of Pennsylvania Press.

Mathieu, P. and Willame, J.-C. (1999) *Conflits et guerres au Kivu et dans la Region des Grands Lacs: entre tensions locales et escalade régionale*, Paris: L'Harmattan.

OECD (2011) 'ODA in the Democratic Republic of Congo', Development Co-operation Directorate. Paris: OECD. www.oecd.org/dac/stats/COD.gif.

——(2012) *Evaluating Peacebuilding Activities in Settings of Conflict and Fragility: Improving Learning for Results*, DAC Guidelines and Reference Series. Paris: OECD Publishing. doi: 10.1787/9789264106802-en.

Pawson, R. and Tilley, N. (1997) *Realistic Evaluation*, Thousand Oaks and London: Sage.

Prunier, G. (2009) *From Genocide to Continental War: The 'Congolese' Conflict and the Crisis of Contemporary Africa*, London: C. Hurst and Co.

Reyntjens, F. (2009) *The Great African War: Congo and Regional Geopolitics, 1996–2006*, Cambridge: Cambridge University Press.

Richardson, K. (ed.) (2009) *Knots, Lace and Tartan – Making Sense of Complex Human Systems in Military Operations Research – The Selected Works of Graham L. Mathieson*, Napels, FL: ISCE Publishing.

Simons, H. (2009) *Case Study Research in Practice*, London: Sage.

Stearns, J. (2011) *Dancing in the Glory of Monsters – The Collapse of the Congo and the Great War of Africa*, New York: Public Affairs.

Stern, E., Stame, N., Mayne, J., Forss, K., Davies, R. and Befani, B. (2012) *Developing a Broader Range of Rigorous Designs and Methods for Impact Evaluations*, report of a study commissioned by the Department for International Development (DFID), London: Department for International Development (DFID). www.dfid.gov.uk/Documents/.../ design-method-impact-eval.pdf, accessed 26 March 2013.

Turner, T. (2007) *The Congo Wars: Conflict, Myth and Reality*, New York: Zed Books.

Van Acker, F. (1999) 'La "pembénisation" du Haut-Kivu: Opportunisme et droits fonciers revisités', in S. Maryse and F. Reyntjens (eds) *L'Afrique des Grands Lacs, Annuaire 1998–1999*, Paris: L'Harmattan, pp.1–35.

White, H. and Phillips, D. (2012) *Addressing Attribution of Cause and Effect in Small n Impact Evaluations: Towards an Integrated Framework*, Working Paper 15, New Delhi: International Initiative for Impact Evaluation.

Willame, J.-C. (1997) *Banyarwanda et Banyamulenge: Violences ethniques et gestion de l'identitaire au Kivu*, Paris: L'Harmattan.

6 Assessing development cooperation in northeast Afghanistan with repeated mixed-method surveys

Jan R. Böhnke
University of York

Jan Koehler
Free University Berlin

Christoph Zürcher
University of Ottawa

1 Introduction

This chapter introduces a longitudinal multi-method approach to assessing the impact of development interventions on peace and security in northeast Afghanistan. Qualitative methods are used to identify a plausible theory of change. Repeated large *n* surveys are used to identify and attribute impacts, while qualitative methods are used to explain the observed changes.

In early 2006, the head of the evaluation unit of the German Federal Ministry of Economic Cooperation and Development (BMZ) unexpectedly approached us to ask if we were interested in developing a method for measuring the impact of development aid in zones in or after conflict and testing this method in northeast Afghanistan, a region in which Germany was leading the international mission. Of course we were interested. This was the beginning of an unusual cooperation between development practitioners in the German government and academics (a political scientist, a social anthropologist and a statistician). We teamed up to find out how to measure the impacts of aid on stability in one region of Afghanistan.

Impact assessments face a challenge that is at the heart of all social science: how can we accurately measure the impact of an intervention? Natural scientists have a laboratory – they can, for example, feed a new drug to a randomly selected group of white mice, and then compare how the treatment group does compared to the control group. But social scientists do not have white mice, development aid in conflict zones is not an intervention as clearly defined as a drug versus a placebo, and Afghanistan is not a laboratory. Learning what works in such settings is a daunting task, as several chapters in this book describe. Even under controlled laboratory conditions it is challenging to choose an adequate method for inferring causality. In zones in or after conflict, getting data and coping with the logistical difficulties adds additional challenges. Yet, learning more about the impact of development aid in conflict zones can help save lives and ensure tax money is allocated effectively. This chapter describes some of the difficulties we faced in conducting a multi-method evaluation in two provinces in north Afghanistan, based on surveys of 2,000 respondents in 80 villages in April 2007 and in March 2009.[1]

The evaluation unit of the BMZ perceived this as a pilot for developing a replicable method for assessing the impact of aid in zones in or after conflict. Furthermore, the project was designed from the beginning as a cooperation between the BMZ's evaluation unit and a university research team. This focus gave more flexibility and control over the evaluation in two ways. First, we were free to choose which aspects of the development aid to include in our assessment. Our choices were therefore driven by theoretical and methodological choices, and not, as might have been, by bureaucratic routines or political reasoning. Second, because the evaluation was seen primarily as a research exercise aimed at developing methods, it was much less politicised than an overall evaluation of the German engagement in Afghanistan would have been. Experiences from other evaluations often show that evaluators may face considerable pressure from policymakers or bureaucracies in such politicised contexts, both while evaluating and in presenting the results. Since our project was designed as research cooperation between two equal partners, we never faced any of these problems.

Development aid, it is hoped, can have a stabilising effect on the situation in conflict zones. Our task was to develop a method that would allow testing this assumption (based on which, as one may remember, donors pour billions and billions of dollars in aid money into conflict zones). In the coming sections, we describe important decisions in developing our approach, and give the rationale for our choices.

2 Analysis of the aid portfolio in northeast Afghanistan

An important first step was to analyse the donor portfolio to identify what kinds of aid activities are actually carried out in the target region, as opposed to activities that are mentioned as priority in policy papers but are not actually carried out. The theory about how change is achieved through aid (described in the next section) must be tested using accurate information about the aid inputs. We used data from a survey conducted by the BMZ which listed 259 projects conducted by German development cooperation actors – state and non-state – in Afghanistan between 2003 and 2006. Given that Germany was the main international player in the region during this period, it was reasonable to assume that this list reflected fairly well the overall development activities. Hence, the initial analysis focused on the German development portfolio. However, the subsequent fieldwork covered all development activities within the target area irrespective of origin of donors or implementing agencies.[2] Most German aid focused initially on developing capacities in Kabul and relatively little aid reached the northeast. Most aid in the northeast targeted the rural population. As is typical for the early stages of aid in a conflict setting, investment in infrastructure and household-level direct aid dominated the portfolio. Capacity-building and institutional development were much less frequent. Some multilateral programmes, however, such as the National Solidarity Programme (NSP), also included an important element of bottom-up institution-building in its constitution of elected Community Development Committees (CDCs).[3] In line with Germany's overall strategy,[4] most bilateral projects went into education, water and road infrastructure.

3 Conflict assessment

After analysing the aid portfolio, the next step was to conduct an up-to-date conflict assessment. We drew on the results of conflict analyses conducted by team members from 2003 to 2007 (see Koehler 2004, 2005; Gosztonyi and Koehler 2010). The impact of development cooperation can only be assessed against clearly defined relevance criteria. In conflict zones, these criteria need to be developed by analysing the conflict and identifying main threats to peace.[5] This includes understanding the specific actors who are engaged in conflict or must be engaged in ending conflict. Conflict zones are characterised by volatility, and not everything in the context is equally relevant to understanding the conflict. A single focus on 'root causes' of a conflict or a long list of factors potentially affecting stability can distort an understanding of the actual dynamic of the conflict in which development cooperation operates.[6]

We analysed the situation in 2006 and the specifics of the region to develop scenarios of possible future developments (which might affect which kind of development interventions would be most relevant during the time of the planned assessment in spring 2007–spring 2009).

Based on this conflict assessment, we concluded that building up governance capacities of the emerging state was a key priority. In order to pacify the region,[7] positive changes in security, material endowments and state legitimacy in rural areas were required. We also deduced that the new central state would need the acceptance and loyalty of a largely sceptical rural population, which by and large seemed to adhere to a 'wait and see who wins' strategy. We identified the development of a rentier state, the corruption by drug money, and the insurgency as the main threats to the emerging Afghan state.[8]

Box 6.1 The framework for the evaluation as derived from the conflict assessment

Strategic priorities: state capacities and security

Afghanistan will not become a stable, self-sustainable and peaceful state without building up a viable administration. Development projects should contribute to strengthening state capacities. Increased state capacities should then be reflected by improvements in security, welfare and state legitimacy.

Threats

The main threat is the insurgency. Also, frontloading of aid may create incentives for the Afghan state to turn into a rentier state and, as a result, the state will grow weaker. Another threat is that the drug economy corrupts the statebuilding process. Drug money strengthens bad local governance, then the central state is unable to convince local power holders to align with it.

Time frame: impact visible within two years

Conflict research shows that a post-conflict zone faces the highest danger of relapsing into war during the first three years after the cessation of hostilities. Hence, development projects should have a visible impact within two years after implementation.

Level: beyond Kabul, in rural areas

Statebuilding must reach out into the provinces. There is a high demand among the rural population for a state that delivers security, visible material improvement, increased good local governance and that helps strengthening conflict-processing capacities at the regional level.

Development intervention

Most programmes in the region are small-scale infrastructure projects targeted at the rural population. To what extent can they help in winning the loyalty of the local population for the statebuilding process?

Based on this conflict assessment, we derived a framework for our evaluation. This framework spelled out an appropriate time frame for the expected impact (two years),[9] narrowed down the development interventions we would look at, specified the geographic scope, identified the main threats to security, and spelled out the strategic priorities for the pacification of the region (state capacity and security).

4 Theories of conflict and change

The portfolio analysis identified the main development activities in the region, and the conflict assessment helped us to define the regional focus, time frame, level and type of observed interventions and the main threats. Next, we needed to specify how development aid might actually contribute to positive change. This is a theory-driven exercise to develop a theory of change regarding aid in conflict settings. We did a close reading of the relevant academic literature and then compared the results of this analysis with the explicit or implicit impact assumptions of development actors operating in fragile or conflict prone environments as described in their policy documents.[10]

A theory of change posits the main hypothesis of the investigation. It is a set of testable assumptions about the causes of the changes that are observed. It proposes the causal chains that bring along those changes which are thought to be helpful for pacifying the conflict zone, and can be plausibly attributed to the ongoing development projects. The theory of change specifies which social changes the research will focus on, and which factors might cause these changes.

How can aid contribute to more stability in conflict zones? It is perhaps too optimistic to assume that the tools that development actors usually have at their disposal will have an immediate effect on the security situation. Development aid in poor post-conflict countries first and foremost intends to increase the provision of basic goods and services for the population. As we saw in northeast Afghanistan, development actors aimed to increase access to food and drinking water, and to rehabilitate or build basic infrastructure. Presumably drilling wells and building bridges will not disarm warlords, and refurnishing schools not increase counterinsurgency capacities of the government. But consider this instance: in the spring of 2006, forces hostile to the Afghan government and international actors increased attacks on schools in northeast Afghanistan. Recently refurnished buildings were burned, and some teachers attacked. In some communities, however, the local population sided with the state security forces in preventing the destruction of their schools by reporting planned attacks to the authorities.[11] Instances such as this demonstrate that the local population, under certain circumstances, chooses cooperation with the emerging and internationally backed state authorities over cooperation with insurgents, despite the risks associated with opposing armed gunmen. In these instances, the benefits that the local communities received from continued cooperation with development actors outweighed the risks of opposing the armed opposition.

This example illustrates that the success of a peacebuilding mission depends to a large extent on how the local population feel about the emerging state as well as their attitudes towards the international military forces and development actors who are supporting this state. Sustainable peace will not be possible as long as substantial segments of the population are neutral or even hostile towards the statebuilding project. Support of the population may not be a sufficient condition for peace; but sustainable peace appears to be unlikely without convincing the population that it is ultimately beneficial for them to become a stakeholder in the peacebuilding process and to engage in prolonged cooperation with the emerging state and its international supporters. The rationale for distributing development aid in post-conflict situations is therefore not only to address the immediate needs of the population, but also to make cooperation with the statebuilding interveners more attractive. Aid, it is hoped, will help to 'win hearts and minds' and increase local support. More support among the local population may then translate into a better security environment, which reduces the costs of international support for the political transition.

But development actors and military forces operating in fragile conflict zones seek not only to gain the acceptance and the cooperation of the local population, they also hope that development aid will increase the legitimacy of the supported government and thus help stabilise a political regime compatible with the interests of the intervening powers.[12] It is believed that aid programmes may help to increase the administrative capacity of the state, which enables the state to better provide basic services to its population. Therefore, often a sizable share of the overall aid allocated to fragile states is earmarked for capacity-building. Development actors have become conscientious to avoid competing with the state. Rather than bypassing the state, they often distribute aid through government institutions, hoping that aid will increase acceptance and legitimacy of state actors. A legitimate and capable state, it is hoped, will command the loyalty of its citizens and withstand insurgents' attempts at claiming power.

> **Box 6.2 A theory of change for aid in northeast Afghanistan**
>
> Development cooperation can facilitate the pacification of conflict zones, because development cooperation has a positive impact on general attitudes towards the peacebuilding mission and because it strengthens the legitimacy of the Afghan state, both of which can reduce the local perception of security threats.

Summing up, while aid is given in conflict zones primarily to protect and improve the livelihoods of people, development and military actors expect other benefits, too. Namely, they hope aid will help reduce the risks for military and development actors in the field, because the material benefits of aid will induce communities to share vital information with the international forces or the official, intervention-backed authorities, rather than with the insurgents. This will make the environment safer and the operations of development actors and counterinsurgency forces more efficient. Furthermore, aid is also thought to convince the population that cooperation with international actors and the emerging state is preferable to cooperating with local insurgents. Aid is thought to foster the legitimacy of the state, either by building the state's capacity for delivering public goods, or by directly delivering pubic goods in the name of the state. A more legitimate state and positive attitudes towards international military and civilian reconstruction and development efforts then add up to an environment with improved security in which the peacebuilding mission stands a better chance of success. International engagement in conflict zones is ultimately based on these assumptions.

The final step, after the portfolio analysis, conflict assessment and identification of the theory of change, was to develop a research design that allows for testing these assumptions and identifying the causal mechanisms that explain the observed impacts. Before we describe this final step, however, we take stock of the limitations of our research design.

5 Knowing the limitations

All evaluations necessarily involve choices about what aspects to include and what to leave out. These choices should be grounded in theory and made explicit. For this evaluation, we decided to focus on villages, because this group makes up the overwhelming majority of the Afghan population, estimated at 74 per cent (OHCHR 2010)[13] and appeared to be the main target group of development interventions in the region.

Since this represents the majority of the Afghan population we assumed that the fate of the international statebuilding mission in Afghanistan would ultimately be determined by whether or not these men and women would accept the new Afghan government as legitimate. Therefore, we focused on the population in rural areas – a focus on urban populations would probably paint a slightly different picture.

We focused on rural households rather than on individuals or nuclear families, because in the context of rural Afghanistan, households pool resources and the head of household represents the attitudes and positions of all household members to the outside world. Since the household is the most relevant sub-village social collective actor, it made sense to survey the heads of households.

We focused predominately on emergency aid and small infrastructural projects (including roads), because such projects are meant to have a relatively quick and visible impact, which should be measurable shortly after implementation. In addition, this type of aid formed the bulk of all aid which reached the communities during this period.

While we felt that the tasks at hand warranted these choices, we were very conscious about the resulting limitations: since we focused on rural communities and small-scale infrastructure projects, we were not well equipped to identify the effects of other types of aid projects (capacity-building in the capital or on the provincial level, for example) although these projects may have an indirect impact on the villages. Also, due to our focus on the household, our interviews were with heads of households, who are, with very rare exceptions, adult men. Hence we did not capture the perceptions of women or youth in the quantitative surveys.

Finally, we chose a short time frame of two years. While donors (and beneficiaries) expect quick results even or especially in conflict zones, we were aware, of course, that some development interventions may take longer before they lead to social changes. While being adequate in terms of achieving the evaluation goal of some stakeholders, we acknowledge that this meant we could not observe long-term effects.

We have argued above that choosing the appropriate level and time frame of analysis is vital in order to arrive at a plausible and relevant theory of change. We have shown that this process rests on three pillars: the goals of the development intervention, predictions of conflict research and case specific conflict analysis. This poses the conceptual demand that for all three perspectives of analysis the level and time frame coincide. Hence, we only focused on predictions of conflict research, results of the conflict analysis and impact expectations of development interventions that relate to quickly visible changes (time frame of analysis) in mostly rural areas (level of analysis).

Though it focused on the rural population in northeast Afghanistan, this approach is not blind entirely to longer-term effects of central or macro-programmes. We also sought to identify and analyse sustainable longer-term effects over the timeline of the research by analysing how far the results of one survey (in this case 2007) predict the results of subsequent surveys (2009). Our methods also aimed to capture indirect effects of programmes targeting, for example, teachers' capacity-building at central or provincial level – whenever these programmes reached our units of analysis (the villages) by changing the curriculum or the quality of schooling.

Other limitations were a consequence of external conditions created by the conflict setting. For example, a near complete lack of basic demographic data[14] required that all data had to be collected by the researchers themselves, which is, of course, time-consuming and expensive. Also, establishing representative samples became difficult since there was no reliable census data and stratified sampling was not possible. Our survey was planned at village level, meaning that we applied random sampling of households in each village. Then, by taking a mixture of 80 randomly and qualitatively selected villages, these results should presumably also be representative for the rural population of the four districts where the communities are located, but it is very likely not large enough to be representative of all of north Afghanistan (for more details see section 8 and Böhnke et al. 2013).

The two provinces we worked in (Kunduz and Takhar) were relatively peaceful in 2006 and remained calm until 2009. During this period there were no large-scale collective violence nor military engagements between armed groups, which could have confounded our results.[15] Insurgent activity was limited to sporadic rocket attacks and improvised explosive devices. ISAF troops were very rarely engaged in actual combat operations. This changed in 2009 when Taliban insurgents began to take control in parts of the region and significantly increased activities in Kunduz and in other Pashtun-populated locations. For our purpose it is important to note that during our observation period (spring 2007 through spring 2009) there was only one large-scale counterinsurgency military operation affecting one of the target districts but not producing any casualties,[16] hence we expect only a very limited bias of our results by regional variations in fighting intensity, civilian casualties, troop deployment patterns, alliance patterns or similar factors, which are hard to control for.[17]

However, limiting our sample to two of the least violent provinces of Afghanistan may have led to results that cannot be generalised to other contexts. We initially played with the idea of including two more provinces from the east of the country, for example Laghman and Nangarhar. However, we anticipated that a deteriorating security situation might make it difficult if not impossible to conduct a follow-up survey in 2009. This prediction turned out to be true. To the best of our knowledge (based on the assessment of our local colleagues working in those provinces) it would not have been possible to work in these provinces in 2009, at least not without endangering the enumerators. Nevertheless, we are aware of the fact that our results pertain to a location which is, for a conflict zone, relatively less violent.

Finally, we opted to collect a random sample of households in every community, for each survey. An alternative would have been to collect panel data – that is to sample the same households for both survey waves. We did not do this because we were afraid of possible high attrition. We anticipated that a deteriorating security situation would have forced many households to flee or be on the move for work. We also wanted to minimise the risks for our respondents. Households who speak too often to foreigners might have been at higher risk of reprisal by insurgents, which could in turn affect responses.[18]

6 The context: northeast Afghanistan

For this study, we monitored 80 Afghan communities located in the provinces of Kunduz and Takhar, in Afghanistan's northeast over a two-year period. Despite the massive engagement of the international community after 2001, development activities were slow to reach outlying Afghan provinces. It was only around 2004 when major agencies, among them the World Bank, UNDP, USAID and the German GTZ, along with numerous international NGOs, started to distribute emergency aid and build infrastructure in the northeast.

Our data indicate that, during our observation period, communities in the northeast received significant benefits from the massive efforts of aid agencies. We asked respondents in 2007 and 2009 whether their community as a whole had been a beneficiary of development cooperation during the last two years in various sectors. With regard to schooling, 46.5 per cent agreed in 2007 and 70.6 per cent in 2009. Numbers for electricity are 14.2 per cent and 19.6 per cent, for roads and bridges 65.9 per cent and 68.8 per cent, and for drinking water 65.9 per cent and 54.7 per cent.

These development programmes were accompanied by military deployments. In order to foster a secure environment for the international reconstruction and rehabilitation effort, ISAF decided to establish so called provincial reconstruction teams (PRTs) in Afghan provinces. By 2004, there were three PRTs in the northeast region, in Kunduz (Kunduz province), Faizabad (Badakhshan province) and in Puli Khumir (Baghlan province). Up until the escalation of Taliban activities around 2009 they were not engaged in direct military action and focused on mere presence, patrols, CIMIC activities and supporting the reconstruction efforts in those comparatively peaceful provinces.

7 Concepts and operationalisation for the quantitative analysis of the survey data

While we used a mixed-methods approach for this evaluation, the backbone of our study was a quantitative analysis of two mass surveys of 2,000 heads of households. We therefore start with a description of our quantitative research, and then turn to the qualitative aspects.

Researchers must define valid measurements for all the concepts they intend to measure. For some concepts, this is a straightforward process. For example, the size of a village can be measured by the number of people living in the village. For other concepts, finding a valid measurement is much more difficult and requires returning to theoretical reasoning. 'Aid' is such a concept, and we will describe in some detail the challenges associated with measuring what seems to be a straightforward notion.

Aid is defined as the independent variable of most interest for our evaluation. There are different ways of measuring development aid, and none is perfect. One way is to simply use the money spent as a measure of aid. There are several problems with this option. For one, it is very difficult to get accurate budget data of all development agencies active in the region. Furthermore, these budgets do not provide figures for specific districts or communities. Finally, different agencies may have very different overhead costs: agency A spends US$1,000 on community A, and agency B spends US$1,000 on community B, but it may be that community A receives a net value of $600, and community B of only $300, due to higher transaction costs in agency A. These differences in overhead costs distort data on the input variable.

Another, alternative way to measure development aid is to actually count projects at the communal level. While logistically demanding, this approach has the advantage that aid is directly attributable to our unit of analysis. For this evaluation, we decided to measure development aid at the receiving end. We counted the number of projects that a community received (number of projects) to use as the independent variable. Information on aid projects was collected from various aid organisations and from the visited villages. The aid projects were then georeferenced and fed into a GIS database.

But the number of projects implemented within or near a given community is only one aspect of aid. It tells us something about the frequency of aid projects, but little about the value of a given aid project to the community. Since we intended to capture the impacts of aid on local attitudes, we employed two more measures of aid, both based on perceptions. These measures reflect the perception of respondents with regard to how much the household or community, in a given sector, had benefited from aid projects. The first of these (direct aid) captures whether individual households directly benefited from aid, for example food aid, training or advice, salary or rent for the household. The second perception-based measure (aid-class) seeks to capture the type and utility of aid to the community, based on respondents' perceptions. Data revealed that communities received quite different mixes of development aid. For example in 2007, 5.9 per cent of the communities received food aid (this aid was, however, disproportionally located in one district only: 112 of 120 cases were in Warsaj); 5.5 per cent training/advice/capacity-building (50 cases in Aliabad; 2 in Imam Sahib; 28 in Taloqan; 32 in Warsaj), 46.5 per cent of communities profited from schooling projects; 14.2 per cent from electricity (269 of 289 cases were in Warsaj); 65.9 per cent from projects related to roads and bridges; while only 2.5 per cent of respondents benefited from projects aimed at creating jobs. Of the respondents, 16 per cent received projects in agricultural extension services; 65.9 per cent reported having received projects related to drinking water and 24.1 per cent related to irrigation (mostly in Imam Sahib). There are thus clearly distinguishable regional patterns: food aid, electricity and jobs are predominately found in Warsaj, whereas irrigation projects are predominately found outside Warsaj.[19] Training and advice is underrepresented in Imam Sahib. All other aid variables seem to be free from relevant regional accumulations.

Although these two variables measure the perception of aid projects, it is still problematic to use these variables in a regression analysis. The answers cannot be easily summed up to a score (measuring a value between 'no aid' and 'aid in all sectors') because this would mean either dropping persons that do not remember some types of projects from the analyses (or declining to answer that question) or to impute their values with statistical methods that again rely on assumptions that are fallible. Entering each of the variables as a predictor in the regression (to estimate specific effects of every aid sector) would on the one hand mean to include many predictors only for this concept and on the other hand interaction effects (i.e., combined effects of different types as well as effects of combinations of aid sectors) would not be investigated because in regression only partial correlations are estimated. One could use interaction effects between the aid sectors to investigate the effects of combinations, but this would increase the number of predictors even further. Therefore we decided to use a Latent Class Analysis (LCA) to explore mixtures of remembered aid sectors.[20]

We entered the respondents' answers from both surveys into the LCA to identify patterns that can be used to describe remembered projects in both waves. If one pattern is irrelevant in one wave, the contingency table between the class membership of respondents and the variable for the next wave would show that no (or nearly no) respondents at one point in time were present in this class. Using LCA on the respondents' answers for both waves revealed six classes, reflecting the mix of projects from which the communities benefited from 2005–2007, according to respondent's perceptions (in both waves, 2007 and 2009, we asked about development aid-induced improvements over the past two years).

Now that we had defined our main independent variable (aid), we needed to operationalise the dependent variables, that is, the factors that we hoped aid would affect. Recall that our theory of change states that 'development cooperation can lead to a pacification of conflict zones, because development cooperation has a positive impact on general attitudes towards the peacebuilding mission and because it strengthens the legitimacy of the Afghan state, both of which can reduce the perceived security threats'.

We therefore needed measures of attitudes and of threat perceptions. *Attitudes towards the activities of the peace builders* were proxied by an index grouping six value statements about respondents' perceptions about state schooling for boys and girls, wage labour for women and men, and the presence of civilian and military actors. *Attitudes towards foreign forces* were proxied by an index (1–10) based on answers to the question: 'How afraid are you of foreign forces' and the rating of 'The presence of foreign troops is threatening local customs and Islamic values in our community.'[21] We proxied attitudes towards the Afghan state (*state legitimacy*) by the rating of the performance of district and provincial governments. Finally, *threat perceptions* were based on membership in threat classes. In order to identify these classes, we used a procedure similar to the one we used for the aid classes. We asked respondents to indicate which actors were threatening to them: 'Please indicate, if you are afraid of the following groups: 1 = not afraid, 2 = somewhat afraid, 3 = very afraid' and also 'refused to answer' and 'don't know' response categories. Respondents could choose from a list of eight actors: criminal groups, external militias, Taliban, local militias (these are militias that typically recruit from communities with which the respondents are familiar), foreign forces, district police, Afghan central security forces and Afghan provincial and district security forces.

Table 6.1 Important variables in quantitative analysis

Independent variables	Important control variables	Dependent variables
Aid: • Number of projects • Perceived aid for the household (food aid, training or advice, salary, rents) • Perceived aid for the community (food aid, training/advice/capacity building, schooling projects, roads and bridges, projects aimed at creating jobs, agricultural extension services, drinking water, irrigation, electrification/power)	• Ethnicity • Material wellbeing (household level) • Location of village • Vulnerability of village	• Attitudes towards development actors • Attitudes towards military actors • Perceived threats from violent actors

In addition to the perception-based fear indicator we also assessed 'objective' security based on geo-referenced violent incidents. Because of issues relating to data quality and finding comparable sources of information, we were not able to construct a robust quantitative indicator from the data but used the information for the qualitative assessment of the security environment of our target villages and districts.

Once we defined independent (aid) and dependent variables (attitudes and threat perceptions), we needed to measure and control for other factors that affect the dependent variables. We created several variables that proxy various characteristics of the households and communities that may also influence attitudes and threat perceptions. We created variables for the ethnic belonging (Pashtu, Uzbek, Tajik, other) of respondents. To control for a household's material wellbeing we asked the respondents to indicate if it was hard for them to buy even simple food products, if they could spend money for clothes and social obligations, if they could buy luxury goods or even anything they want (material wellbeing). Based on this, we created an index which reflects the self-reported material situation of the household. Other control variables measure whether a community was remotely located, whether it was vulnerable to disasters (mudslides, for example), and in which district it was located. Finally, we controlled for the respondents' individual perceptions of the security situation by asking respondents to rate whether security, in their opinion, had increased or decreased during the last two years (security change). Table 6.1 gives an overview of the main concepts used in the quantitative analysis.[22]

A core problem of impact assessments is that one has to establish that the intervention is actually causally related to the dependent variable. This would be easy to establish if both groups (those receiving the intervention versus those who do not) were similar in all other aspects *but* the intervention. In an experimental setting randomisation is used to create groups that are at least approximately similar in all aspects but the intervention. Nevertheless, this goal of similar groups is not easy to reach in a real world setting. On the one hand it is difficult even with experiments to observe groups where all respondents' characteristics are equally distributed across groups, since this is a statistical property that only works with large groups and repeated experiments (Hsu 1989; Krause and Howard 2003). On the other hand, specific practical problems arise with view to experiments outside a laboratory context. It is, for example, ethically difficult not to deliver aid to control groups. Also, structural factors such as low quality information in implementation areas or programme roll-out plans of donors make it difficult to plan even a stratified design (cf. Chapter 7 of this book). Another strategy therefore is to statistically control factors that could also be causing changes in the dependent variable and to try to construct comparison groups in a way that selection biases are kept at a minimum (Leeuw and Vaessen 2009: 23–24). In this case, the term 'intervention groups' is only used as a reference term to differentiate between those respondents whose villages received aid and those whose villages did not, and not in the classical sense that we allocated respondents to certain interventions. Mean differences between intervention groups are assessed after controlling for proxy variables. In our project we tried to assess the influence of context factors in our regression models, which provide information on the differences between groups after controlling for the effects of other variables. The biggest problem with this approach is the potential influence of other unobserved variables. We assume that these unobservable variables were causing differences between the districts in our sample. Hence, we also tested in our regression models whether the district of an interview predicts trends that differ between districts and that may have an effect on the dependent variable.

In summary, when developing a regression model it is important to identify clearly the dependent and independent variables, but also to scrutinise the underlying assumptions to exclude other possible causal relations and endogenous factors that could lead to false conclusions about the effect of the independent variable. Therefore, we had to establish that the distribution of our main independent variable (aid) was not influenced by other variables, introducing endogeneity problems.

In terms of possible selection biases of a causal model with aid as independent variable there are two major risks. First, there is the possibility that aid goes where people have positive attitudes towards the intervention anyway and security is already good. It is also possible that the opposite is true: that aid is put where it is dangerous and people do not like the intervention or the state (in order to win the population over; this has been extensively discussed under the headline of potentially doing harm by setting perverse incentives; cf. Gosztonyi and Koehler 2010). This would, of course, render the model useless because in both cases those who receive and those who do not receive are pre-chosen on the dependent variable of the model. Hence, no credible comparison group could be constructed.

This option we excluded qualitatively for the time frame 2005 to 2009 by analysing the roll-out and implementation strategies of the (few) major development actors in our four target districts. Those programmes followed needs assessments and implementation logics not informed by an analysis or, indeed, systematic knowledge of security issues or pre-existing attitudes of target villages and districts. This did change, however, during the year 2009 with the strengthening of the Taliban insurgency and the increasing influence of counterinsurgency thinking among the state and interventionists. Additionally, this was tested quantitatively as described below. Attitudes or security had no major influence on the allocation of aid projects in any of the two waves.

Second, selection bias aside, there is still the credible risk of self-selection for those programmes that follow participatory and competitive procedures in identifying beneficiaries. Such programmes, most importantly the Provincial Development Funds, did, indeed, increase their operation in mid 2007 and did have some visibility in the target districts during the time of observation (Koehler and Zürcher 2007c). The competitive and highly formalised selection procedure (one of the authors participated in a number of these sessions in 2007 and 2009) did not have a bias towards either security or attitudes. However, we cannot exclude that some degree of self-selection existed since completely hostile communities may have censored their participation in the process a priori (some Taliban-affected communities did, however, apply with varying degrees of success).

Our main proxy for the independent variable was measured on the village level: the number of projects per village (in 2007 in 77 villages; in 2009 in 80 villages). To check statistically whether the number of projects was predicted by other variables, which would introduce other causal paths than our main hypothesis, we used bootstrapped Poisson regressions. Since the outcome is a count variable, Poisson regressions were more appropriate than other models such as linear regressions, and bootstrapping was used to reduce reliance on statistical assumptions in this small sample case. We first conducted regressions in sets of variables to identify the strongest predictors from theoretical sub-domains (e.g., structural variables such as the district, remoteness of the village; attitude variables such as attitudes towards foreign forces or development actors). In a second step we combined significant predictors from these models in a final model to identify their joint predictive strength.

Significant predictors of the number of aid projects per village in 2007 were village size, share of literate people in the village and mean irrigated land, of which the latter two remained significant when used together in a model. Significant predictors in 2009 were district, number of projects in the village in (2007), attitudes toward development actors (2007), mean household resources (2007) and mean perceived level of aid (2009). Only the number of projects received in 2007 remained a significant predictor when used together in a model.

Significance of predictors is only one way to look at the associations between variables. More interesting in this case is the predictive strength of the indicators. This is for two reasons. First, in a small sample case like ours, the statistical power might not be high enough to identify relevant associations between variables. Second, it would be unrealistic to assume that in such a study no relationships would exist between the variables in question, so information on their actual predictive value is necessary to assess how strongly they could have influenced the results. When samples are small this is an even more conservative test, since using several variables in small samples to predict an outcome can lead easily to over-determination (and therefore high predictive values).

In Poisson regression models pseudo-r^2 values can be used to assess the predictive value of a combined set of predictors. For 2007 we found a pseudo-r^2 of 0.07. For the 2009 model the pseudo-r^2 value was 0.15. Given the number of predictors and the number of observational units both values can be classified as low. Based on these extensive checks, we therefore concluded that the available data does not provide us with strong predictors of aid allocation and endogeneity problems with these variables would be low if present at all. Additionally, most of the variables that were tested as predictors of aid allocation were also used as control variables in our final regression models. This limits their possible influence on the results further (cf. Angrist and Pischke 2009: 51ff.).

8 Data collection and analysis

Our analysis required a huge amount of mostly original data, and we relied on various methods for collecting data. First, we conducted a mass survey in 2007 and in 2009. We surveyed 2,034 households in 77 communities in 2007 and 2,132 households in 80 communities in 2009. The communities were located in four districts in northeast Afghanistan: Imam Sahib, Aliabad, Warsaj and Taloqan within the provinces of Kunduz and Takhar. Half of the communities were selected by random sampling. All known communities of a district were coded with subsequent numbers. A random number processor was then used to identify ten communities in each of the four target districts. The remaining 50 per cent were selected according to their diversity on five criteria: 1) size; 2) remoteness; 3) estimated natural resource base (access to irrigated or rain-fed land, access to pastures, forest); 4) estimated vulnerability to natural disasters; 5) ethnic and religious composition. Within the communities, households were sampled randomly both in 2007 and 2009. The size of the sample varied according to the size of the community in order to ensure that the sample was representative for the community as a whole. In 2007, 2,034 heads of households were interviewed, and 2,132 in 2009.

The implementation of a survey in regions in which no population data are available on the community level is challenging because researchers cannot devise a sampling plan beforehand. Before conducting interviews in a community, the interview teams held an initial meeting with the village *shura* (village council) members, elders and other local representatives. During that meeting, they established the number of households in the village. This information was necessary since we employed a sampling frame over the villages that kept the sampling error constant with regard to the household number of every village (sampling with finite sample correction, see Fowler 2002 for details). Once the teams had this information, they calculated the number of interviews that were needed for this village.

Before implementing the survey, we made sure that the questionnaire was peer-reviewed by country experts. Furthermore, we carefully followed the process of translating the questions into Dari making sure that the translation 'meant' what we had in mind. Specific phrases had to be adapted to local usages and local meanings. The enumerators then received intensive training. A one-week training and preparation workshop was held in Kabul from 21–28 February 2007 and was repeated in February 2009. Finally, we ran a pre-test with 35 respondents. The survey was designed to generate data on objective indicators of development cooperation and local capacities. Furthermore, we also asked about subjective perceptions of respondents on topics such as the coverage and usefulness of development cooperation projects within the community, or the perception of everyday security.

We also trained profilers to collect important background data on the communities and on the districts, such as, for example, the number of schools or the access to markets. We also commissioned semi-structured reports to be filled in by trained local correspondents four times a year. These so called quarterly reports record major events and significant changes, for examples major new development initiatives, outbreaks of violence, military operations and natural disasters. This sort of data cannot be captured in surveys or profiles. We used these data to check whether our units were indeed similar, or whether there were large differences with regard to important contextual factors that might explain differences in the subsequent analysis.

Furthermore, we conducted in-depth qualitative case studies, mainly in communities that showed untypical high or low values on the dependent variables (outliers). For these case studies, we relied on standard qualitative methods including expert interviews, group interviews, key informant interviews and ethnographic participatory observation.

9 Inferring causality: statistics and qualitative analysis

Equipped with a theory and enough data, we were now in a position to search for causal relationships between aid and its anticipated impacts. The bulk of the analytical work was done through statistical methods. We used various types of regression analysis to search for associations between different types of aid and threat perceptions and attitudes towards aid worker, foreign forces and the Afghan state. But we also backed up and refined our results with qualitative data, because for many complex social situations valid information is not easily obtained via standardised questionnaires and statistics. Often more contextual qualitative methods are required to understand what actors do and why. As described above, the qualitative data was collected by expert reports on the communities, and by fieldwork, conducted by team member Jan Koehler. Two extended field visits were conducted by a team of local and external researchers to visit a selection of communities and trace specifically interesting cases/stories with key informants.

Qualitative data are used in three vital ways in this research. As shown above, we use systematic qualitative research in the initial setup, most importantly for the conflict analysis. The conflict analysis is descriptive, uses analytical tools such as resource, actors and institutional analysis and makes inductive use of case studies that capture the most important constellations and dynamics of conflict (Gosztonyi and Koehler 2010; Koehler and Zürcher 2007d).

Qualitative analysis is further used as part of the field research. We have shown above that local knowledge and analysis of data obtained during fieldwork is vital to better understand the quality and robustness of the causal model that is tested statistically.

Lastly, case studies and background knowledge on the villages and districts were necessary to interpret results and to make sense of sometimes counterintuitive findings that found either unexpected causal mechanisms or semantic differences in concepts we used.

To give an example of the former, according to our quantitative data, well over 90 per cent of all respondents said in 2007 that their security had vastly improved during the past two years, and foreign forces were credited with this development. Individual and group interviews supported this surprising finding. These interviews also helped us to better understand the causal relations. The overwhelming majority of Afghans had suffered from the violent reign of many second and third tier warlords; the presence of the international military force was enough to deter theses militias, hence Afghans attributed gains in security to foreign forces. Using additional qualitative data to corroborate statistical findings and identify causal relations behind statistical correlations proved to be a very valuable tool. Box 6.3 summarises some of our findings.

Box 6.3   Some findings: the impact of aid in Afghanistan

Development aid had a small impact on the attitudes of the rural population towards international actors (both civilian and military) and the Afghan state. This impact vanished when the population perceived that their security situation was deteriorating. Communities that received more aid had more positive attitudes about the legitimacy of the Afghan state.

Attitudes towards Western actors, both military and civilian, were predominately correlated with the threat perceptions of Afghans. Those who felt more secure had more positive attitudes towards international actors. Addressing the immediate security concerns of Afghans is thus the single most effective way of winning acceptance of the local population.

We found no evidence that small infrastructure development projects increased the acceptance of foreign troops. The acceptance of foreign troops was driven predominately by their success or failure to provide everyday security.

In volatile, insecure conflict zones, acceptance cannot be stockpiled, but needs to be earned constantly. Our data show that high levels of acceptance in 2007 did not translate automatically into high levels of acceptance in 2009.

Moreover, aid only has its (small) positive impact on acceptance if it is perceived by many as being useful. Our data show that it is not the number of projects within a given community, but the perceived usefulness, which explains the effect of aid on acceptance.

An example of semantic issues explaining results is the apparent disconnect between continuous positive security assessments of households and villages while fear levels with regard to armed groups increased dramatically between the two waves. In the eyes of most Afghans in our research area, insecurity relates to a more general situation of warlike collective violence. Fear of gunmen, on the other hand, is concrete. Fear of local armed strongmen does not, however, necessarily indicate that those strongmen are seen as illegitimate leaders causing local insecurity. When people perceive them as socially embedded and think they help keeping (warlike) insecurity out of their districts people often accept a degree of abuse of power (Koehler 2012).

Finally, qualitative research can be directly integrated into statistical assessments, for example in the form of coded semi-structured guideline interviews with the same village functionaries across the sample or coded experiences taken from the village histories compiled. Constructing quantitative indicators from qualitative interviews is in process but has not been used for the observation-period drawn upon in this chapter (for this approach see Koehler et al. 2011).

10 Lessons

This chapter described one approach for conducting an impact assessment in conflict zones. The impact assessment was designed by a small research team, and was implemented in collaboration with a team of researchers and enumerators in Afghanistan. The project ran for approximately 34 months, including the preparation phase, from 2007 to 2009. We started with a portfolio analysis in order to get an overview of development interventions in our target region. We then conducted a conflict assessment that pointed to the main threats for stability in the region. Based on portfolio analysis and conflict assessment, we developed the framework for the impact assessment, which specified key parameters of the assessment, such as time, regional scope, development interventions and target groups to be observed and indicators for change. Next we formulated a theory of change, based on a reading of the relevant literature. This theory spelled out how aid might have an impact on the changes in which we are interested. We then defined the concepts and measures. Once we had collected our primary data (in two waves, so that we had the opportunity to compare over time), we analysed the data. Statistical results were corroborated, refined and put in context with the help of additional qualitative data.

An evaluation project of this scope is a very long process full of unexpected adventures. This concluding section highlights some of the lessons we have learned with regard to the implementing process itself, and underlines the point that process results from a formative evaluation can be extremely valuable for future implementation of aid projects as well as evaluations.

First of all, the various logistical difficulties of such a project cannot be overemphasised. Difficulties with regard to transportation, communication and security were to be expected. Other challenges arose unexpectedly. For example, we were surprised to learn that large parts of rural Afghanistan are literally uncharted territory: many villages had no univocal official name, or various names were used for the same village, and even the borders of villages were often not clearly defined. Maps were rare and not up-to-date; we found that the Soviet military maps of the 1970s and 1980s of a scale of 1:50,000 were still the most detailed and reliable topographic references. Administrative borders were not yet in place, or were being redrawn. We also had to deal with the challenge that demographic and other basic statistical data are hardly available in Afghanistan – and if available it is mostly unreliable. All of this makes conducting surveys highly problematic. In logistically less challenging countries, researchers typically develop a questionnaire and experienced local enumerators then conduct the survey, making sure that the sample is representative for the chosen unit. In a country such as Afghanistan (and we assume that this is the case for many poor countries in or after war), researchers have to establish their own basic data (for example, village lists and population figures) before they can devise a sampling strategy. We ended up preparing our own maps (based on Soviet maps) and using GPS to locate our target communities. While this was feasible, it was also time-consuming. Researchers preparing an impact assessment in such regions are well advised to plan for a substantial preparation period, and to anticipate that most of the needed data must be collected on the ground.

Just as we underestimated the challenges of uncharted territory, we dramatically overestimated the quality of the data that is available on development aid projects. Data that has been provided by various state and non-state agencies was often of very poor quality, and not all organisations seem to record data or were willing to share it with us. Most organisations also do not collect geo-referenced data about the location of their projects. This is specifically the case when donors rely exclusively on local implementing partners who may or may not identify exact project locations correctly. Many organisations also keep only aggregated information for the records and do not archive exact project locations. In the end, we had to collect our own data (numbers of projects) and to rely on perception based measures of aid. We continue to dream about accurate, geo-referenced aid data that can be used to track aid flows to province, district and community level. If the international community is serious about rigorous impact evaluations, then it must pressure donors and implementing actors for much higher standards for recording and sharing data!

Another lesson is that researchers should not underestimate the many conceptual difficulties involved in impact assessments. It is not only difficult to gather data on the key variables 'aid' and 'security', it is often also a conceptual problem to define measurement for these variables. Above, we have described in some detail how we constructed measurements for aid, based on the number of projects that a community received and on perceptions of aid for the household and for the community. Clearly there are alternatives, and researchers should be transparent about their delimitations with regard to their concepts and measurements. Aid is not the only difficult concept, of course. Other concepts are no less difficult to define and measure. We could easily write lengthy academic papers on the many challenges involved in defining good measures for concepts such as security, fear, value threat, material household resources or positive attitudes. It is important that researchers acknowledge that finding valid measures is a time consuming activity that is best done in workshops with both statisticians and regional experts.

As described above, this impact assessment was organised as an equal cooperation between independent researchers and the evaluation unit of the Ministry for Economic Co-operation and Development. We think that such an organisation has some advantages over other forms of organisation. Getting access to data and receiving logistic support for conducting fieldwork in difficult regions can be an incentive for researchers. As a result, they bring in their methodological skills and considerable amounts of unpaid research time. We saw that such cooperation can help to control costs, and increase quality. Second, organising an impact assessment as cooperation with independent researchers can help to shield the researchers from political pressure, which is likely to be high in evaluations of highly politicised issues.

Finally, there is the question of method replication. The approach that we have developed in this project relies on a bundle of methods.[23] These can be adapted to different contexts, which makes our approach – in theory – replicable beyond Afghanistan. It should be noted, however, that the presented approach is time-consuming and labour intensive. This not only refers to the data gathering and data analysis, but also to the development of tools for data gathering. Developing (or adapting) questionnaires and semi-structured interview guidelines is time-consuming. It also requires that the researchers are familiar with the political, social and cultural context of the target regions, otherwise the concepts and questions will not 'work' in the given context which renders the data useless.

The evaluation team must also be comfortable with using both qualitative and quantitative methods, combining advanced statistical methods and fieldwork. One of the most challenging but also rewarding tasks in the framework of a multi-method evaluation is the organisation of an ongoing dialogue and exchange between statistical results and evidence from qualitative data, such as interviews and observations in the field. Such a dialogue needs to take place from project design to the final analysis: knowledge about local understanding for certain concepts has to be taken into consideration when developing the survey tools; results from surveys need to be interpreted in the light of local context, and perhaps local idiosyncratic events. Data gathered from qualitative sources need to be coded in order to be used for further statistical analysis. In doing so, data will be aggregated, which implies that information is lost; hence it is important that researchers also store the original qualitative data for future reference.

Summing up, we think that our approach can be successfully adapted to other contexts, yet there are requirements which must be met: team members should be trained in qualitative and quantitative methods; sound knowledge on the local context is required; the dialogue between qualitative and quantitative methods needs to be structured; it should be taken into due consideration that such a complex endeavour is time-consuming and will not produce quick results. In planning such evaluations, the evaluation units should acknowledge that the earlier the evaluation team is involved in the mission on the ground, the easier (and more efficient) it is for the evaluators to collect the right data later on. Accompanying evaluations are arguably easier to do than *ex post* evaluations. But even under the best of circumstances, complex impact evaluations are highly demanding on time, skills and resources. One way to deal with these demands is fostering cooperation between development organisations and research institutions. An example of such an approach has been portrayed in this chapter.

Notes

1 The evaluation described in this chapter is a result of a four-year cooperative research project conducted by the German Federal Ministry for Economic Co-operation and Development (BMZ), evaluation division, Free University of Berlin's research centre 700 and the University of Ottawa. We have documented our methodological approach in a separate report that contains a full account of our research strategy, the questionnaires, coding rules, model specifications and additional descriptive data in Zürcher and Koehler (2007). An updated version of this report will be made available as a SFB 700 Working Paper in early 2013 (Böhnke et al. 2013). Results of the evaluation are published in Böhnke et al. (2010). In planning this research, we prepared an inception report that contains a conflict assessment of the target area, a brief analysis of German development projects in the region, and a preliminary outline of the methods to be developed (see Koehler and Zürcher 2007b). Other publications related to this project are Koehler/Zürcher (2007a); Kohler (2008); Böhnke et al. (2009).
2 It would have been impossible to get access to a comprehensive list of ongoing development programmes from all donors active in this part of Afghanistan prior to the fieldwork. All attempts made to administer such information in a central database – by UNAMA, by ISAF or by the Afghan government – did not produce reliable results. Hence, we decided to collect the data in-field both at village and district level from the beneficiaries as well as from the agencies active in our target districts.
3 For a detailed analysis of the concept and effects of this World-Bank initiated nationwide programme see Nixon (2008).
4 For the priority sectors of German governmental development aid see Bundesregierung (2007). In the rural target region up until 2010 the most visible development projects of the German governmental aid related to the Development Oriented Emergency and Transitional Aid (DETA) with a focus on demand-oriented quick impact rural infrastructure.
5 In the development literature this process is often referred to as the identification of so-called 'peacebuilding needs' that the instruments of development aid can influence (see Leonhardt et al. 2007).
6 For a discussion of structural versus dynamic concepts of stability, cf. Koehler and Zürcher (2003).
7 For our purposes here we use a minimal definition of peace as the absence of warlike forms of collective violence.
8 Based on findings in Koehler and Zürcher (2007d).
9 This time frame follows the DETA-logic and BMZ implementation logic of that time: disaster and humanitarian aid is followed by emergency aid for three years; hence, emergency aid effects should be visible roughly after two years.
10 For details on this approach see Böhnke et al. (2013).
11 We recorded one such case in Taloqan city in 2006. In rural areas with weak state presence and stronger insurgents exposure we recorded cases of in which local communities either negotiated separate security arrangements with the Taliban (Chahar Dara District and parts of Aliabad district) or asked the Taliban to leave the district altogether (Kalafgan district).

12 We simplify here in order to highlight the main expectations on causal relations between aid and security on the side of the interveners. Convergence of interest over what to achieve and vision of how to achieve it cannot be assumed for the different intervening states or even for different agencies of one state. Afghanistan is an especially messy case as to the number of intervening powers (e.g., 49 countries and 10 international organisations participating at the International Donor Conference in London in January 2006; 50 force-contributing countries to ISAF in 2012) and mandates (e.g., the US-led coalition of Operation Enduring Freedom operation on the basis of Article 51 of the UN charter on the right of countries to defend themselves in contrast to the specific UN mandate of the International Security Assistance Force in support of the Afghan statebuilding and reconstruction effort). Also for the sake of simplification here we do not differentiate between the conceptually different security of the population, the state and the interveners. We elaborated on this issue elsewhere (see Koehler 2008).

13 This estimate is based on a 14-province survey. However, demographic data on Afghanistan is chronically unreliable. Other estimates put the number at 79 per cent (CSO 2009: 7); the most recent official estimate indicates a strong trend towards urbanisation (that could, however, rather reflect a broader definition of what is considered urban) and estimates the urban population at 31.3 per cent (CSO 2013).

14 The last census was conducted in 1979 under difficult security conditions; even this census is considered highly unreliable. Since then dramatic demographic changes have taken place due to 30 years of war and political instability.

15 The first wave of suicide attacks occurred, however, in Kunduz in 2007 and insurgents activities changed in quality between 2007 and 2009: the insurgents changed from operating as small clandestine cells to active groundwork in potentially sympathetic communities, thus preparing for taking control of some strategically important territory and escalating the violent challenges to the government and foreign forces (which, indeed, happened from late 2009 to 2011; see Koehler 2012).

16 Operation Sweep in late 2008 as a show of force to the increasing Taliban presence in areas West of the Kunduz river; the operation did not meet any armed resistance.

17 Between April 2004 and April 2009, the time when our survey was completed, only 2.18 per cent (1,145 reported events) of all security incidents reported by ISAF took place in the north of Afghanistan (the Regional Command North). Between April 2009 and December 2010, 4.8 per cent (998) of all security incidents took place in the north. Broadly speaking, the number of security incidents per months for the period April 2009–December 2010 has more than doubled compared to the period of April 2004–March 2009 (data from Wikileaks Afghan War Diaries, available at wikileaks.org). We also observe a disproportional increase of fear with regard to foreign forces in the district affected by the sweep operation.

18 Focal points in some of our target villages related this risk to us and asked to meet with the foreign member of the field team only outside the village. The local members of the team did, however, always manage to negotiate their way into all target communities.

19 These regional patterns emerge from the different geography and development history of the districts: Warsaj is a mountainous area with plenty of water but – until recent community-driven development programmes (here: NSP) – hardly any electricity; Imam Sahib is agriculturally one of the richest districts of Afghanistan with lots of irrigated land. Taloqan and Aliabad both have irrigated lowland and rain-fed hill-agriculture.

20 Latent Class Analysis (LCA) is a statistical tool to explore data for mixtures in categorical data. LCA has the advantage over factor analysis/cluster analysis that no scaling properties have to be assumed. LCA estimates different classes of units of analysis that can be characterised by a common pattern of category probabilities. The easiest case is the so-called 'one class solution' that corresponds to the usual sample-mean based analytic methods. In this solution it is assumed that all units of analysis stem from the same distribution. In most cases this mean-based solution does not yield the most accurate

description of the data. In LCA solutions with an ascending number of classes are estimated and the solution which indicates the best fit with the least number of parameters is the number of classes to be used to describe the data most effectively. These classes can be seen as the relevant combinations of remembered aid sectors.
21 Particularly for the more sensitive questions running pre-tests in villages close to the training location was important to understand how well the questions work and are acceptable to the respondents.
22 The identification of independent and dependent variables follows from the theory of change; the identification of relevant intervening variables follows from local knowledge and the conflict analysis.
23 We are aware of some recent impact evaluations implemented under comparable fragile conditions that make use of some similar methods applied in our research: Beath et al. (2012) used an experimental design by matching villages in order to evaluate the impact of a specific programme on attitudes in a selection of districts in Afghanistan; Fearon et al. (2009) used a field experimental design to investigate the impact of a specific community driven development programme on social cohesion after the civil war in Liberia; Humphreys et al. (2012) used a randomised experiment design to assess the aggregate impact of a community-driven development programme on social cohesion, local accountability and welfare in DR Congo. Those evaluations share the focus on a specific programme; they are not accounting for the impact of an intervention as a whole (and controlling for other programmes running parallel proofs to be one of the more difficult tasks). While there are some impact assessments using test-like statistical procedures to attribute observed changes the systematic use of qualitative and quantitative methods is still clearly a very rare occurrence. Local in depth knowledge is rarely combined with the scrutiny of robust statistics.

Bibliography

Angrist, J. D. and Pischke, J.-S. (2009) *Mostly Harmless Econometrics: An Empiricist's Companion*, Princeton, NJ: Princeton University Press.
Beath, A., Christia, F. and Enikolopov, R. (2012) 'Winning Hearts and Minds through Development? Evidence from a Field Experiment in Afghanistan', *Policy Research Working Paper, July 2012*, Washington, DC: World Bank.
Berman, E., Shapiro, J. N. and Felter, J. H. (2009) *Can Hearts and Minds Be Bought? The Economics of Counterinsurgency in Iraq*, http://econ.ucsd.edu/~elib/ham.pdf, accessed 14 March 2013.
Böhnke, J., Koehler, J. and Zürcher, C. (2009) 'Evaluation von Entwicklungszusammenarbeit zur Stabilisierung in Post-Konflikt-Zonen: Anwendung eines Mixed-Method Surveys in Nordost-Afghanistan', *Zeitschrift für Evaluation* 8: 215–235.
——(2010) *Assessing the Impact of Development Co-operation in North East Afghanistan 2005–2009*, Bonn: Bundesministerium für Entwicklung und Wirtschaftliche Zusammenarbeit, BMZ.
——(2013) *Assessing the Impact of Development Co-operation in North East Afghanistan: Approaches and Methods* (SFB Working Papers 43), Berlin: Sonderforschungsbereich 700 'Governance in Räumen begrenzter Staatlichkeit', www.sfb-governance.de/publikationen/sfbgov_wp/wp43_en/wp43.pdf?1362403520, accessed 8 March 2013.
Bundesregierung (2007) *Das Afghanistan-Konzept der Bundesregierung*, Berlin: Bundesregierung.
CSO (2009) *Statistical Yearbook 2008–09: Population*, Kabul: Central Statistics Organisation. http://cso.gov.af/Content/files/Population%20Full%20chapter.pdf, accessed 9 January 2013.

——(2013) *Settled Population of Afghanistan by Civil Division, Urban, Rural and Sex 2012–13*, Kabul: Central Statistics Organisation. http://cso.gov.af/Content/files/Settled%20Population%20by%20Civil%20Division.pdf, accessed 8 March 2013.

Fearon, J. D., Humphreys, M. and Weinstein, J. M. (2009) 'Can Development Aid Contribute to Social Cohesion after Civil War? Evidence from a Field Experiment in Post-conflict Liberia', *American Economic Review: Papers and Proceedings* 99(2): 287–291. http://pubs.aeaweb.org/doi/pdfplus/10.1257/aer.99.2.287, accessed 16 October 2012.

Fowler, F. (2002) *Survey Research Methods*, 3rd edn, Thousand Oaks, CA: Sage.

Gosztonyi, K. and Koehler, J. (2010) *PCA Analysis North Afghanistan, Kabul, Berlin*, Berlin: Gesellschaft für Technische Zusammenarbeit, ARC-Berlin.

Hsu, L. M. (1989) 'Random Sampling, Randomization, and Equivalence of Contrasted Groups in Psychotherapy Outcome Research', *Journal of Consulting and Clinical Psychology* 57(1): 131–137.

Humphreys, M., de la Sierra, R. S. and van der Windt, P. (2012) *Social and Economic Impacts of Tuungane, Final Report on the Effects of a Community Driven Reconstruction Program in Eastern Democratic Republic of Congo*, June 2012, New York: Columbia University. www.oecd.org/derec/unitedkingdom/drc.pdf, accessed 4 October 2012.

Koehler, J. (2004) *Assessing Peace and Conflict Potentials in the Target Region of the GTZ Central Asia and Northern Afghanistan Programme to Foster Food Security, Regional Co-operation and Stability*, Berlin: ARC and GTZ.

——(2005) *Conflict Processing and the Opium Poppy Economy in Afghanistan*, PAL Internal Document Series, Jalalabad: Programme for Alternative Livelihoods in Eastern Afghanistan. www.gtz.de/de/dokumente/en-DrugsandConflictAfghanistanPAL.pdf, accessed 8 July 2006.

——(2008) *Auf der Suche nach Sicherheit – Die internationale Intervention in Nordost-Afghanistan*, SFB 700 Working Papers 17, Belin: Research Centre (SFB) 700. www.sfb-governance.de/publikationen/sfbgov_wp/index.html, accessed 24 November 2012.

——(2012) *Social Order within and beyond the Shadow of Hierarchy: Governance Patterns in Afghanistan*, SFB-Governance Working Papers Series 33, Berlin: Research Centre (SFB) 700. www.sfb-governance.de/publikationen/sfbgov_wp/index.html, accessed 24 November 2012.

Koehler, J. and Zürcher, C. (2003) *Institutions and the Organisation of Stability and Violence*, in J. Koehler and C. Zürcher (eds) *Potentials of Disorder*, Manchester and New York: Manchester University Press, pp. 243–265.

——(2007a) *Assessing the Contribution of International Actors in Afghanistan: Results from a Representative Survey*, Berlin: Freie Universität Berlin, SFB 700. www.sfb-governance.de/en/publikationen/sfbgov_wp/wp7_en/index.html, accessed 14 March 2013.

——(2007b) *Assessing the Impact of Development Co-operation in North East Afghanistan, Prestudy*, BMZ Evaluation Working Papers, Bonn: BMZ.

——(2007c) *Quick Impact Projects in Nordost-Afghanistan : Studienkennziffer SP 30S 7 006*, unpublished final draft, Berlin: ARC-Berlin, BMVg.

——(2007d) 'Statebuilding, Conflict and Narcotics in Afghanistan: A View from Below', *International Peacekeeping* 14(1): 62–74.

Koehler, J., Gosztonyi, K. and Böhnke, J. (2011) 'Assessing Conflict and Stability in Afghanistan: A Methodological approach', paper presented at 'Violence, Drugs and Governance: Mexican Security in Comparative Perspective', Stanford University, 4 October 2011. http://iis-db.stanford.edu/evnts/6716/20130513_StabilityConflict_Final_FINAL_Koehler_Gosztonyi_Boehnke.pdf, accessed 24 July 2013.

Krause, M. S. and Howard, K. I. (2003) 'What Random Assignment Does and Does Not Do', *Journal of Clinical Psychology* 59(7): 751–66.
Leeuw, F. and Vaessen, J. (2009) *Impact Evaluations and Development*, Nonie Guidance on Impact Evaluation. http://siteresources.worldbank.org/EXTOED/Resources/nonie_guidance.pdf, accessed 5 October 2012.
Leonhardt, M., Leonhardt, K. and Strehlein, C. (2007) *Peace and Conflict Assessment (PCA): Ein methodischer Rahmen zur konflikt- und friedensbezogenen Ausrichtung von EZ-Maßnahmen*, Eschborn: BMZ, GTZ. www.giz.de/Themen/de/SID-66D8741A-9B24C07B/dokumente/de-crisis-pca-2008.pdf, 23 October 2012.
Nagl, J. A., Petraeus, D. H. and Amos, J. F. (2007) *The US Army/Marine Corps Counterinsurgency Field Manual*, US Army field manual no. 3–24, Marine Corps warfighting publication no. 3–33–5, Chicago: University of Chicago Press.
Nixon, H. (2008) *The Changing Face of Local Governance: Community Development Councils in Afghanistan*, Kabul: Afghan Research and Evaluation Unit (AREU). www.areu.org.af/Uploads/EditionPdfs/802E-Changing%20Face%20of%20local%20Governance-WP-print.pdf.pdf, accessed 9 February 2013.
OHCHR (2010) *Human Rights Dimension of Poverty in Afghanistan*, Kabul: United Nations Office of the High Commissioner for Human Rights. http://unama.unmissions.org/Portals/UNAMA/human%20rights/Poverty%20Report%2030%20March%202010_English.pdf, accessed 14 September 2012.
Zürcher, C. and Koehler, J. (2007) *Assessing the Impact of Development Co-operation in North East Afghanistan: Approaches and Methods*, Evaluation Working Papers, Bonn. www.bmz.de/en/zentrales_downloadarchiv/erfolg/BMZ_WP_Methodenbericht_AFG.pdf, accessed 19 February 2013.

7 Impact evaluation for peacebuilding[1]
Challenging preconceptions

Marie Gaarder
World Bank[2]

Jeannie Annan
International Rescue Committee

1 Introduction

The premise of this book is that evaluating interventions in situations of conflict and fragility requires special consideration. Many take this premise further to argue that impact evaluation – evaluation that accounts for the counterfactual in order to attribute impact – is simply not possible, or perhaps not ethical, in these situations. Some evaluators and practitioners in this field raise four main concerns: 1) it is unethical to identify a comparison group in situations of conflict and fragility; 2) it is too operationally difficult to do so; 3) impact evaluations do not address the most important evaluation questions; and 4) they are too costly. In this chapter, we argue that it is both possible and important to carry out impact evaluations even in settings of violent conflict, and we present some examples from a collection of impact evaluations of conflict prevention and peacebuilding interventions. We examine the practices of impact evaluators in the peacebuilding sector to see how they address evaluation design, data collection and conflict analysis. Finally, we argue that such evaluations are crucial for testing assumptions about how development interventions affect change – the so-called 'theory of change' – which is important when we are interested in the results on the ground.

2 Defining impact evaluations

Impact evaluation, as defined in this chapter, refers to evaluations that draw from a set of methods designed to establish a counterfactual or valid comparison, to the intervention in question. The objective is to measure the net impact of the intervention, which in theory is the difference in outcomes for those receiving the intervention compared to what the outcomes would be for the same participants without the intervention. Since it is not possible to measure this difference in practice, impact evaluation methods are all designed to create a comparison group that resembles the participant group as closely as possible. This methodology can be used to explore attribution at any level throughout the results matrix, be it outputs or short- and long-term outcomes and impacts.

Impact evaluation methods include experiments – randomised controlled trials (RCTs) in which subjects are randomised to receive a certain version of an intervention (the 'treatment' as it is known from medical trials) or not, and cluster randomised controlled trials in which groups of subjects (as opposed to individual subjects, such as schools, villages or households) are randomised – and 'quasi-experiments'. The key difference between experiments and quasi-experiments is the use of random assignment of the target population to treatment or control in experiments. Instead of random assignment, quasi-experimental designs typically allow the researcher to establish a comparison group that is as similar as possible to the intervention group using either programme eligibility criteria or statistical methods to control for confounding variables. One important practical implication of this difference is that randomisation requires planning and starting the evaluation prior to the initiation of the intervention for which we want to measure impact, as units of assignment can only be randomised *ex ante*, which may not always be politically feasible or operationally realistic. Quasi-experimental approaches do not have this specific limitation but suffer from other shortcomings, such as potential selection bias due to differences in time-varying unobservable characteristics (Baker 2000; White 2011; World Bank 2013).

The impact evaluations we discuss in the first part of this chapter are large n impact evaluations, meaning that the design is based on data collected over a large sample, usually of individuals. In the second part, we will briefly address the subject of small n attribution analysis, and what it may imply for evaluations in conflict prevention and peacebuilding.

On its own, a large n impact evaluation explores the effect (or lack thereof) of a certain intervention or activity. The counterfactual quantitative analysis of impact should be supplemented by factual analysis, such as of programme beneficiary targeting effectiveness, implementation and process documentations, and qualitative data (which can be derived from a large variety of methods) in order to help develop the initial theory of change, dissect the differences in findings between different settings and to further understand why the results were what they were. The importance of including both counterfactual and factual analysis is exemplified by the International Initiative for Impact Evaluation's (3ie) requirement of the use of mixed methods for the evaluations they fund (White 2009).

3 Addressing concerns about impact evaluations in conflict prevention and peacebuilding

Conflict-affected settings make conducting impact evaluations challenging. To address the objections that impact evaluation of peacebuilding interventions cannot be done, and to document the type of methodologies that have been more prominently used, Samii et al. (2012) conducted a thorough literature search to identify all the impact evaluations that have been conducted (and including some ongoing studies) of what they call stabilisation interventions. Their search and review covers impact evaluations of peacebuilding/stabilisation interventions by any donor or government. They found that there are roughly two dozen impact evaluations, some ongoing, across seven categories of stabilisation interventions. While the search did not fulfil all the criteria to qualify as a systematic review, it was extensive covering multiple databases as well as direct contact with the researchers to identify ongoing studies. The largest number of impact evaluations has been of ex-combatant reintegration programmes and of peace dividends (community-driven reconstruction) programmes. The impact evaluations they found were conducted in Afghanistan, Burundi, Democratic Republic of Congo, the Aceh region of Indonesia, Israel and Palestine, Liberia, Rwanda, Sierra Leone, Sri Lanka and northern Uganda.[3]

The Samii et al. (2012) search results demonstrate that impact evaluation of peacebuilding interventions is indeed possible in conflict-affected settings in a number of circumstances. This insight then brings us to a second type of concerns relating to the worth of impact evaluations. What sort of insights can these types of evaluations bring that other types cannot?

This chapter addresses major concerns and questions about the ethics, feasibility and value added of impact evaluations in conflict-affected settings. It builds among others on the review of the two dozen screened studies from the Samii et al. (2012) paper, insights from a survey we administered to the authors of the included studies (see Appendix B) and explores 1) ethical concerns about impact evaluations in conflict prevention and peacebuilding; 2) adaptations of designs and data collection methods in conflict-affected situations; 3) evaluations as interventions, and the implications for the risks and reliability of results; and 4) the importance and value-added of impact evaluations.

4   Ethical concerns about impact evaluations in conflict prevention and peacebuilding

The descriptors of large n impact evaluations in conflict-affected settings raise several ethical concerns. There is the concern that impact evaluation designs require that only some individuals receive the intervention.[4] This is considered an ethical problem and some claim that for certain peacebuilding interventions, it simply is not feasible to involve some individuals and not others. These objections are not unique to evaluations in conflict-affected settings, although the risks in these settings may be heightened. We will see that just as possibilities for ethical evaluations abound in other types of development interventions, they also exist in conflict-affected settings. Randomisation or quasi-experimental designs do not necessarily drive the fact that only some individuals receive the intervention; they are particularly well-suited when for financial or logistical reasons the implementation and roll-out is slow or staggered, or when comparable groups are left out for other reasons. This is the reality of most development interventions, as well as those in fragile settings.

Part of what underlies the ethical concern about impact evaluations is the premise that assignment to a comparison or control group implies 'not receiving a benefit'. This is not necessarily the case for two reasons. First, the comparison group can be receiving a treatment with which another competing intervention is being compared. For example, in the case of an impact evaluation of an agricultural training programme for ex-combatants in Liberia (Blattman and Annan 2011) questions about whether to invest in capital or skills in agricultural programming arose as some of the results suggested that the private returns to capital could be higher than those for skills. In a future impact evaluation one could compare the impact of providing capital versus skills without the necessity of a control group that does not receive any programme interventions.

Second, it is important to examine the assumption that receiving a development intervention, or more of one, is always a benefit. However, the effectiveness and impact of most development interventions have yet to be proven (Center for Global Development 2006). When a genuine state of uncertainty exists about the benefits of an intervention, so that in theory it could be harmful or ineffective, there is an urgent need for it to be critically examined. This state of uncertainty, known as 'equipoise' in the medical literature, is considered a necessary ethical condition for the use of a control group which is reflected (with a couple of important caveats) in the Declaration of Helsinki on the use of placebo controls (World Medical Association 2001; Lau et al. 2003).When there is no known effective medical treatment, a new drug might produce better, worse or the same results as no treatment, and so there is no ethical conflict in trials where this equipoise is present.[5] An evaluation discussed in further depth in Section 6.1 provides a case in point. Discussion groups as a tool to reduce ethnic conflict was tested in the DRC context, and found to increase rather than decrease intolerance (Paluck 2010).

Another concern raised is about randomising a programme's activities across possible beneficiaries instead of selecting according to other criteria (e.g., those who first apply or those easiest to access). In a conflict-affected setting, prioritising certain beneficiaries could be important for defusing volatile situations or prioritising quick wins. On the other hand, in cases where a programme cannot be implemented across all individuals immediately, randomisation of eligible individuals can in fact be more ethical and politically feasible than determining who benefits first and who later, especially in a sensitive situation where particular choices can be construed as being politically motivated.

While the ethical concerns may sometimes be misplaced or exaggerated for the reasons just described, it is nevertheless critically important to always carefully consider the potential ethical issues that may arise when designing and conducting impact evaluations. Guidelines exist to help determine when not to do an impact evaluation for ethical reasons, and there exist a number of strategies to alleviate ethical concerns. Many agencies and universities have formal ethical clearance procedures, and the standards typically include 1) ensuring informed consent; 2) guaranteeing the confidentiality of participant data; 3) limiting the burden associated with study participation; and 4) making sure that no one is denied essential services for the purpose of the evaluation (USDA 2005; Friedman 2011).

5 Adaptations of designs and data collection methods in conflict-affected situations

5.1 Establishing the counterfactual

In designing an impact evaluation in fragile or unstable contexts, it is important to carefully consider how to establish a counterfactual, analysing what is ethical and feasible in the particular context. While one might have expected to see mainly quasi-experimental designs used for impact evaluations of conflict prevention and peacebuilding interventions, given that these methodologies avoid many of the challenges of randomisation, the majority of impact evaluations of these interventions still use experimental designs (Samii et al. 2012). This section provides a few illustrative examples of how different researchers established a counterfactual using experimental and quasi-experimental designs.

The first example is of individual randomisation. In Blattman and Annan's (2011) study of a reintegration programme for ex-combatants in Liberia, demand exceeded supply of spaces in the programme so registrants were admitted to the programme by individual lottery. The programme team publicised the intervention in their target communities to identified 'risky' populations and screened people interested in registering, identifying 1,330 eligible participants. The random assignment was stratified by gender, military rank and location, using a computer programme. From an ethical point of view, given that space in the programme was limited, the equal chances of participating that the lottery awarded within each stratum was arguably the fairest and most transparent approach. An exception to the random assignment was made for those who previously held a rank of general in an armed group. Because they were considered high-risk by the programme implementers, all who met this criterion were assigned to the programme and were excluded from the study.

The second type of example is group-based randomisation. Many peacebuilding interventions are implemented in groups or communities, which requires group-based, instead of individual-based, randomisation. For example, for a community-driven programme aiming to improve social cohesion, economic welfare and democratic governance in Liberia studied by Fearon et al. (2008), the NGO randomly assigned 42 communities to receive the programme out of 83 eligible communities. The lottery was conducted in a public place, with chiefs representing each community in attendance. In a similar community-driven project in Sierra Leone, a pool of communities was selected from two districts that had regional, political and ethnic diversity, high levels of poverty and little NGO presence. From those districts, an eligible pool of communities of the appropriate size for the project were chosen and then randomly assigned into treatment (118) and control (118) communities using a computerised random number generator (Casey et al. 2011).

An additional example of group-based randomisation is Paluck's evaluation of a reconciliation radio programme in Rwanda, which used matched-pair randomisation at the level of listening groups. Communities were first sampled to represent political, regional and ethnic breakdowns. Then communities were matched to the most similar community

> according to a number of observable characteristics, such as gender ratio, quality of dwellings, and education level. Then, one community in each pair was randomly assigned to the reconciliation programme and the other to the health programme. This stratification of sites helped to balance and minimize observable differences between the communities ex ante.
>
> (Paluck 2009a: 577–78)

The third type of example is of quasi-experimental designs. Where randomisation is not feasible or ethical, quasi-experimental designs may be used to create a suitable counterfactual. For example, to examine the impact of a reintegration programme on ex-combatants in Burundi, Gilligan et al. (2010) used a disruption in the roll-out of a programme to construct a counterfactual. Three NGOs were given contracts in three different regions to provide benefits to ex-combatants. However, due to external factors, one of the NGOs delayed providing services for a year. Because the disruption was unrelated to choice of entry by participants or implementers, this comparison group theoretically avoids the traps of self-selection or targeting bias. However, the participants in the delayed area may be systematically different from individuals in the other two areas. To account for the potential imbalance on important covariates, the authors matched the 'treatment' and 'control' groups on individual (e.g., age, economic variables and combatant variables) and community characteristics (e.g., war violence and population density) as well as propensity score.

To estimate the effects of the Demobilisation, Disarmament, Rehabilitation and Reintegration (DDRR) programme in Liberia on incomes and chances of employment, Levely (2012) used propensity-score matching based on age, gender, rank and county. As pointed out by the authors, propensity-score matching does not entirely solve the identification problem, as it does not account for potential self-selection on unobservable characteristics. Nevertheless, it does provide a more accurate estimate by accounting for observable variables.

Sometimes the experimental conditions are determined by nature or by other factors out of the control of the experimenters but imitate a randomised process to the extent that they are called natural experiments. In an evaluation of peace workshops for youth in Sri Lanka (Malhotra and Liyanage 2005), those who came from the same schools as workshop participants and had been nominated to attend the workshops but had not been able to participate due to budget cuts that year were treated as a natural control group.

An underused quasi-experimental design is the Regression Discontinuity Design (RDD) which uses programme eligibility criteria (e.g., an eligibility cut-off score such as a poverty-line) to establish the counterfactual. The Samii et al. (2012) search uncovered no existing RDD impact evaluations in the fields of conflict prevention and peacebuilding. One could, however, imagine a scenario where a programme in this field had rated districts in a country by a fragility index, or by some index related to risk of (re)outbreak of violence. If the programme decided that only districts with a score above a certain level qualified for their programme, then the districts that were close to, but below, the cut-off point and hence did not take part in the programme would be very similar to those who were just above it and hence received it, and could act as a control group.

We have described ways of establishing a counterfactual when eligible individuals are excluded from the treatment or the treatment is delayed or rationed. However, the peacebuilding interventions whose effectiveness we would like to measure are often of a nature that does not easily permit the identification of a control or comparison group because in theory they should be available to everyone at the same time. This could be the case, for example, when using the media to deliver peace messages, as above, or when a service such as social reintegration services for ex-combatants is in theory available to all. As long as the uptake of the service or intervention is less than 100 per cent, there still exists the possibility to create a comparison group. This method is called an 'encouragement design' because it requires that a randomly selected group of beneficiaries receive additional encouragement, typically in the form of additional information or incentives, to take up the offered service (or use more of it). As long as information on relative uptake is available along with the measured outcomes, the encouragement design allows estimation of the effect of the intervention as well as the effect of the encouragement itself. The creation of listening groups has already been mentioned (Paluck 2009a) as one type of encouragement. Other types could include an informational brochure about a service which is available or subsidising the service fee or sign-up costs of a service for a limited period.

5.2 Adaptation and flexibility throughout the evaluation process

The unpredictability of the situation in which many peacebuilding and conflict prevention impact evaluations take place sometimes calls for flexibility in the design and implementation of the evaluation.

Despite serious challenges to data collection in conflict-affected environments, all but one of the impact evaluations summarised by Samii et al. (2012) involved collecting primary data. It appears that the dearth of useful administrative data in these settings leaves little option but to collect primary data. The review reported, however, that, relative to the comparison group of impact evaluations carried out in other sectors, the impact evaluations appeared to be based on smaller average sample sizes (2.5–4 times smaller), which may limit the analysis, for example of differential effects on sub-groups.

We asked the researchers of the conflict prevention and peacebuilding studies whether and how the research teams adapted the data collection methods for the conflict-affected settings. Of the survey responses that reported some adaptations, the types of modifications can be roughly divided into four categories: 1) adaptations to the sample; 2) timing; 3) question formulation and focus group composition; and 4) the enumerators' experience and training.

First, adaptation of sample size, either by design or due to unforeseen events, was a recurring response. In the evaluation of the Community Development Fund in Sudan, the researchers reported that they lost 60 per cent of the sample communities due to the (re)outbreak of war (Paluck 2009b), whereas in the impact evaluation of Afghanistan's National Solidarity Programme (NSP), the districts in which the security of the enumerators and participants was at risk were excluded from the intervention and evaluation (Beath et al. 2010). The fact that the research was not being done in the hostile Pashtun communities clearly affects and limits the generalisability of the findings, and so it is important to be careful about how one reads the evidence. As described above, in the evaluation of ex-combatant agriculture and psychological training programme in Liberia, the team decided to exclude high ranking commanders from the evaluation in order to avoid potential conflict caused by randomising them into both treatment and control. The programme was concerned that commanders who were randomised into the control group may cause problems for the overall programme. Therefore, all commanders were provided access to the programme and were excluded from the evaluation. The validity of the evaluation findings is therefore limited to the ex-combatants of lower ranks.

Second, the timing of surveys is one of the most commonly-cited adjustments made. The researchers involved in the evaluation of the peace education programme for Israeli and Palestinian youth reported having had to adjust the timing of data collection due to the conflict (Biton and Solomon 2006). In the evaluation of the Rwandan radio programme, the team had planned follow-up interviews in prisons, which were among the experimental sites. The timing of these had to be changed due to a sudden move to release prisoners (Paluck 2009a). Similarly, in an ongoing evaluation of the community monitoring for better health programme in Burkina Faso (World Bank 2012), the research team had to halt data gathering in the Sahel because of problems with Tuaregs who were engaged in violent conflict in neighbouring Mali. They were however able to gather the data at a later stage. It is worth reflecting on the fact that the measured size of effects is likely to change over time, and may take a non-linear shape, hence a great deal of caution is necessary when interpreting the findings for policymaking purposes. This will be particularly important in situations when the window of opportunity for data collection is limited.

Third, researchers described issues over what questions could be asked due to conflict-related sensitivities. In the evaluation of the Community Driven Development interventions in Sierra Leone, they explored whether they could ask about ongoing tensions, or directly about people's role in the conflict. The team spent time discussing with those working in the communities and piloting questions. They found little reluctance to talk about the conflict and found that it did not seem to raise tensions. However, they decided not to ask about some areas of current tensions, such as marital infidelity, as they were warned that this could spark tensions (Casey et al. 2011). In the civic education programme in Southern Sudan, the focus groups were designed to prevent more conflict. Where the social divisions were based on sect, single-sect discussion groups were organised. Where conflict was based on the affiliation to ethnic/tribal groups, the groups included members of only one ethnic group (Paluck 2009b).

Finally, researchers frequently mentioned the experience and background of the enumerators as a factor that had been taken into account when designing data-collection strategies. For both the studies of the Burundi ex-combatant reintegration programme (Gilligan et al. 2010) and of the peacebuilding and democracy promotion efforts in Liberia (Mvukiyehe and Samii 2010, 2011), the authors reported having recruited specially trained enumerators who had either done social work or human rights advocacy. It was deemed important that the research staff were sensitive to issues of trauma and trained to handle themselves in sensitive situations. For the evaluation of an IRC Community Driven Reconstruction programme in northern Liberia, the authors reported that the use of staff from a local organisation, consisting almost entirely of ex-combatants, as enumerators had been helpful. In the case of the Afghanistan evaluation, female enumerators who were able to decide the most appropriate means of selecting participants carried out the focus groups and interviews among the female population. In the case of the evaluation of peacekeeping in Côte d'Ivoire (Mvukiyehe and Samii 2009), the enumerators were intensively trained in human subjects and survey techniques for a week. For the evaluation of the reconciliation radio programme in Rwanda (Paluck 2009a), the research assistants represented both Hutu and Tutsi backgrounds, which in itself gave a message of tolerance and may have helped in downplaying ethnicity issues when approaching the communities.

5.3 Evaluations as interventions: implications for reliability and risk

All evaluations in which primary data are being collected through human interaction could in themselves be seen or perceived as a type of intervention. This fact has potential implications both for the reliability of the evaluation results and for the safety of the evaluation personnel and those being evaluated. In addition, the perceived or real threat to safety is likely to be negatively correlated with the reliability of the results, as has been acknowledged in the new OECD guidance for *Evaluating Peacebuilding Activities in Settings of Conflict and Fragility* (OECD 2012). The guidance states that 'evaluations of interventions in the field of conflict prevention and peacebuilding expose – in contrast to almost all forms of evaluation – both evaluators and evaluated to real risk'. The guidance goes on to discuss the implications:

> First, the threat of violence may constrain the evaluators' ability to raise issues, collect material and data, recruit and retain local staff, meet interlocutors, publish findings, and disclose sources. Defending the integrity of evaluation findings in highly politicized and even dangerous settings can pose problems for evaluation teams, particularly where evaluation findings may potentially be misused by different parties to a conflict or harm those involved. Second, the risk of harm may mean that the information obtained is biased, incomplete and/or (voluntarily or involuntarily) censored. Consequently, evaluations must address the operational and methodological consequences of the risk of violence. More specifically, in order to deal with this challenge, it is advisable that the evaluation itself include a conflict analysis in order to assess the intervention and to ensure that the evaluation process and product is conflict sensitive.
>
> (OECD 2012: 28)

Impact evaluations, to a greater extent than other evaluation methodologies, rely on the collection of primary data from a large number of units both in a treated and a comparison population. This means that evaluation teams may have increased exposure to the above-mentioned risks.

Carrying out evaluations in conflict-affected settings can potentially cause harm to participants of the evaluation team (which under field visits may include implementation staff) and the local population interviewed. For example, in a community driven reconstruction evaluation in the DRC,

> the harsh conditions produced great costs to enumerators with high incidence of sickness including malaria and cholera. Although safety regulations were in place in all areas, one of the teams was involved in a tragic accident in which a child died…Despite the precautions undertaken we did encounter some security issues: 31 villages were not visited due to security risks; one team was ambushed and had to hand over their equipment; and one IRC staff member was abducted (and subsequently released unharmed).
> (Humphreys et al. 2012: 34–35)

Carrying out evaluations in conflict-affected settings could furthermore potentially adversely affect intergroup relations and the course of intergroup conflict. While examples were not found of this having happened, an ongoing study in Côte D'Ivoire (not included in the Samii et al. 2012 review) made evaluation design adjustments to minimise the risk of exacerbating existing conflict. The evaluation, which looks at the impact of couples discussion groups in addition to a savings intervention to combat intimate partner violence (Gupta and Annan, ongoing), included women who would not otherwise have been included in the sample. They were interviewing women in savings groups, but were only interested in women who had partners because the outcomes of interest were about partner relations and decision-making. Given that the villages were in areas where there had been high ethnic tensions and conflict, the programme team felt that if they separated the women and interviewed some and not others, there was the potential to create conflict and suspicion. They therefore decided to also administer a shorter survey to non-partnered women.

Broadly speaking, there are three reasons for evaluation teams to conduct conflict analyses: 1) to assess the relevance and impact of the programme; 2) to assess the risks of negative effects of conflict on the evaluation design and process; and 3) to assess the risks of the evaluation exacerbating conflict (conflict-sensitivity) (DFID 2002). When reviewing the conflict assessments reported in the summarised studies or commented upon in the survey responses, we found a varied approach. Some teams reported having relied on the assessment of the programme implementing agency and partners in the country. In other cases, an assessment of risk to subjects was conducted as part of the institutional review board (IRB) approval process. A number of the studies derived insights from baseline studies that included questions about conflict experience, regular programme reviews of the methods and measures with a 'do no harm' approach in mind, survey piloting and discussions with people working in similar communities, as well as behavioural monitoring. All of these approaches indicate an adapted use of conflict assessment. A finding of some concern is that none of the studies or of the survey respondents indicated that they had given any thought to the potential of adverse effects from the publication and dissemination of their results and findings.

Determining what is good enough in terms of conflict assessment is a difficult question and a balancing act between time, resources and a priori knowledge of risk. The instability of conflict-affected settings poses significant challenges to the rigour of evaluation design and the quality of data collected. Evaluations in these settings also introduce risks and potential harm to evaluators and the evaluated. Drawing from experiences of evaluators in these contexts, below are a set of questions about ethical and feasibility issues that research teams should consider:

- Does the evaluation factor in time for delays, which are more likely to occur in unstable conditions?
- Does the sample size factor in the potential for higher attrition due to potential security issues, migration or ethical concerns?
- Have the potential ways that the evaluation may introduce risk and harm to participants, interviewers and implementing partners been adequately considered and have strategies been devised to mitigate these risks and harm?
- Have interviewers been trained in ethical data collection and conflict-sensitive approaches to study participants? Have the characteristics of the interview team been thought through in light of the conflict (i.e., ethnicity, age, gender, status)?
- Is there a security protocol or guidelines for evaluation staff? Do evaluation staff fall under any organisational protection for security?
- Who carries the legal responsibility for the risks taken? Have the researchers partnered with an organisation able to bear the risks?
- Have methods of monitoring the potential ethical and conflict-related issues throughout data collection process been considered and planned?
- Does the evaluation team have strong key informants who can provide thoughtful analysis about the security situation and the research implications at the design phase and throughout the evaluation?
- Is a flexible approach to the evaluation in place such that adjustments can be made throughout the process in light of potential harm, security or other programmatic issues?
- Is the responsibility of the dissemination and communication of the findings clarified, is there a communications plan in place and is it conflict-sensitive?

We have seen that impact evaluations are feasible to carry out in diverse and challenging circumstances, but require precautionary measures, flexibility and conflict-sensitivity on the part of the evaluators. Having acknowledged the challenges and resources impact evaluations in these contexts take, the next section attempts to address the core question of the value of impact evaluations.

6 Why are impact evaluations important?

6.1 Testing theories of change

While large n impact evaluations of peacebuilding are possible, they are also difficult, so the question remains: why do we need them? The answer is that only impact evaluations allow us to measure net impact and thus attribute the effects of the intervention. As a result, only impact evaluations allow us to test whether the intervention and its various inputs and outputs lead to the hypothesised changes, outcomes and impacts in our theory of change (White 2009). The simplest case for this claim is the before–after fallacy. Consider measuring an outcome both before the programme and after the programme. Typically if there is an improvement, the evaluator (and programme manager) considers the intervention a success. But over the period of any programme, many other factors come into play, not least of which all the other programmes that are being implemented in the same country. Without a valid counterfactual, there is no way of knowing whether the improvement can be attributed to the programme's activities or may have happened in spite of these.

In conflict-affected settings, the before–after fallacy may be even more misleading, as the general situation may actually deteriorate over the period of the programme. The before–after measurement would show the outcomes worsening, but a comparison to a counterfactual could very well reveal that the programme prevented the outcomes from worsening to an even greater extent – a crucial result for a peacebuilding programme. Similarly, a before–after measurement could show an improvement that is entirely due to other factors and may indeed mask unintended negative consequences of the programme in question – again a crucial result for peacebuilding programmes.

So, when returning to the question of the importance of impact evaluation, we suggest focusing on the two key distinguishing features/qualities/characteristics, namely the need to account for other possible confounding factors and to focus on results rather than the intentions. While we stand to be corrected, our impression is that most disagreements and discussions about the importance of impact evaluations, the way we have defined these in the chapter, revolve around the need for a control or a comparison group to account for confounding factors. We will not deal with this larger debate here but refer to recent literature (Stern et al. 2012).

A limitation to quantitative impact evaluation often cited is the fact that large n impact evaluations can only be applied in large n situations, therefore significantly limiting the questions that can be addressed. While large n situations can be possible to implement even in what may seem like small n situations, such as when a nationwide policy is being implemented from which no one is or can be excluded (we have argued earlier in this chapter that even in this case an encouragement design can help us give a dose-response perspective of the policy in question), quite often they are not. In these cases, rather than to move on and look for the next question that is evaluable by large n methods, we call for small n attribution analysis and will revert to these in the next sub-section. First, however, we present the type of learning and insights that can be gained by large *n* impact evaluations.

The results of several large *n* impact evaluations of peacebuilding interventions provide compelling evidence that many key assumptions and theories of change about conflict prevention and peacebuilding need to be tested. This section presents examples of impact evaluations whose findings challenge the theories that personal beliefs and prejudices need to change in order to change behaviour; that discussion and debate necessarily leads to improved tolerance; and that Community-Driven Development (CDD) or Community Driven Reconstruction (CDR) projects, at least in the way these have tended to be implemented, improve social cohesion.

Two studies by Elizabeth Levy Paluck test psychological theories of attitude and behaviour change from media interventions designed to help rebuild communities following conflict. In Rwanda, she evaluated a reconciliation-themed radio soap opera (Paluck 2009a) and in eastern Democratic Republic of Congo (DRC), she evaluated a radio talk show that was aired in conjunction with a talk show (Paluck 2010).

The first evaluation tested conflicting psychological theories about the relationships between personal beliefs, societal norms and behaviours, and how those can be influenced by media. In Rwanda, the NGO La Benevolencija produced a radio soap opera called *Musekewaya* (*New Dawn*) that was designed to promote reconciliation by playing out a story that includes similar sources of tensions and violent outcomes as the 1994 Rwandan genocide,[6] but that speaks out against violence and includes characters banding together across ethnic groups (which were proxied by 'communities' as the government forbade the use of the word 'ethnic'). Although the radio programme was aired nationwide, Paluck created a pair-wise matched cluster randomised controlled trial using an 'encouragement' design. She established listening groups to encourage the beneficiary, or treatment, group to listen to the *New Dawn* programme and to concurrently encourage the control group to listen to an alternate radio programme on health.

Since the ultimate goal of the programme was to reduce intergroup conflict, the questions the experiment tried to answer were first, can such a radio programme influence both personal beliefs and prejudices as well as perceived societal norm? And second, is a change in personal beliefs a necessary precondition to influence behaviour? While psychological theories conflict, 'theories of media persuasion claim that beliefs are influenced by media cultures and programs' (Paluck 2009a: 575). The findings were startling; the perceptions of social norms as well as behaviours changed significantly in the treatment group with respect to intermarriage, open dissent, trust, empathy, cooperation and trauma healing, while the programme did not significantly change listeners' personal beliefs.

The second evaluation tested the effectiveness of discussion to reduce conflict. In the DRC, a radio soap opera *Kumbuka Kesho* (*Think of Tomorrow*) emphasised conflict reduction through community cooperation. While the radio programme was aired in all the experiment's regions, Paluck again used an encouragement design, this time by pair-wise matching regions and randomly choosing one broadcast region in each pair to air a talk show directly following the soap opera, and the other the soap opera only. The talk show was designed to encourage listeners' reactions and discussions. While there is a resurgence in the use of discussion as a policy tool to reduce conflict (evidenced by the proliferation of terms such as 'deliberation', 'dialogue', 'participatory' and 'community driven' in the literature on interventions designed to promote peace) psychological research has also flagged potential hazards of discussions including opinion polarisation, social pressure and cognitive errors (Paluck 2010). Paluck carried out this research to learn more about the success of discussion-based conflict-reduction programmes. The findings were sobering: those listeners who were encouraged to discuss through the additional talk show did indeed discuss more, but were also found to become more intolerant and less likely to aid disliked community members.

A third group of evaluations examined the effectiveness of CDD projects to strengthen social cohesion. A commonly proposed theory is that of the importance of social cohesion, or the (re)building of interpersonal or intergroup networks, trust, and reciprocity, as a crucial factor for peacebuilding and conflict prevention. In a recent talk at the launching conference for the High Commissioner on National Minorities (HCNM) Guidelines on Integration in Diverse Societies, Stefan Wolff answered his rhetorical question about what it is about social cohesion that is so important for successful conflict prevention in the following way:

> One of the fundamental ideas underlying the notion of conflict prevention in diverse societies is that different population segments can resolve any differences by recourse to institutional processes rather than violence. For such institutional processes to be effective, a viable and resilient state is required, whose fundamental constitutional principles are broadly accepted and respected across all segments of societies. If this is the case, societies may well be diverse across any number of indicators, including, ethnicity, language, and religion, but they will also be characterised by a sufficient level of social cohesion.
>
> (Wolff 2012: 1)

Efforts to strengthen social cohesion have increased among development organisations, most often operationalised through CDD or CDR projects. In a systematic review of interventions to promote social cohesion in sub-Saharan Africa, including in several conflict-affected countries (King et al. 2010), the authors outlined the theory underlying CDD interventions:

> [P]rojects promote social cohesion by supporting and building community capacity for decision-making and collective action through a process of participation. The hypothesis is that, by handing over control of decisions and resources to the community, the sub-projects will better meet communities' needs and enhance ownership, and that the experience of being involved in this participatory process will empower communities, improve capacity for local development and improve social cohesion.
>
> (King et al. 2010: 347)

Drawing upon the available evidence from impact evaluations that fulfilled a set of quality criteria, the review finds that the evidence of pro-social effects from CDD-type interventions is weak. More surprisingly, a negative effect on individuals' perceptions of intergroup relations is found across the three studies that measured this factor.[7]

The preceding examples of how impact evaluations have been used as tools to test and critically examine commonly held assumptions about how development interventions affect change were all based on large n impact evaluations. But what happens when we have a question about results and impact of an intervention, be it a policy reform or a service delivered, on the ground (on the so-called 'beneficiaries') and do not have a large number of units of assignment? The next section discusses the use and commonalities of small n impact evaluations.

6.2 Small n *impact evaluations*

What distinguishes impact evaluation from other types of evaluation is that it relies on a counterfactual analysis to attribute an effect to a particular intervention or set of interventions, or said differently: to make causal inferences. We further distinguish between large n impact evaluations which involve tests of statistical significance between outcomes for treatment and comparison groups, with n referring to the unit of assignment, and small n impact evaluations carried out when a treatment and comparison group of sufficient size cannot be identified, be it individuals, communities or countries, and thus where tests of statistical significance are not possible.

While there exists considerable consensus among impact evaluators conducting large n impact evaluations as to what constitutes a high quality impact evaluation, no such consensus exists for small n impact evaluations. In a recent paper by White and Phillips (2012), they examine various small n evaluation approaches that have been used and find that a methodological core which could provide a basis for consensus exists:

> This common core involves the specification of a theory of change together with a number of further alternative causal hypotheses. Causation is established beyond reasonable doubt by collecting evidence to validate, invalidate, or revise the hypothesized explanations, with the goal of rigorously evidencing the links in the actual causal chain.
>
> (White and Phillips 2012: 18)

These types of approaches they refer to as process- or mechanism-based approaches. They go on to summarise the main difference between large and small n evaluations in the following manner: 'Whereas experimental approaches infer causality by identifying the outcomes resulting from manipulated causes, a mechanism-based approach searches for the causes of observed outcomes' (White and Phillips 2012: 18). The small n evaluations will typically gather information on both the 'what' and the 'why', but are at risk of suffering from substantial biases likely to arise from the collection, analysis and reporting of qualitative data.

Quite often, however, when large *n* impact evaluation is not possible, evaluators revert to process evaluations[8] or impact assessments based on association[9] rather than to small *n* attribution analysis, not out of methodological disagreement but rather due to a whole range of supply and demand limitations (related to time and resources, evaluation skills, etc.; see Chapter 8 in this book).

An illustration of an evaluation that used elements of the methodologies referred to as small *n* attribution analysis to critically assess important theories of change is the evaluation of Norwegian peace efforts in Sri Lanka (see Chapter 4 in this book). Among the main objectives of the Sri Lanka evaluation was to assess results achieved through the Norwegian facilitation of the peace process. This is a case where the total population (N) is 1 (and small *n* can obviously not be larger than large N). In other words, there was only one peace negotiation process going on with Norwegian involvement in Sri Lanka, and that was what the researchers set out to evaluate. Clearly, no large *n* impact evaluation was feasible. What about small *n* attribution analysis? One of the main challenges to attributing results to the Norwegian facilitation efforts is that the 'treatment', Norwegian facilitation, cannot be assumed to be an independent variable – rather the Sri Lankan and international actors chose to contact Norway, or did not object to this, requesting it to play the role as facilitator (and Norway chose to accept). It is likely that assumptions about what role Norway could or would play will have influenced the decision of approaching Norwegian policymakers. Indeed, according to the report:

> Norway was chosen as a facilitator, not only for its expertise, but also because it was a small power without geo-strategic interests and colonial baggage. Being a less powerful player, Norway felt it had to consult the US and India, the former as the world's superpower and the latter as the regional hegemon.
> (Goodhand et al. 2011: 73)

Assuming the Norwegian treatment as exogenous would have led to overplaying the role of agent, as opposed to context and path-dependence being crucial factors. Indeed, the provocative title of the evaluation report, 'pawns of peace', alludes directly to the endogeneity issue.

The methods chosen by the team include features designed to explicitly assess the plausibility of causal claims; the common feature of small *n* attribution analysis. In particular, the 'inside-out' and 'outside-in' approaches that they seek to combine allows them to critically assess whether it is realistic to believe that if Norway had acted differently then different outcomes would have ensued at various points in time, given the structural constraints in which key actors operated. The study is also very explicit about the many data collection constraints and biases they faced, including missing key informants, secrecy and safety issues, conflicting and unreliable accounts, and not being able to interview a number of key informants in person due to visa problems. The main strategy used to deal with these challenges was that of triangulation.

7 Conclusion: high risk, high return?

Carrying out impact evaluations in conflict-affected settings can be risky and methodologically challenging, although we have discussed ways in which the evaluation designs and data-collection practices can be adapted and risks reduced to make their implementation feasible. Impact evaluations are also costly, due to the reliance on data from large samples to achieve statistical power, ranging from as little as US$50,000 for quasi-experimental impact evaluations with pre-existing survey data to more than US$1 million for large multi-year RCTs with several rounds of survey data gathered. For both of these reasons, the returns to the studies in terms of learning and programmatic improvements should also be high for the effort to be worth it.

We have argued that if we are interested in the actual development effects of interventions and programmes on the people they are supposed to benefit, rather than whether the programme was implemented as planned, and if we want to know whether this effect was due to, or despite, the intervention in question, then a well-designed and executed impact evaluation is the most reliable approach. The potential usefulness and importance of impact evaluation is well exemplified by the way impact evaluations have tested and challenged many of the key assumptions and theories of change that underpin conflict prevention and peacebuilding activities.

Important insights have therefore been gained and it is important that this knowledge feeds back into the way we design and implement conflict prevention and peacebuilding programmes, as well as the way we carry out programme-theory evaluations. To date, evidence of putting learning into practice from impact evaluations is limited. Out of the 13 programmes in which survey respondents had been involved, two were rated as not having led to any learning, three as having contributed to programme improvements or general learning around a programme type, and in all remaining eight cases the respondents said any learning impact was unclear or 'too early to tell'. It may be that learning happens without the knowledge of the researchers, and clearly learning takes time. Especially when trying to draw lessons that have validity beyond a single programme, country and point in time it is necessary to build up a body of evidence and systematically review it. Nevertheless, the survey responses are a good reminder that dissemination and learning from evaluation work, the *raison d'être* of these risky and challenging endeavours, cannot be taken for granted. Whether the high risk leads to high returns remains a question for further research.

Appendix A

Studies reviewed in the Samii et al. (2012) paper

	Article	*Category*	*Country*	*Status*	*IE Type*	*Counterfactual*
1	Annan and Blattman (2011)	Ex-combatant reintegration	Liberia	Ongoing	RCT	Randomised control group

Impact evaluation for peacebuilding 147

	Article	Category	Country	Status	IE Type	Counterfactual
2	Beath et al. (2010)	Peace dividends	Afghanistan	Completed	RCT	Randomised control group
3	Blattman (2011a)	Peace structures	Liberia	Ongoing	RCT	Randomised control group
4	Blattman (2011b)	Victims of war	Uganda	Ongoing	RCT	Delayed treatment control group
5	Blattman (2011c)	Victims of war	Uganda	Ongoing	RCT	Randomised control group
6	Casey et al. (2011)	Peace dividends	Sierra Leone	Completed	RCT	Randomised control group
7	Fearon et al. (2009)	Peace dividends	Liberia	Completed	RCT	Randomised group assignment of villages
8	Fearon et al. (2008)	Peace dividends	Liberia	Completed	RCT	Randomised control group
9	Glennerster and Miguel (2010)	Peace messaging	Sierra Leone	Ongoing	RCT	Randomised control group
10	Paluck and Green (2009)	Peace messaging	Rwanda	Completed	RCT	Clustered random assignment
11	Paluck (2009a)	Peace messaging	Sudan	Ongoing	RCT	Clustered random assignment with factorial model
12	Paluck (2009b)	Peace messaging	Rwanda	Completed	RCT	Randomised assignment of clusters with matching
13	Pugel (2007)	Ex-combatant reintegration	Liberia	Completed	RCT	Randomised selection of 20-person clusters
14	Paluck (2010)	Peace messaging	DRC	Completed	RCT	Randomised assignment of clusters with matching
15	Barron et al. (2009)	Peace dividends	Indonesia	Completed	Quasi-experimental	Matched control group
16	Biton and Solomon (2006)	Consensus and dialogue	Israel	Completed	Quasi-experimental	Matched-pair randomisation of classes in selected schools/ natural
17	Gilligan et al. (2010)	Ex-combatant reintegration	Burundi	Completed	Quasi-experimental	Natural control group with matching
18	Humphreys and Weinstein (2007)	Ex-combatant reintegration	Sierra Leone	Completed	Quasi-experimental	Matched control group

	Article	Category	Country	Status	IE Type	Counterfactual
19	Kondylis (2007)	Victims of war	Rwanda	Preliminary	Quasi-experimental	Natural control group
20	Levely (2012)	Ex-combatant reintegration	Liberia	Completed	Quasi-experimental	Matched control group
21	Malhotra and Liyanage (2005)	Consensus and dialogue	Sri Lanka	Completed	Quasi-experimental	Natural control group
22	Mvukiyehe and Samii (2009)	Peace dividends	Côte d'Ivoire	Preliminary	Quasi-experimental	Natural control group
23	Mvukiyehe and Samii (2011)	Community security initiatives	Liberia	Preliminary	Quasi-experimental	Matched clusters (communities)
24	Mvukiyehe and Samii (2010)	Ex-combatant reintegration, peace dividends	Liberia	Completed	Quasi-experimental	Cluster matched sampling

Appendix B

Online survey sent to the lead authors of the studies reviewed in the Samii et al. (2012) paper

1. Please list briefly the impact evaluations (IEs) you have conducted in conflict-affected settings, and indicate whether you were involved in the design of the intervention in any of these (e.g., a pilot intervention that was evaluated).
2. Did the conflict or sensitive situation make you and your team adapt the evaluation design in any way (e.g., change of geographic focus, drop baseline, adapt timing of surveys, etc.)? If yes, please provide details.
3. More particularly, did you and your team adapt the data-collection methods in any way due to the situation in which the evaluation was going to be carried out (e.g., smaller sample size, only administrative data, use of particularly trained enumerators, etc.)? If yes, please provide details.
4. In retrospect, would you have done anything differently with respect to the evaluation design and data collection? If yes, please provide details.
5. Did you make use of a formal strategic level (or country level) conflict analysis or assessment in designing the evaluation and surveys? If yes, please specify whether the assessment was based on any specific template or tool or guidelines.
6. Considering that an evaluation in which primary data is being collected could in itself be seen or perceived as a type of intervention, did you conduct any conflict assessment (e.g., PCIA, do no harm) in designing the evaluation and surveys?
7. In any of the conflict assessment work, did you identify possible unintended consequences (positive or negative) of your evaluation or survey plans? If possible adverse consequences were identified, how did you address these?
8. Did you get an IRB approval?[10] Was the IRB process beneficial to you? Did you make any changes as a result of going through the IRB process? Please provide details.
9. As far as you are aware, did the evaluation(s) you were involved in lead to any learning or improvement in intervention implementation or policies?
10. Please list other researchers you know about who have carried out IEs in this area, preferably with the relevant reference. This will help us identify whether we have missed anyone out.
Any other information you deem important for the purposes of the described chapter?

Notes

1 We would like to thank a number of people for their input into this chapter. Dr Anette Brown, Deputy Director, and Daniela Barba, Research Assistant, at the International Initiative for Impact Evaluation (3ie) have provided helpful suggestions and given us access to the database and literature survey which formed the basis for the Samii et al. (2012) survey. Dr Julia Leininger at the German Development Institute, Professor Christoph Zürcher at the University of Ottawa, Assistant Professor Cyrus Samii at New York University, Professor Macartan Humphreys at Columbia University and the editors of this book have reviewed and provided invaluable comments to previous versions of the chapter. Finally, a number of the lead investigators of the impact evaluations discussed in the paper took the time to respond to our survey and we are very grateful for being able to draw on their experiences.
2 Marie Gaarder was Director, Evaluation Department, Norwegian Agency for Development Cooperation at the time of writing the chapter.
3 Appendix A lists the included studies.
4 For the purpose of discussion, we use the term 'individuals' for the unit of analysis, although households or communities or other entities may also be the unit of analysis. As it turns out, the vast majority of IEs of peacebuilding interventions do use individuals as the unit of analysis (Samii et al. 2012).
5 It is worth noting that development interventions may differ slightly from the medical 'equipoise' case of a zero probability event, in the sense that the development practitioners tend to hold priors of an intervention being beneficial but with some remaining doubts.
6 The Rwandan genocide was the 1994 mass murder of an estimated 800,000 people in the East African state of Rwanda. It was the culmination of longstanding ethnic competition and tensions between the minority Tutsi, who had controlled power for centuries, and the majority Hutu peoples, who had come to power in the rebellion of 1959–1962 (Wikipedia, accessed 31 October 2012).
7 The review indicates that this finding may be partly explained by the fact that broad and substantive participation, including in actual decision-making, was often lacking and suggests that the implementation of the CDD interventions may have been flawed.
8 What distinguishes impact evaluations from process evaluations – evaluations of how the implementation was carried out – is that the benchmark against which we compare in process evaluations is not a counterfactual scenario but rather non-tested (or in the best-case scenario previously tested) assumptions of what underlies a 'good process'.
9 Association claims are very widespread in the small n evaluation world, as is raised in Chapter 8 in this book. These are claims of having contributed to an outcome (or sometimes even claiming attribution) by having contributed an input or claiming to have done so (e.g., by having been present at the same time). This approach does not explore alternative causal hypothesis, the minimum criteria for small n attribution analysis, and is clearly not good enough.
10 An institutional review board (IRB), also known as an independent ethics committee (IEC) or ethical review board (ERB), is a committee that has been formally designated to approve, monitor, and review biomedical and behavioural research involving humans. IRBs are responsible for critical oversight functions for research conducted on human subjects that are scientific, ethical and regulatory.

Bibliography

Annan, J. and Blattman, C. (2011) *Reintegrating and Employing High Risk Youth in Liberia: Lessons from a Randomized Evaluation of a Landmine Action Agricultural Training Program for Ex-combatants*, Evidence from Randomized Evaluations of Peacebuilding in Liberia: Policy Report 2011, 1, New Haven: Yale and IPA.

Baker, Judy. L (2000) *Evaluating the Impact of Development Projects on Poverty: A Handbook for Practitioners*, Washington, DC: World Bank.

Barron, P., Humphreys, M., Paler, L. and Weinstein, J. (2009) *Community-Based Reintegration in Aceh: Assessing the Impacts of BRA-KDP*, Washington, DC: World Bank. www.columbia.edu/~lbp2106/docs/arls/FINAL_BRA-KDP_WB.pdf.

Beath, A., Christia, F., Enikolopov, R. and Kabuli, S. A. (2010) *Randomized Impact Evaluation of Phase II of Afghanistan's National Solidarity Programme (NSP): Estimates of Interim Program Impact from First Follow-up Survey*. www.nsp-ie.org/reports/BCEK-Interim_Estimates_of_Program_Impact_2010_07_13.pdf.

Biton, Y. and Solomon, G. (2006) 'Peace in the Eyes of Israeli and Palestinian Youths: Effects of Collective Narratives and Peace Education Program', *Journal of Peace Research* 43(2): 167–180. http://jpr.sagepub.com/cgi/doi/10.1177/0022343306061888.

Blattman, C. (2011a) *Uganda: Enterprises for Ultra-poor Women after War* (in progress). http://chrisblattman.com/projects/wings.

——(2011b) *Uganda: Post-war Youth Vocational Training* (in progress). www.chrisblattman.com/projects/nusaf_yo.

——(2011c) *Peace Education in Rural Liberia. Innovations for Poverty Action* (in progress). www.poverty-action.org/project/0139.

Blattman, C. and Annan, J. (2011) *Reintegrating and Employing High Risk Youth in Liberia: Lessons from a Randomized Evaluation of a Landmine Action Agricultural Training Program for Ex-combatants*, Evidence from Randomized Evaluations of Peacebuilding in Liberia: Policy Report 2011, 1, Interventions for Policy Action (IPA), New Haven: Yale University.

Casey, K., Glennerster, R. and Miguel, E. (2011) 'Reshaping Institutions: Evidence on External Aid and Local Collective Action', National Bureau of Economic Research Working Paper no. 17012. www.nber.org/papers/w17012.

Center for Global Development (2006) *When Will We Ever Learn? Improving Lives through Impact Evaluation*, Report of the Evaluation Gap Working Group, Washington, DC: Center for Global Development.

DFID (Department for International Development) (2002) *Conducting Conflict Assessments: Guidance Notes, Issues*, London: Department For International Development. www.conflictsensitivity.org/sites/default/files/Conducting_Conflict_Assessment_Guidance.pdf, accessed 6 January 2013.

Diamond, A. and Hainmueller, J. (2007) *The Encouragement Design for Program Evaluation*, IFC. www.ifc.org/ifcext/rmas.nsf/AttachmentsByTitle/Encouragement/$FILE/The+Encouragement+Design+for+Program+Evaluation.pdf.

DiNardo, J. (2008) 'Natural Experiments and Quasi-natural Experiments', in S. N. Durlauf and L. E. Blume (eds) *The New Palgrave Dictionary of Economics*, 2nd edn, Basingstoke: Palgrave Macmillan.

Fearon, J., Humphreys, M. and Weinstein, J. M. (2008) *Community-Driven Reconstruction in Lofa County*. www.columbia.edu/~mh2245/FHW/FHW_final.pdf.

——(2009) 'Can Development Aid Contribute to Social Cohesion after Civil War? Evidence from a Field Experiment in Post-conflict Liberia', *American Economic Review: Papers and Proceedings* 99(2): 287–291. http://pubs.aeaweb.org/doi/pdfplus/10.1257/aer.99.2.287, accessed 16 October 2012.

Friedman, J. (2011) *Development Impact Blog: The Ethics of a Control Group in Randomized Impact Evaluations – the Start of an Ongoing Discussion*. http://blogs.worldbank.org/impactevaluations/node/598, accessed 31 March 2013.

Gilligan, M., Mvukiyehe, E. and Samii, C. (2010) *Reintegrating Rebels Into Civilian Life: Quasi-experimental Evidence From Burundi*, Washington, DC: United States Institute of Peace. www.columbia.edu/~cds81/docs/bdi09_reintegration100701.pdf.

Glennerster, R. and Miguel, E. (2010) *The role of information and radios on political knowledge and participation in Sierra Leone*, Cambridge, MA.: Poverty Action Lab (in progress). www.povertyactionlab.org/evaluation/role-information-and-radios-political-knowledge-and-participation-sierra-leone.

Goodhand, J., Klem, B. and Sørbø, G. (2011) *Pawns of Peace: Evaluation of Norwegian Peace Efforts in Sri Lanka, 1997–2009*, Oslo: Norad evaluation 5/2011.

Gupta, J. and Annan, J. (ongoing) *Evaluating an Economic and Empowerment Intervention on the Prevention of Partner Violence*, IRC project.

Hossain, M., Zimmerman, C., Kiss, L. and Watts, C. (2010) *Violence Against Women and Men in Côte d'Ivoire: A Cluster Randomized Controlled Trial to Assess the Impact of the 'Men and Women in Partnership' Intervention on the Reduction of Violence Against Women and Girls in Rural Côte d'Ivoire – Results from a Community Survey*, London: London School of Hygiene and Tropical Medicine.

Humphreys, M. (2008) *Community-Driven Reconstruction in the Democratic Republic of Congo*, Baseline Report, Washington, DC: Columbia University and the International Rescue Committee.

Humphreys, M. and Weinstein, J. M. (2007) 'Demobilization and Reintegration', *Journal of Conflict Resolution* 51(4): 531–567. http://jcr.sagepub.com/cgi/doi/10.1177/0022002707302790.

Humphreys, M., de la Sierra, R. S. and van der Windt, P. (2012) *Social and Economic Impacts of Tuungane: Final Report on the Effects of a Community Driven Reconstruction Program in Eastern Democratic Republic of Congo*, Washington, DC: Columbia University. www.oecd.org/countries/democraticrepublicofthecongo/drc.pdf.

King, E., Samii, C. and Snilstveit, B. (2010) 'Interventions to Promote Social Cohesion in Sub-Saharan Africa', *Journal of Development Effectiveness*, 2(3): 336–370.

Kondylis, F. (2007) 'Agricultural Outputs and Conflict Displacement: Evidence from a Policy Intervention in Rwanda', *Households in Conflict Network Working Paper* 28. www.csae.ox.ac.uk/conferences/2007-edia-lawbidc/papers/046-kondylis.pdf.

Lau, J. T. F., Mao, J. and Woo, J. (2003) 'Ethical Issues Related to the Use of Placebo in Clinical Trials', *Hong Kong Medical Journal* 9(3): 192–198.

Levely, I. (2012) *Measuring Intermediate Outcomes of Liberia's DDRR Program*, IES Working Paper 2/2012, Prague: Institute of Economic Studies, Faculty of Social Sciences Charles University in Prague.

Malhotra, D. and Liyanage, S. (2005) 'Long-Term Effects of Peace Workshops in Protracted Conflicts', *Journal of Conflict Resolution* 49(6): 908–924. http://jcr.sagepub.com/cgi/doi/10.1177/0022002705281153, accessed March 2013.

Mvukiyehe, E. and Samii, C. (2009) *Laying a Foundation for Peace? Micro-Effects of Peacekeeping in Cote d'Ivoire*, paper prepared for the 2009 American Political Science Association Conference, Toronto. https://files.nyu.edu/cds2083/public/docs/unoci/mvukiyehe_samii_unoci090801.pdf, accessed 20 May 2013.

——(2010) *Quantitative Impact Evaluation of the United Nations Mission in Liberia: Final Report*, Typescript, Washington, DC: Columbia University, https://files.nyu.edu/cds2083/public/docs/lib/unmil_final100209.pdf, accessed 20 May 2013.

——(2011) *Peace from the Bottom Up: A Randomized Trial with UN Peacekeepers*, Paper presented at the FBA Peacekeeping Working Group, Stockholm, 11–12 February.

OECD (2012) *Evaluating Peacebuilding Activities in Settings of Conflict and Fragility: Improving Learning for Results*, DAC Guidelines and Reference Series. Paris: OECD Publishing. doi: 10.1787/9789264106802-en.

Paluck, E. L. (2009a) 'Reducing Intergroup Prejudice and Conflict Using the Media: A Field Experiment in Rwanda', *Journal of Personality and Social Psychology* 96(3): 574–587. www.ncbi.nlm.nih.gov/pubmed/19254104.

——(2009b) *Entertainment, Information, and Discussion: Experimenting with Media Techniques for Civic Education and Engagement in Southern Sudan*, Memo presented at the Experiments on Government and Politics (EGAP) Conference at the Institution for Social and Policy Studies, Yale, 24–25 April 2009. http://isps.research.yale.edu/conferences/EGAP/egap/download/Paluck_4.25.09_MEMO.pdf.

——(2010) 'Is It Better Not to Talk? Group Polarization, Extended Contact, and Perspectives Taking in Eastern Republic of Congo', *Personality and Social Psychology Bulletin* 36(9): 1170–1185.

Paluck, E. L. and Green, D. P. (2009) 'Deference, Dissent, and Dispute Resolution: An Experimental Intervention Using Mass Media to Change Norms and Behavior in Rwanda', *American Political Science Review* 103(4): 622. www.journals.cambridge.org/abstract_S0003055409990128.

Pugel, J. (2007) *What the Fighters Say: A Survey of Ex-combatants in Liberia*, Monrovia, United Nations Development Programme. www.lr.undp.org/UNDPwhatFightersSayLiberia-2006.pdf.

Samii, C., Brown, A. and Kulma, M. (2012) *Evaluating Stabilization Interventions*, Working draft 2.0, 16 August 2012.

Stern, E., Stame, N., Mayne, J., Forss, K., Davies, R. and Befani, B. (2012) *Developing a Broader Range of Rigorous Designs and Methods for Impact Evaluations*, report of a study commissioned by the Department for International Development (DFID), London: Department for International Development (DFID). www.dfid.gov.uk/Documents/.../design-method-impact-eval.pdf, accessed 26 March 2013.

USDA, Food and Nutrition Service (2005) *Nutrition Education: Principles of Sound Impact Evaluation*, Washington, DC: USDA. www.fns.usda.gov/Ora/menu/Published/NutritionEducation/Files/EvaluationPrinciples.pdf.

White, H. (2009) *Theory-Based Impact Evaluation: Principles and Practice*, Working Paper 3, New Delhi: International Initiative for Impact Evaluation.

——(2011) *An Introduction to the Use of Randomized Control Trails to Evaluate Development Interventions*, Working Paper 9, New Delhi: International Initiative for Impact Evaluation.

White, H. and Phillips, D. (2012) *Addressing Attribution of Cause and Effect in Small n Impact Evaluations: Towards an Integrated Framework*, Working Paper 15, New Delhi: International Initiative for Impact Evaluation.

Wolff, S. (2012) *Integration and Conflict Prevention in Diverse Societies, The Ljubljana Recommendations of the OSCE High Commissioner on National Minorities in the Post-Soviet Context*, Launching Conference HCNM Guidelines on Integration in Diverse Societies, 7 November 2012. www.stefanwolff.com/talks/integration-and-conflict-prevention-in-diverse-societies, accessed 19 November 2012.

World Bank (2012) *Impact Evaluation of the Burkina Faso Community Monitoring for Better Health and Education Service Delivery Project*, ongoing evaluation presented at a World Bank seminar 10 July 2012. http://web.worldbank.org/WBSITE/EXTERNAL/EXTDEC/EXTDEVIMPEVAINI/0,,contentMDK:23238146~menuPK:7637304~pagePK:64168445~piPK:64168309~theSitePK:3998212,00.html, accessed 6 January 2013.

——(2013) *Evaluation Designs* (webpage), http://web.worldbank.org/WBSITE/EXTERNAL/TOPICS/EXTPOVERTY/EXTISPMA/0,,contentMDK:20188242~menuPK:415130~pagePK:148956~piPK:216618~theSitePK:384329,00.html, accessed 30 March 2013.

World Medical Association (2000) 'Declaration of Helsinki: Ethical principles for Medical Research Involving Human Subjects', *JAMA* 284: 3043–3045.

——(2001) *Note of Clarification on Paragraph 29 of the WMA Declaration of Helsinki*, Geneva: World Medical Association.

8 Evaluating statebuilding support[1]
Learning from experience or judging from assumptions?

Jörn Grävingholt
German Development Institute

Julia Leininger
German Development Institute

1 Introduction

Statebuilding has become a major concern of donor countries in recent years. Several conceptual studies and policy documents devoted to the aim of increasing aid effectiveness in fragile states have been produced within the OECD's Development Assistance Committee (DAC), the World Bank and the wider development community.[2] All these documents confirm the urgency of effective statebuilding in countries affected by fragility, conflict and violence. They also confirm the complexity of statebuilding interventions – an amalgam of activities that aim to foster institutions based on legitimate politics, support the provision of citizen security, contribute to processes and institutions of justice, support foundations for thriving economic activity and help improve state revenue and services.[3]

At the same time there is broad agreement in both the academic and the practitioners' community that statebuilding is first and foremost an endogenous process that takes place within a society, is driven by actors and interests from within this very society and can only to a limited degree be influenced from outside.[4]

Yet the questions of where the exact limits of external influence lie, and how statebuilding support is best designed and delivered in order to be effective, are still underexplored. Impact evaluations of statebuilding support conducted on behalf of those agencies that offer such kinds of assistance are supposed to provide answers – supplying reliable knowledge about 'what works and what doesn't' to help aid practitioners to improve their interventions. But, as the following analysis shows, this is not always the case.

In a recent study for the Danish Ministry of Foreign Affairs a team of researchers from the German Development Institute, including the authors of this chapter, reviewed about 130 evaluations in the field of international statebuilding support with a view to distil the most relevant findings from many years of development practice (Grävingholt et al. 2012a). Our analysis found a 'high convergence of evaluation results and recommendations' across many studies on diverse countries. Yet a closer look at the methodologies employed in those studies raised some concern. In fact, it made us suspect that the observed convergence of findings was not so much proof of the robustness of the conclusions as it was a reflection of widespread methodological weaknesses, which were reproducing common, although not necessarily correct, 'conventional wisdom'.

These observations provide the starting point for this chapter. It analyses and discusses the design of major statebuilding evaluations, their methodological rigour and the generalisability of their findings. We aim at assessing the quality of the methods and research techniques used in evaluations of statebuilding support and, by extension, the methodological validity of their findings and conclusions. Reservations concerning the 'methodological validity' of findings do not per se mean that these findings are necessarily factually 'wrong'. Rather, our doubts relate to flaws in the logic of the arguments that lead to certain findings. This raises questions about how much confidence we can place in their findings and whether these findings can and should be used to establish policy guidance.

In addition to this introduction the chapter is divided into five parts. The second section introduces basic standards for evaluation against which the studies under review are measured. These standards include: 1) mapping out a theory of change; 2) devoting attention and effort to the adequate understanding of the intervention's context; and 3) evaluating impact rigorously using a credible counterfactual. We identify two levels at which evaluations of statebuilding interventions have to prove their value: the internal validity at all stages of the evaluation and the generalisability of its results. The second section also discusses the limits to fully applying these standards in the specific circumstances that characterise fragile states The third section introduces the empirical basis for our analysis, describing the number and types of studies that were included in our review. The fourth section presents our findings at each of the two levels identified above. The fifth discusses structural factors that might help explain what we consider to be a disconcerting overall picture emerging from our analysis of statebuilding evaluations. The sixth section provides conclusions of the chapter.

2 Standards for evaluating statebuilding support

There can be no doubt that the support of statebuilding is one of the most complex types of development interventions conceivable.[5] Peaceful and functioning states are complicated outcomes that result from long and winding political processes within societies. By no means is it trivial for a society to develop the type of polity that provides citizens with basic services, successfully monopolises the use of violence to the benefit of the public good and musters support for its institutional continuation.[6] The emergence of such states cannot be guaranteed *ex ante* and their survival, where they do emerge, is far from secure in all but the happiest cases.[7]

The magnitude of the statebuilding task has sometimes prompted an attitude of pre-emptive surrender among both aid practitioners and evaluators when it comes to demonstrating positive achievements or explaining failure. Given the complexity of statebuilding, this reasoning goes, we cannot reasonably expect evaluations to be able to trace any ultimate outcome back to any specific intervention and hence evaluations should refrain from this task. Evaluations should rather be more modest, confine themselves to less ambitious aims and avoid sophisticated designs and techniques.

While we recognise the concerns about complex intervention logics that inform this opinion, we do not share the conclusion that the usual standards of what constitutes convincing empirical evidence cannot be applied in settings of state fragility. In fact, as long as a practice exists of giving support with the intention to cause a particular effect in a social system, the question of whether this support has really had the desired effects or not is an inevitable question to ask. And answering this question will require following basic principles of causal inference established in social science. Hence we argue that there is only *one* legitimate standard against which the validity of findings can be measured, and this standard must be applied even in difficult contexts.

At the same time it is obvious that all empirical social science research has to cope with problems of incomplete data and unreliable information. Arguably even worse, it also has to live with countless implicit assumptions about causes and effects. These are built into its models that are in many cases at best plausible and widely observed, yet hardly ever proven to be universally true. Good evaluation research aims to inform policy decisions that have fundamental effects in real life, such as deciding whether to support a first attempt at free and fair elections, establish a peace commission, or fund reintegration programmes for former combatants. Given the potential consequences that such decisions may have, policy research and recommendations should come with clear statements about their scope and limitations. Highly dynamic political contexts complicate the task of constructing plausible counterfactual scenarios for comparative purposes and making valid inferences. Yet while these limitations should inform our ways of drawing conclusions and instil modesty, they should not prevent us from trying to apply the best methods possible. To the contrary, given the many qualifications we need to make in fragile states with respect to the validity of findings, the gains from applying the best method available to our objects of study is likely disproportionately higher than it would be in rather stable political contexts.

In sum, we argue that the basic standards for evaluations in the field of statebuilding in fragile states must not be different from those in other areas of evaluation. The degree to which we can feasibly abide by these standards may be lower in some respects, in particular with regard to data collection. But it is important to be aware that not meeting basic evaluation standards will inevitably come at the cost of reduced validity and generalisability of findings and should hence be made explicit wherever conclusions are drawn from the empirical material.

In an influential article in the *Journal of Development Effectiveness*, Howard White (2009) has recently proposed a list of six key principles for theory-based impact evaluation: 1) map out the causal chain (programme theory); 2) understand context; 3) anticipate heterogeneity; 4) use a credible counterfactual for rigorous evaluation of impact; 5) conduct rigorous factual analysis; and 6) use mixed methods (White 2009: 274).

While we agree with the importance of all of these principles, numbers 1, 2 and 4 seem to us to be of utmost relevance and can be interpreted as incorporating the others.[8] Our reduced list of principles thus reads:

1) map out the causal chain (programme theory);
2) understand context;
3) use a credible counterfactual for rigorous evaluation of impact.

Programme theory (also theory of change or intervention logic), according to White, links inputs of statebuilding interventions to outcomes and impacts. If the documentation of a statebuilding intervention does not provide an explicit theory of change, evaluators must (re)construct the assumed causal changes. In order to assess intended and unintended effects, it is furthermore necessary to analyse the facts and understand the specific context of fragility in which the statebuilding support takes place. A counterfactual is often constructed using a control group in an experimental or quasi-experimental analysis. However, we apply a broader understanding. In this chapter, counterfactual analysis also refers to thought experiments. A thought experiment provides alternative explanations for policy results of statebuilding interventions.

Our analysis of statebuilding evaluations uses these three main principles and discusses their application at two complementary levels. First, we will analyse the internal validity of findings, i.e., the reliability of results generated from individual country cases. Second, we will address external validity, i.e., the question of how generalisable findings are from one country to other cases and how convincingly broader conclusions are when based on multiple cases.

3 Sample: empirical basis for the analysis

The analysis presented in this chapter is based on a sample of 38 evaluation studies, listed in Table 8.1, that assess international activities which are explicitly and primarily aimed at addressing issues of statehood/fragility, peace and security or governance.[9] For the purpose of our analysis, we define evaluations as studies initiated by a donor or group of donors to learn more about the impact of their interventions, and conducted by independent evaluators with the consent and support of those donors, thus ensuring maximum access to relevant programme information. Only those studies that are based on empirical data collection and analyse that information according to a methodology that is made explicit are included.[10] With one exception, our survey focuses on studies published in the period from 2005 to 2011.[11] Our research yielded about 130 studies that met this broad set of criteria. For an in-depth analysis, we applied a second step that narrowed this large sample down to 38 studies by identifying two sub-types:[12]

1) Thematic studies based on the analysis of more than one country (including lessons-learnt studies that summarise findings from such studies).

Table 8.1 Sample of analysed evaluation studies[a]

Fragility type and country	Number of evaluations[b]
Failed states	
Afghanistan	9
DRC	4
Somalia	3
Sudan[c]	4
Weak states	
Haiti	6
Liberia	2
Sierra Leone	6
Challenged performer	
Sri Lanka	4
Total	38

[a] A compilation of the analysed evaluations can be found in Annexes A and B of Grävingholt et al. (2012a) on www.netpublikationer.dk/um/11152/pdf/effective_statebuilding.pdf.
[b] This account includes individual studies of joint evaluations.
[c] Comprises North and South Sudan prior to the creation of South Sudan in 2011.

Source: own compilation, typology of state fragility based on Grävingholt et al. (2012b).

2) Country studies from countries that have received a high degree of international attention in recent years allowing individual studies to be triangulated with studies by other donors or on other sectors in the same country so as to allow for a more complex picture and to cross-check findings.

Based on the relevance of statebuilding and the breadth of donor engagement reflected in thematic and country evaluations, we found about 15 fragile states that would have qualified for in-depth analysis. In a last step, we identified countries with different levels of fragility. We assumed that the effectiveness of statebuilding support depends on the type of fragility context in which it is offered. In order to differentiate types of fragility contexts, we relied on a recent typology of state fragility proposed by Grävingholt et al. (2012b). We narrowed our analysis to the following eight country cases, which represent the three most common types of state fragility in our sample: Afghanistan, Democratic Republic of Congo (DRC), Somalia and Sudan in the group of 'failed states'; Haiti, Liberia and Sierra Leone in the 'weak state' category; and Sri Lanka as a 'challenged performer' with relatively high levels of capacity but low state authority (see Grävingholt et al. 2012b).[13]

4 Assessment of evaluation methodology in international statebuilding support

We identified many evaluations that use well-designed data collection techniques such as document analysis, interviews or surveys. However, only a few studies reflect on and address the key issues such as attribution problems or the choice of methods, raised by the current international debate on evaluation design and methods (see Garcia 2011). Above all, there is virtually no reference at all to addressing the attribution gap between specific donor interventions and observed changes in statebuilding. Also, basic features of scientific research, such as the replicability of results, the validity of data, the isolation of variables in complex causality chains or the construction of counterfactuals and baseline data, are hardly ever addressed. In most of the evaluations using multiple case studies, cases were selected in an ad hoc way and without applying accepted standards. In sum, we find astonishingly few studies that are able to make truly convincing statements about the impact – positive and negative – of development assistance on statebuilding. Interestingly, other meta-evaluations screening the (internal and external) evaluations that have been produced in the past come to the same conclusion as our report. They identify a lack of rigorous methods in evaluating effective statebuilding support, and yet, rather than criticising the methodological or conceptual approaches, they still summarise their main results and recommendations.

The vast majority of evaluations assessed rely on a 'conventional approach' (see Box 8.1) which uses qualitative methods for data collection and analysis, rather than advanced statistical methods or a mix of the two. Some major evaluations are based on (small n) 'multiple-country' analysis and sum up the findings of studies of up to ten countries. These studies are typically confronted with a large diversity in terms of the implementation context and the quality and quantity of data on the projects and strategies under review, making comparisons between cases or specific approaches difficult. As a consequence, most multi-country evaluations do not include a truly comparative analysis of the cases. As a result of these methodological weaknesses, these evaluations tend to reproduce (rather than challenge) conventional wisdom and seem to be overly focused on the views of development experts and their immediate counterparts. The extent to which evaluations on countries as diverse as Haiti, Sierra Leone, Sri Lanka or Sudan closely resemble each other in terms of evaluation design, major findings and recommendations, is striking. Drawing on our analysis, we argue that this convergence is the result of built-in constraints on evaluators that result in reproducing unchallenged assumptions about how best to support statebuilding. As a consequence we also have doubts about the cost-efficiency of this approach as it consumes remarkable resources without truly generating new knowledge to inform policymaking in fragile contexts.

> **Box 8.1 Taking the conventional approach to evaluation to its limits**
>
> *Aiding the Peace: A Multi-donor Evaluation of Support to Conflict Prevention and Peacebuilding Activities in Southern Sudan 2005-2010* (Bennett et al. 2010b) is an example of the methodological strengths, but also the weaknesses, of conventional approaches to evaluation.
>
> A team consisting of 16 international and Sudanese experts carried out 1) a conflict analysis (by means of a literature review); 2) an analysis of the aid portfolios and policies of the donors who commissioned the evaluation, combined with preliminary interviews; and 3) an analysis of existing evaluations. This was followed by 4) field verification work in Southern Sudan, covering seven of the ten states (but not representative in statistical terms) and using semi-structured interviews as well as some focus group discussions. Findings were triangulated and cross-referenced according to a work plan designed by the evaluation team and outlined in the report. Also, there was extensive quality control, with draft reports being presented to a reference group in southern Sudan as well as to a group of three independent academics.
>
> The evaluation belongs without any doubt to the top tier of our analysed sample in terms of methodological soundness. It is also fairly transparent in describing the methodology and its limitations, for instance by mentioning the limited coverage of field trips. There is no reason to call the professional judgement of team members into question. Still, it remains difficult for the reader to trace findings and recommendations back to specific empirical observations, and the question arises whether the wealth of information generated by the team could not have been collected and analysed more systematically.

In sum, we identified two specific types of methodological problems in the evaluation of statebuilding support which will be elaborated in the following two sections: the lack of reliable data and the lack of rigorous comparative analysis across country cases.

4.1 Validity of data and findings

Robust attribution of positive or negative changes in statebuilding to international interventions requires valid data. Validity means that the data provided to represent the measured phenomena are reliable and comparable across cases in a constant and consistent manner. This precondition of using valid data applies to any kind of robust evaluation, regardless of whether it is based on quasi-experimental methods, case studies or a comparative approach. The scope of these data must go beyond narrow project documentation and include more general, context-oriented information, in particular data on possible alternative explaining factors of statebuilding processes (White 2009). If the causal mechanisms of statebuilding are to be identified in a credible way, information about the evaluated external engagement and the country context must be provided – not only at the moment of evaluation but at all stages of the analysed process. It is particularly important that factual analysis provides baseline data on the situation of the fragile state before (or at least at the beginning of) the intervention in question. Generating data about a specific project and its context is a fundamentally important task of evaluators. However, fragile contexts complicate the gathering of data as access to areas, respondents or reliable statistics are often severely limited.[14]

In the meta-analysis of statebuilding evaluations we observe inconsistencies in donors' provision of data and evaluators' abilities to systematically reconstruct and generate relevant information. The evaluators often rely on incomplete project documentation. Consequently, most evaluations are based on a limited set of data and do not meet the standard of validity. Moreover, the analysed data are frequently not classified with regard to their function in the analysis. Although some evaluations refer to different types of data as for example 'perception data, validation and documentation' (UNDP 2006: 79), they fail to spell out the purpose of these different kinds of data, why and how they are interlinked with the broader picture of the overall assessment of statebuilding support. With regard to the operational context, evaluations make no reference to different types of fragility contexts and the implications this context has for data collection. Thus the challenges in evaluating fragile contexts seem to be almost the same, no matter if these states vary with regard to their capacity, authority or legitimacy. In sum, the extensive use of project documentation and limited access to alternative sources of information perpetuate a self-referential system that unquestioningly reflects the discourse of the donor community rather than developments in fragile states.

Evaluators use two techniques to generate and assess data – analysis of project documentation and interviews during field trips. Any of the analysed evaluations starts with the analysis of project documentation. In most cases evaluators undertook field trips to gather more data and generate new information in interviews. Against this general background we identify several problems in generating and analysing data in our sample of evaluations on statebuilding support.

Problems with programme theory and context analysis

Analysis of project documentation is – as usual (White 2009: 276) – the starting point of all evaluations in our sample. Generally, project documentation is used to identify the theory of change (or intervention logic) of statebuilding support and to link donor activities to conflict assessments or strategy papers. Reconstructing intervention logics is a major task of all evaluations because many programmes of statebuilding support lack transparent and accessible intervention logics. In some cases, donors either do not have or do not provide sufficient information for evaluators to trace the explicitly or implicitly intended theory of change (Channel Research 2011). In other cases, project documents diverge and present inconsistent theories of change. Statements such as the following from Norad's evaluation of statebuilding support are therefore all too common: 'the team faced [significant obstacles] to begin pasting together the programme logic' (Norad 2009: 6). Difficulties in identifying donors' underlying logics hamper or even impede the attribution of international support to statebuilding outcomes.

The majority of evaluations focuses on programme documents, ignoring additional information which could shed light on the activities of other donors and the country context. By integrating knowledge about other donors' activities, evaluations could learn from each other. A comparison of different interventions' outcomes and impacts would help evaluators better understand the limits of a programme or instrument. This would also improve generalisability, allowing donors to compare similar strategies and instruments in different country contexts and ask what worked in one context, what in the other? They would also have a stronger basis to determine what seemed to work independently of the specific context. Despite these potential benefits, evaluations of specific donor (or international organisation) programmes are often very much concentrated on the documents and strategic guidelines provided by this individual state or organisation. As a case in point, ADE's evaluation of the European Commission support to conflict prevention and peacebuilding hardly mentions activities, conceptual or strategic papers by other donors and international organisations – even though it acknowledges that 'the Commission channelled half of its total financial support to CPPB [conflict prevention and peacebuilding] through international organisations' (ADE 2010: 56). ADE's evaluation is furthermore one of many examples of the lack of context analysis and the integration of additional information from academic literature.

Profound and factual analysis of the context is still the exception and not the norm in the evaluation of statebuilding support. However, data problems are mostly recognised by evaluators. For instance, evaluators often stress the lack of up-to-date data (Vaillant et al. 2010: 64) or emphasise the limits of data generation in fragile contexts: 'No primary data collection or commissioned studies were undertaken, and the limited extent to which the team has been able independently to verify the evidence needs to be borne in mind when reading the report' (Bennett et al. 2010a: 2). However, evaluations replicate findings from a recent OECD monitoring of international engagement in fragile states (OECD 2011b). Here, the OECD makes a strong point that donors rarely use assessments of context conditions in fragile states for programming. In an analogous manner, context analysis is rarely used to reconstruct baseline data and to build consistent alternative theories of change. Profound factual analysis of the context is still the exception rather than the norm in the evaluation of statebuilding. In evaluations that do provide context and conflict analysis, their findings are often not systematically linked to statebuilding programmes and thus add limited value to the impact analysis (see, for instance, Bennett et al. 2010a; UNDP 2010: 9).

But there are also exceptions to the rule. Thanks to the integration of political analysis, the evaluation of support to conflict prevention in southern Sudan identified important drivers of conflict which were ignored in donors' programmes (Bennett et al. 2010b). Böhnke, Koehler and Zürcher pursued an innovative way of generating additional knowledge about the statebuilding context in Afghanistan:

> [W]e commissioned semi-structured reports to be filled in by trained local correspondents four times a year. These so called quarterly reports record major events and significant changes, for examples major new development initiatives, outbreaks of violence, military operations and natural disasters. This sort of data cannot be captured in surveys or profiles. The quarterly reports may also be used to construct time series on a limited range of variables.
> (Böhnke et al. 2010: 8)

These commissioned reports formed part of a sophisticated evaluation design which consistently applied mixed methods.

Problems with field trips and knowledge basis of evaluations

Field trips are an essential part of all major evaluations. Exposure to the context and reality of the project is crucial for an evaluator's ability to gain sufficient in-depth knowledge and to discover alternative causality paths. They are, of course, often affected by the specific challenges of travelling in conflict-ridden or extremely fragile settings, with security issues playing an important role. In many cases, however, the duration of evaluation field trips is very limited. While the practice of extended or repeated field research is common in some areas of the social sciences – with stays of several months or even years[15] – evaluations, as a rule, do not follow this approach, and the average evaluation mission leans towards the other extreme lasting just one or two weeks. Such cursory visits do not seem to allow sufficient time for exposure to the international engagement's context. As a result, most evaluations do not integrate local knowledge beyond the reach of the assessed programme. Budget and time constraints are the most common reasons given for short field trips.

Problems of data generation through interviews

Interviews are another key source of information in evaluation reports. They can provide new information on projects to reconstruct baseline data, and provide perceptions about programmes' performance and results, and indicate important political and social events and developments. Four types of interviews, with different degrees of standardisation, predominate in evaluations: 1) semi-standardised interviews with one interviewee, which are the most widely used type of interviews; 2) focus group interviews, which gather 10–20 people; 3) consultations with groups that are not focused and resemble talks about specific topics; and 4) highly standardised surveys which cover more than 50 respondents.

It is difficult to spot the specific purpose and function of interviews in the respective evaluations because they rarely make questionnaires available and do not clarify the relationship between interviews and the aim of the specific evaluation.[16] It remains therefore vague how triangulation of information works. Evaluations rarely specify how interviewees fit in the theory of change of a specific programme or in an evaluator's reconstructed theory of change. The selection of interview partners is therefore mostly atheoretical. Conventionally, interviews focus on the inner circle of statebuilding programmes – those persons directly involved in the intervention being reviewed (for instance, OECD 2009, 2010: 2; Bennett et al. 2010a). They always address desk officers from headquarters, project staff, sometimes delegates from other donors and international organisations and local or national authorities from partner countries who are involved in the evaluated programme. In evaluation studies this reads typically as follows:

> A field visit (8–12 February 2010) to Juba and Torit County, Southern Sudan in order to conduct semi-structured interviews with UNDP staff and former staff members, who were responsible for implementing these projects and subsequent activities, local counterparts, stakeholders and members of the donor community.
>
> (UNDP 2010: 9)[17]

At the same time, a high number of interviews does not guarantee a large and representative scope of interviewees from different spheres and sectors of a society. For instance, the evaluation of DFID's programme in the Democratic Republic of Congo is based on 89 interviews. But the vast majority (63 interviews) were conducted with donor agencies, 18 with DRC ministries and three with representatives of the Congolese civil society (Vaillant et al. 2010).

Availability of interviewees is another problem of data generation in fragile contexts (e.g., Willitts-King et al. 2007). Since most evaluations focus on the inner cycle of statebuilding support programmes they encounter typical problems of the donor community. High fluctuation of staff is common in fragile contexts because incentives to stay in insecure settings are low. Institutional memory is further limited because of low levels of institutional capacity, which complicate the filing of project information. Against this background it is difficult for evaluators to identify a sufficient number of interviewees who are informed about the past and present of a programme. One evaluation even reports that they could not interview a single representative of the most relevant group of interviewees – the key decision-makers in the Ministry of Foreign Affairs during the ten-year period – despite significant efforts (Norad 2009: 6).

Although evaluations frequently face problems of availability of key interviewees they do not regularly pursue alternatives such as interviews with former programme staff via phone or email. Sometimes, evaluators go beyond the inner cycle of projects and visit individual academic institutions, civil society organisations or target groups, but as a general observation, it does not appear to be common practice to systematically explore local knowledge sources. Even where this is done, target groups are rarely integrated in a systematic manner. As a result it is difficult to credibly determine whether or not target groups actually benefit from projects. Such a narrow use of interviews might in some cases serve to re-establish projects' theory of change or baseline data but it aggravates or even impedes the construction of counterfactuals. If evaluators aim at integrating counterfactuals, they have to broaden and sophisticate the selection of interviewees by identifying control groups who are not linked to the project. Moreover, they could broaden an evaluation's scope by using surveys of target groups.

Problems and opportunities of using surveys to establish counterfactuals

Surveys with more than 50 respondents and standardised questionnaires are one of the widely used techniques to generate additional data (for instance, UNDP 2006; IEG-World Bank 2006; ADE 2010). They provide information about projects of international statebuilding support and their context beyond project documentation. A general objective of surveys is to identify perceptions of programme staff, programme stakeholders, target groups and beneficiaries about donors' performance and project effectiveness. Similar to semi-structured and focus group interviews, surveys were most often conducted with project staff in the field, whose return rates are usually quite high (above two-thirds in most cases). It is surprising, however, that target groups and beneficiaries play a minor role in evaluation surveys. What is more, almost no evaluation extends surveys to control groups, which would be a standard approach to credibly construct a counterfactual.

Against this background, one evaluation mentioned earlier stands out, that tries to assess impact of foreign aid in Afghanistan (Böhnke et al. 2010). In the context of a joint research project of the Federal Ministry for Economic Co-operation and Development (BMZ) and the Free University Berlin, the authors developed a method for assessing the impact of development cooperation in conflict zones, which is then applied to northeast Afghanistan. They conducted two mass surveys at target group level in 2007 and 2009, with around 2000 Afghan respondents from 80 villages. The report uses innovative instruments to measure the spatial distribution of aid, based on a mix of donor-generated data and household surveys.

The approach has its strength in looking at the input–impact relation from a highly aggregated (although geographically limited) perspective. The measures used to represent the variables of interest are somewhat ambitious but acceptable. As a consequence of the aggregate perspective, however, it is not possible (and not intended) to attribute aid interventions (and, consequently, impact) to individual donors. Also, the approach cannot be easily scaled up geographically as it requires broad resources in terms of time and interviewers involved. However, surveys could be conducted jointly for evaluations of several aid instruments simultaneously, thus producing economies of scale.

4.2 Generalisation of results

The usual purpose of impact evaluations is to provide insights that allow aid practitioners to improve their interventions. For this to be possible it is not enough that findings are valid for the concrete case of evaluation at hand. The same setting of intervention in which an evaluated programme was realised will never exist again. Even within one country, the context at early stages of an intervention and the situation captured by an ex-post evaluation of the same intervention usually differ substantially. Useful learning thus requires that findings are generalised beyond concrete cases. However, whether generalisations make sense or not, whether they are useful or not, depends largely on the methodology chosen to ensure generalisability. Social science research has developed standards that facilitate (or complicate) the task of drawing general lessons on the basis of a limited number of cases (Brady and Collier 2004). Comparable data, truly comparative research designs (such as systematic most-different-cases designs, qualitative comparative analysis or statistical regressions) and a careful selection of cases are the most important elements of a research strategy that aims to ensure generalisability.

The sample surveyed in our study includes, besides individual country case studies, a considerable number of cross-country (small n) comparisons with up to ten countries under scrutiny.[18] As a rule, these studies employ common Terms of Reference and sometimes a common research or evaluation design to all the cases. At the same time, they are typically confronted with important challenges that mirror the standards introduced above:

- Almost none of the comparative studies we found base the selection of countries or projects on a clear conceptual or methodological argument.[19] The most common rationales for case selection refer to data availability or access to information, while a few studies mention the need to cover a certain range of situations and conditional factors. In other cases, the objects of evaluation are usually selected by the donors on grounds unrelated to methodological reasoning. Chapman and Vaillant (2010: 2) openly concede that the 'diversity of fragility makes drawing out common trends and linkages between different contexts challenging'.
- Most cross-country evaluation designs do not exhaust the opportunity for a truly comparative analysis of cases. This is aggravated by the fact that country case studies are often carried out by local teams, sometimes under the direction of one member of the core evaluation team, but with limited contact to other country teams. As a consequence, lessons drawn from such multiple-case evaluations are usually limited to the (unsystematic) aggregation of individual findings.
- Systematic comparisons across country cases are made additionally difficult by a large diversity in terms of the quality and quantity of project documentation and data sources. Only a few evaluations report results from quantitative in-case methods (e.g., randomised samples, standardised interviews or surveys, standardisation of qualitative data, statistical analysis of quantitative data provided by governments or third parties) that would help overcome some of the limitations inherent in case comparisons. Instead, most evaluations are at best based on descriptive statistics rather than advanced statistical methods.

5 Structural reasons for lack of methodological rigour

Our findings that evaluations of international statebuilding support are weak in methodological terms come amid an ongoing debate about robust programme evaluation in international development cooperation. Already in 2006, the Center for Global Development, Washington, DC, suggested common transparent and reproducible 'quality standards for rigorous evaluations' be established (Savedoff et al. 2006: 5). Although these calls for more rigorous evaluation reached the OECD DAC and soon translated into a first international agreement on appropriate evaluation standards (OECD 2008), they did not result in a marked improvement in evaluation quality.[20] In this section, we discuss potential reasons for the current lack of methodological rigour in three intersecting areas: the design of intervention programmes; the Terms of Reference agreed with the evaluators; and the quality of international guidelines for evaluation in fragile contexts.

5.1 Programme design

Programme design can have tangible effects on the quality of *ex post* impact evaluations in many ways. Most importantly, programmes need to be designed in ways that allow measuring the dependent variable of an intervention at an initial point in time ('baseline') and tracking its further development. Additionally, project documents should provide a clear picture of which interventions (type and size) were undertaken at which point in time, thus tracking the main independent variable. Information on other context variables that might have influenced the outcome is also needed. Finally, an explicit theory of change and clearly defined objectives are helpful to identify those variables that need to be tracked throughout the project implementation phase. Its existence is also important for efforts to construct credible counterfactuals. Evaluations rely on the quality of project data and implementation standards. Hence, programme evaluations cannot be better than the programme design itself.

Our review confirms that poor programme design does indeed account for some of the most basic problems of evaluation quality, and several evaluators mention this in their reports. Typically, programmes were not designed to undergo systematic evaluation and hence lacked sufficient and useful baseline data. Project documentation was inconsistent and programmes had no transparent, discernible theories of change. In the case of Norad's engagement in the Haitian peacebuilding process, for instance, evaluators concluded, 'there was an *absence of implementation logic*. There was also a lack of any reference to a structured conflict analysis or theory of change for Haiti in Norwegian interventions' (Norad 2009: 6, emphasis in original).

Clearly, many actors in the field of statebuilding support shy away from bold statements about how their relatively small contributions are expected to improve the resilience of fragile states. Yet, while modesty is certainly in order when it comes to assessing the chances of success, no statebuilding support activity or even larger country strategy should come without a clear explication of the causal chain that links interventions to the ultimate hoped for outcome.

5.2 Terms of Reference

Sophisticated and clear Terms of Reference are another precondition of robust evaluation of international statebuilding support. In other words, if commissioning agencies encourage, or even demand, the use of rigorous methods, it is more likely that these standards are met. Our review yields a mixed picture in this regard. As far as one can tell from those evaluation studies that provide their Terms of Reference, these are often sensitive to such problems of evaluation design as the reconstruction of baseline data, the identification of a theory of change and the assessment of impact (e.g., Chapman and Vaillant 2010). This is particularly the case in those evaluations that were conducted as part of the testing period of the OECD Working Draft Guidance on Evaluating Conflict Prevention and Peacebuilding Activities (OECD 2008).

Beyond such general principles, however, the incentives given in the Terms of Reference for evaluators to apply rigorous methods are very limited. In the studies under our review, we found almost no references to robust evaluation methods made in the Terms of Reference.[21] Typically, Terms of Reference call for particular techniques of data collection and processing (e.g., interviews, analysis of documents, field trips) instead of specifying certain methodological standards (see, e.g., Bennett et al. 2010a: A1) or, less frequently, make very generic references to methods (such as 'use of mixed methods').

Leaving the choice of method to the evaluators may seem to be an adequate division of labour between commissioning agencies and implementing evaluation experts. Yet most Terms of Reference do not in fact leave that much choice because they predefine certain aspects of the evaluation approach, such as the number of evaluators per country (in a cross-country design), the number of days in the field, the amount of resources available for different types of tasks. Commissioning agencies demonstrate that they usually have a certain methodological design already in mind when evaluators come on board – a generic 'standard' design which the latter will usually find hard if not impossible to alter fundamentally. This has severe implications for evaluation findings. As Khagram and Thomas (2010: 104) noted recently, 'How evidence-based assessment is understood and practiced will dramatically shape how evidence is generated.'

5.3 International guidelines

While programme design and Terms of Reference appear to be two major arenas where much room for improvement exists, the question remains whether better international guidelines for conducting evaluations in contexts of conflict and fragility could also help improve evaluation quality. The OECD working draft *Guidance on Evaluating Conflict Prevention and Peacebuilding Activities* was published in 2008 and several evaluations in our sample were explicitly meant as part of the 'testing period' of this endeavour to formulate problem-specific evaluation guidelines.[22] Do these guidelines make a difference? Or reversely, are the weaknesses identified almost across the board in our review also reflected in this draft guidance? Our short answers to these questions are yes and no, respectively. The draft guidance does indeed provide important state of the art knowledge about high-quality evaluation. It emphasises the need to identify theories of change,[23] discusses the problem of lacking baseline data and demands the triangulation of collected data (OECD 2008: Annex 6).

Only a minority of evaluations undertaken after 2008 and reviewed by us make explicit reference to the draft guidance. Yet where it was applied, evaluations were more sensitive to core evaluation principles. Particularly the joint evaluations of international engagement in DRC, South Sudan and Sri Lanka offer a separate conflict analysis and mapping as well as analysis of donor engagement (Chapman et al. 2009; Bennett et al. 2010b; Channel Research 2011). In line with the draft guidance, the three evaluations aim at identifying theories of change of donor interventions and linking them to the other relevant conflict factors in the respective country.

In fact, however, none of the three evaluations was able to trace a consistent intervention logic because of a lack of transparency, lack of data, change of programme and staff turnover.[24] Thus, Chapman et al. (2009) conclude:

> More *explicit* theories of change will help to explain how assistance will actually deliver intended [conflict prevention and peacebuilding] outcomes. This should describe the kinds of change in attitudes or behaviour that are expected to arise from the intervention and at what level (for example, within or between different parties to the conflict, at local level or more widely), and what assumptions and risks are likely to affect this outcome and how these may be mitigated.
>
> (Chapman et al. 2009: 53)

In sum, it appears that mainstreaming the task of rigorous learning in both programme designs and the Terms of Reference of their evaluations continues to be the prime challenge. The draft guidance was a workable document with the potential to raise the quality of evaluations, but the realities of both programmes and evaluations impeded its full use. It will remain to be seen if the recently adopted official guidance on evaluating peacebuilding activities can avoid the same fate.

6 Conclusions

This chapter set out to assess the quality of the methods and research techniques used in evaluations of statebuilding support in order to examine the validity of findings and policy recommendations.

In conclusion, we find that surprisingly few studies take key issues of the current international debate on the design and methods of impact evaluation into account. Most fail to explicate a theory of change, to construct a credible counterfactual and to make use of quantitative methods where possible to achieve these aims. As a consequence, these evaluations' findings are weak and tend to reproduce the conventional wisdom underlying development interventions in fragile states in the first place instead of testing implicitly assumed causality chains.

In our observation, few studies are able to make truly convincing statements about the *positive* impact of development assistance on statebuilding. Most are stronger in pointing out negative outcomes without, however, providing evidence that the alternatives they call for would have worked better. In addition, many evaluations are overly focused on the views and opinions of the development experts' community and their immediate counterparts, leaving aside the perspective of larger parts of the population, which might, in fact, question the evaluator's conclusions.

However, since 2008, continuous exchange between donor agencies, evaluators and recipients about evaluation standards has been providing a basis for improving methodological rigour in the assessment of statebuilding support in fragile contexts. It will be the task of all involved parties in an evaluation process to implement existing guidelines and agreements to ensure basic principles of quality research are applied. In order to meet international evaluation standards, more time and resources must be allocated during programme design and from the very beginning of the evaluation process. Despite all practical difficulties associated to evaluating statebuilding interventions and mentioned above, both evaluators and commissioning agencies could do more to increase their chances of gathering reliable data and drawing more convincing conclusions from them.

Notes

1 This chapter is based on a report commissioned by the Danish Ministry of Foreign Affairs (Grävingholt et al. 2012a). We are indebted to our co-author of that report, Christian von Haldenwang, who contributed major ideas to the arguments made in both the report and this chapter. We gratefully acknowledge insightful comments to earlier drafts received from Jörg Faust, Melody Garcia and Ole Winckler Andersen and the research assistance provided by Maren Jaschke, Johannes Thema and Antonia van Delden.
2 These studies include, among others, the 2011 policy guidance *on Supporting Statebuilding in Situations of Conflict and Fragility* (OECD 2011a), the World Development Report 2011 (World Bank 2011) and the 'New Deal For Engagement In Fragile States' adopted by donor and recipient country governments at the 4th High Level Forum on Aid Effectiveness in Busan (International Dialogue on Peacebuilding and Statebuilding 2011). See the INCAF website for a full list of relevant OECD publications, www.oecd.org/dac/incaf.
3 This is an intentional paraphrase of the five peacebuilding and statebuilding goals agreed among the participants of the International Dialogue (2011) in the 'New Deal'.
4 The OECD (2011a: 20) refers to statebuilding as 'an endogenous process to enhance capacity, institutions and legitimacy of the state driven by state-society relations...It is axiomatic that statebuilding is primarily a domestic process that involves local actors, which means that the role of international actors is necessarily limited.'
5 We use the following, broad definition of statebuilding support: 'International support to statebuilding...refers to international actors' strategies and projects which by design or by their nature are expected by those actors to assist the endogenous process of statebuilding' (Grävingholt et al. 2012a: 7).
6 The concepts underlying this explication of major state functions are: state capacity, authority and legitimacy (see Carment et al. 2008; Call 2011; Grävingholt et al. 2012b).

7 A recent literature devoted to the historical challenge of stable, peaceful and democratic statehood includes, inter alia, Acemoglu and Robinson (2006); North et al. (2009).
8 We assume that recognising heterogeneity (3) is a precondition for understanding the context of a statebuilding intervention and rigorous evaluation is impossible without a rigorous factual analysis (5) as well as the use of mixed methods (6).
9 We do not include primarily academic literature although many academic studies deal with statebuilding and peacebuilding in a general manner, often even based on country cases. We were not able to identify any purely academic studies that take a systematic empirical look not only at the dependent variable (i.e., the country situation) but also at the independent variable (i.e., donor interventions) and thus satisfy our requirements of being systematic and empirical in a way that would allow learning from experience.
10 These conditions serve to exclude studies that do not fulfil minimum requirements of empirical social science research.
11 The one exception is the 2004 'Joint Utstein Study of Peacebuilding' (Royal Norwegian Ministry of Foreign Affairs 2004). This document was included because of its multi-donor, cross-country character and the international attention it received.
12 This rationale follows the observation that only few studies address the issue of state-building impact head-on. Findings on individual sectors or aspects of statebuilding will therefore have to prove their reliability and usefulness against the background of the broader country context. This way, we aim to avoid the typical micro–macro fallacy of seemingly successful 'projects' without measurable systemic impact.
13 Grävingholt, Ziaja and Kreibaum's typology differentiates degrees of fragility with regard to three dimensions of statehood, namely state capacity, state authority and state legitimacy.
14 The World Development Report 2011 underlines this problem stating that '[o]ne of the greatest challenges in researching lessons on violence prevention and recovery is the lack of available quantitative and qualitative data, due to challenges of security and access, along with low statistical capacity. Even in the World Bank's comprehensive data sets, countries most affected by violence often register empty data columns. Polling, household surveys, and evaluations of the impacts of policies and project interventions are also limited in violence-affected countries and regions' (World Bank 2011: xix).
15 Morton Bøås' work on Liberia could be taken as an example of this kind of research (see, for instance, Bøås and Stig 2010). Many Masters' or PhD theses are based on extended field research stays in fragile or post-conflict settings. Yet, evaluations, as a rule, do not follow this approach.
16 UNDP (2006) is an exception because it classifies the interviews with regard to their function in the analysis (UNDP 2006: 86).
17 UNDP's evaluation of conflict prevention and peacebuilding in Southern Sudan gives a good example with regard to the transparency of interview groups' representativeness. The evaluation provides a table with different types of interview groups and whom they represent in the donor community and society.
18 Examples include Royal Norwegian Ministry of Foreign Affairs (2004); IEG-World Bank (2006); UNDP (2006); ADE (2010); Chapman and Vaillant (2010); OECD (2010).
19 Exceptions are Böhnke et al. (2010), discussed below, who evaluate the impact of development cooperation in Afghanistan, and a review carried out by the World Bank Independent Evaluation Group (IEG) on the Bank's support to low-income countries under stress (IEG-World Bank 2006), which relies on random sampling of projects in parts of the review.
20 In 2008, donor governments agreed on preliminary draft guidance for a testing period. Final guidance was adopted in 2012 (OECD 2012).
21 Obviously, this statement extends only to those evaluations that report their Terms of Reference.

22 As mentioned above, the official OECD guidance for *Evaluating Peacebuilding Activities in Settings of Conflict and Fragility* was published in 2012. As this chapter analyses the effect of guidelines on evaluations conducted in the period up to 2011, we refer to the previously published draft guidance.
23 The draft guidance defined a theory of change as 'a term closely related to implementation logic that is often used...to describe the links between inputs, the implementation strategy and the intended outputs and outcomes. It describes the assumed or hoped causal relationship between the activity or policy and its (intended) effects on larger peace-making goals' (OECD 2008). This is in line with White's definition, which we provided earlier in this chapter.
24 In the case of the DRC evaluation, the authors gave up on constructing a theory of change altogether as they found it too hard to distil an overarching theory from programme documentations that more often than not failed to establish explicit links to peacebuilding at all (Channel Research 2011: section 2.4).

Bibliography

Acemoglu, D. and Robinson, J. A. (2006) *Economic Origins of Dictatorship and Democracy*, Cambridge: Cambridge University Press.
ADE (2010) *Thematic Evaluation of European Commission Support to Conflict Prevention and Peace Building: Concept Study*, Brussels: European Commission.
Bennett, J., Alexander, J., Saltmarshe, D., Phillipson, R. and Marsden, P. (2010a) *Country Programme Evaluation Afghanistan*, Evaluation Report EV696, London: Department for International Development.
Bennett, J., Pantuliano, S., Fenton, W., Vaux, A., Barnett, C. and Brusset, E. (2010b), *Aiding the Peace: A Multi-donor Evaluation of Support to Conflict Prevention and Peacebuilding Activities in Southern Sudan 2005–2010: Final Report – December 2010*, Howe: ITAD Ltd.
Bøås, M. and Stig, K. (2010) 'Security Sector Reform in Liberia: An Uneven Partnership without Local Ownership', *Journal of Intervention and Statebuilding* 4(3): 285–303.
Böhnke, J., Koehler, J. and Zürcher, C. (2010) *Assessing the Impact of Development Co-operation in North East Afghanistan 2005–2009*, Bonn: Bundesministerium für Entwicklung und Wirtschaftliche Zusammenarbeit.
Brady, H. E. and Collier, D. (eds) (2004) *Rethinking Social Inquiry. Diverse Tools, Shared Standards*, Lanham: Rowman and Littlefield Publishers.
Call, C. T. (2011) 'Beyond the "Failed State" Toward Conceptual Alternatives', *European Journal of International Relations* 17(2): 303–326.
Carment, D., Samy, Y. and Prest, S. (2008) 'State Fragility and Implications for Aid Allocation: An Empirical Analysis', *Conflict Management and Peace Science* 25(4): 349–373.
Channel Research (2011) *Amani Labda, Peace Maybe: Joint Evaluation of Conflict Prevention and Peace Building in the Democratic Republic of Congo: Synthesis Report*, Brussels: FPS Foreign Affairs, Foreign Trade and Development Cooperation.
Chapman, N. and Vaillant, C. (2010) *Synthesis of Country Programme Evaluations Conducted in Fragile States*, London: Department for International Development.
Chapman, N., Duncan, D., Timberman, D. and Abeygunawardana, K. (2009) *Evaluation of Donor-Supported Activities in Conflict-Sensitive Development and Conflict Prevention and Peacebuilding in Sri Lanka: Main Evaluation Report*. www.oecd.org/dataoecd/63/50/44138006.pdf.

Garcia, M. M. (2011) *Improving Donor Support for Governance: The Case for More Rigorous Impact Evaluation*, DIE Briefing Paper 2011 (11).

Grävingholt, J., Leininger, J. and von Haldenwang, C. (2012a) *Effective Statebuilding? A Review of Evaluations of International Statebuilding Support in Fragile Contexts*, Evaluation Study 2012/3, Copenhagen: Ministry of Foreign Affairs of Denmark.

Grävingholt, J., Ziaja, S. and Kreibaum, M. (2012b) *State Fragility: Towards a Multidimensional Empirical Typology*, DIE Discussion Paper 3/2012, Bonn: DIE.

IEG-World Bank (World Bank Independent Evaluation Group) (2006) *Engaging with Fragile States: An IEG Review of World Bank Support to Low-Income Countries under Stress*, Washington, DC: World Bank.

International Dialogue on Peacebuilding and Statebuilding (2011) *A New Deal for Engagement in Fragile States*, Paris: OECD.

Khagram, S. and Thomas, C. W. (2010) 'Toward a Platinum Standard for Evidence-Based Assessment by 2020', *Public Administration Review* 70: 100–106.

Norad (Norwegian Agency for Development Cooperation) (2009) *Evaluation of Norwegian Support to Peacebuilding in Haiti 1998–2008*, Evaluation Report 5/2009, Oslo: Norad.

North, D. C., Wallis, J. J. and Weingast, B. R. (2009) *Violence and Social Orders: A Conceptual Framework for Interpreting Recorded Human History*, Cambridge: Cambridge University Press.

OECD (2008), *Guidance on Evaluating Conflict Prevention and Peacebuilding Activities – Working Draft for Application Period*, Paris: OECD Publishing. www.oecd.org/dac/evaluation/dcdndep/39774573.pdf, accessed 20 May 2013.

——(2009) *Statebuilding in Fragile Situations – How Can Donors 'Do No Harm' and Maximise Their Positive Impact? Country Case Study Afghanistan*, Paris: OECD Publishing.

——(2010) *Do No Harm: International Support for Statebuilding, Conflict and Fragility*, Paris: OECD Publishing. doi: 10.1787/9789264046245-en.

——(2011a) *Supporting Statebuilding in Situations of Conflict and Fragility: Policy Guidance*, DAC Guidelines and Reference Series, Paris: OECD Publishing.

——(2011b) *International Engagement in Fragile States: Can't We Do Better?* Conflict and Fragility Series, Paris: OECD Publishing.

——(2012) *Evaluating Peacebuilding Activities in Settings of Conflict and Fragility: Improving Learning for Results*, DAC Guidelines and Reference Series. Paris: OECD Publishing. doi: 10.1787/9789264106802-en.

——(2013) *ODA Statistics – Democratic Republic of Congo*, Paris: OECD Publishing. www.oecd.org/dac/stats/COD.gif, accessed May 2013.

Royal Norwegian Ministry of Foreign Affairs (2004) *Towards a Strategic Framework for Peacebuilding: Getting Their Act Together. Overview Report of the Joint Utstein Study of Peacebuilding*, Oslo: Royal Norwegian Ministry of Foreign Affairs.

Savedoff, W. D., Levine, R., Birdsall, N. et al. (2006) *When Will We Ever Learn? Improving Lives through Impact Evaluation. Report of the Evaluation Gap Working Group*, Washington, DC: Center for Global Development.

UNDP (2006) *Evaluation of UNDP Support for Conflict Affected Countries*, New York: UNDP.

——(2010) *Southern Sudan. Local Governance in Complex Environments, Project Assessment*, New York: UNDP.

Vaillant, C., Condy, A., Robert, P. and Tshionza, G. (2010) *Country Programme Evaluation. Democratic Republic of Congo*, Evaluation Report Ev704, London: Department for International Development.

White, H. (2009) 'Theory-based Impact Evaluation: Principles and Practice', *Journal of Development Effectiveness* 1(3): 271–284.

Willitts-King, B., Mowjee, T. and Barham, J. (2007) *Evaluation of Common/Pooled Humanitarian Funds in DRC and Sudan*, submitted to OCHA ESS. https://ochanet.unocha.org/p/Documents/CHF_evaluation_report.pdf, accessed May 2013.

World Bank (2011) *World Development Report 2011: Conflict, Security, and Development*, Washington, DC: World Bank.

9 Systems thinking in peacebuilding evaluations
Applications in Ghana, Guinea-Bissau and Kosovo

Diana Chigas
CDA

Peter Woodrow
CDA

1 Introduction

The Reflecting on Peace Practice Program[1] is dedicated to improving the effectiveness of peace practice. We have been exploring how a project, programme or initiative can reach beyond its stated goals to make a significant contribution to transforming the broader conflict, or 'peace writ large'.[2] Our engagement with systems thinking approaches has been prompted by the questions this programme set out to answer: how do peacebuilding programmes and activities fit into the larger picture, and how can we use our limited resources to generate the largest possible positive impacts on conflicts? In this context, the Reflecting on Peace Practice Program has been experimenting with the application of systems thinking to peacebuilding practice and evaluation, as systems thinking promotes an understanding of complex change that is crucial when working in conflict zones. Systems thinking tools can be used to assess impacts, even when direct or linear causal relationships cannot be established. This can be done despite the difficulty in isolating the effects of programmes from the various actors with which they interact and from other factors that influence a conflict. This chapter explores how this systems perspective has been applied to three evaluations of peacebuilding work carried out by the Reflecting on Peace Practice team.

2 What is systems thinking?[3]

Systems thinking is a way of understanding reality that emphasises the relationships among a system's parts rather than the parts themselves. Following this view, systems thinking holds that the whole is more than the sum of its parts – in other words, that the ability to see the whole of a phenomenon in its broader context will provide insights that cannot be gained by looking at each of its component parts individually. Systems thinking provides language and tools for expressing what many practitioners already know about conflict contexts and peacebuilding interventions: that the 'parts' of the conflict system, including issues, actors, attitudes, behaviours, institutions, interact with each other to form a complex dynamic that is not linear – or at least not as linear as suggested by the predominant frameworks and tools for programme management, such as the log frame.

A key insight of systems thinking is that cause and effect are not unidirectional or immediate. Rather, one factor can have indirect effects on a range of other factors, sometimes after considerable delays in time. For instance, the failure of a government to provide security has consequences beyond the immediate physical threats to the population. Insecurity influences economic productivity and, over time, the climate for investment, which affects growth rates, government revenues and so on, and these, in turn, can further undermine the government's ability to provide security. Such effects can be unrelated to the scale of a basic cause (Patton 2011; Williams and Hummelbrunner 2011).

These principles of systems thinking can help us to understand conflicts in a more complex and dynamic way, and thus facilitate more robust design of conflict interventions. In addition, a systems view allows us to see that an intervention in a conflict system becomes a part of that system and cannot be fully understood separately from its interactions with other parts of the system. Glenda Eoyang, a human systems dynamics practitioner, summarises the implications of these realities for evaluators:

> These temporal and dynamical [sic] characteristics challenge many of the assumptions of the traditional evaluator. [...] An evaluator may be able to assign an arbitrary beginning and end date of an intervention, but the system itself recognizes no such boundaries in time. For this reason, the whole concept of projected and predictable outcomes is an artificial construct when evaluating performance in a CAS [complex adaptive system].
>
> (Eoyang and Berkas 1999)[4]

3 Why systems thinking?

We did not originally intend to apply or test the relevance of systems thinking in evaluation of peacebuilding programming. Rather, the findings from our previous research[5] and learning from our experience in field applications drove us to look to systems thinking for ways to deal with a number of challenges raised by practitioners and policymakers concerning the evaluation of peacebuilding programming, especially in relation to understanding the relevance and impacts of programmes at the 'peace writ large' level.[6] Four such challenges have been posed.

First, our work in the field supported the findings of earlier work (summarised in *Confronting War*) that peacebuilding programmes often 'miss the mark' – that is, they do not address things that really make a difference in the conflict (Anderson and Olson 2003: 24). This stems largely from shortcomings in the way practitioners and policymakers conduct conflict analyses and whether and how they integrate their analyses into programme planning (Woodrow 2006). Moreover, while the OECD DAC guidance, *Evaluating Peacebuilding Activities in Settings of Conflict and Fragility* (hereinafter, 'DAC Guidance'), identifies *relevance* as one of the criteria for evaluating peacebuilding activities (OECD 2012), it does not provide guidance on evaluation methods that can be used to obtain credible and useful findings about relevance.[7] Other frameworks outline processes for assessing 'peacebuilding relevance' but also provide little guidance on methods for evaluating programmes in terms of 'peace writ large' (see Paffenholz 2006; Paffenholz and Reychler 2007).[8]

Second, as noted in *Confronting War*, 'All of the good peace work being done should be adding up to more than it is. The potential of these multiple efforts is not fully realized' (Anderson and Olson 2003). In other words, individual programmes – and even all the efforts put together – are not adding up to real progress towards peace. Even when programmes are individually effective in achieving their desired outcomes, one cannot assume that cumulative changes in the conflict system will result. Some practitioners and evaluators have thus advocated reducing expectations of evaluations by only asking for assessment of outcomes that can be logically linked to the programme (see Spurk 2008). Others recommend focusing on strategic-level evaluations linking multiple interventions to the broader conflict, rather than attempting to attribute impacts to individual projects (Smith 2004). Yet the question of the disconnect between the outcomes of individual programmes and their significance for peace remains.

Third, despite the widely accepted finding of CDA's Do No Harm Program (a predecessor to the Reflecting on Peace Practice Program) that all forms of assistance, and those who provide it, become part of the conflict context and system, programmes continue to be conducted and evaluated as if they are somehow 'outside' of the system they engage. Unintended outcomes and impacts of programmes on conflict are rarely evaluated, and there is little guidance on how to do so (Goldwyn and Chigas 2013).

Finally, the difficulty of evaluating peacebuilding impacts and, perhaps more importantly, practitioners' resistance to doing so, suggest a need to adapt evaluation approaches and methods to the conflict context. Practitioners are concerned about the impacts of their work at the 'peace writ large' level, but often question the feasibility of evaluating these impacts and the appropriateness of the usual approaches to assessment (Anderson and Olson 2003: 9). Practitioners often feel that it is unfair to evaluate projects based on effects beyond the immediate target population, as their efforts often operate in limited geographic areas or with limited constituencies. Those working at these levels argue that accountability for 'peace writ little' (effects at the community level or upon direct beneficiaries of the project) would be more reasonable than attempting to trace causal chains from a community programme to impact at the societal level ('peace writ large').

Practitioners further note real challenges in relation to the timing of impacts. Evaluations are typically performed at a fixed point in time, usually towards the end or immediately after project/programme completion. Such evaluations can be misleading, as they may find no discernible impacts, when, in fact, impacts occur much later. Or, conversely, an evaluation may find impacts that subsequently are not sustained or are reversed. In other words, practitioners see a disconnect between the real dynamics of peace programming and the widely used tools for programme planning, management and evaluation, such as the logical framework or results chain, because such models seem ill-suited to understanding inputs, outputs, outcomes and impacts in contexts characterised by high uncertainty, dynamism and unpredictability (see Rogers 2008: 39; Patton 2011: 126).

Systems thinking can help to deal with these challenges, in particular to assess relevance, identify and assess the theory of change of an intervention, assess effectiveness and determine actual or potential impacts in complex environments. Our staff have used systems thinking frameworks in evaluations of programmes in Ghana and Guinea-Bissau, and in a more general study of peacebuilding programming in Kosovo. These evaluations found systems thinking useful in situating the interventions within the larger conflict context and for drawing conclusions about the programme's relation to 'peace writ large'. Section 4 examines how systems thinking tools were used for assessing *relevance* in Ghana, while Section 5 explores use of systems tools for evaluating *effectiveness* and *impacts* in Guinea-Bissau and Kosovo.

4 Evaluating relevance using systems mapping: the conflict prevention and resolution portfolio of UNDP Ghana

The criterion of *relevance* is 'used to assess the extent to which the objectives and activities of the intervention(s) respond to the needs of beneficiaries and the peacebuilding process – that is to say, whether they address the key driving factors of conflict revealed through a conflict analysis' (OECD 2012: 65). In other words, are the design and implementation of the intervention based on an accurate, up-to-date conflict analysis, and do the goals and objectives address peacebuilding needs or points of leverage? (Rogers 2012).[9] Relevance is critical for understanding the impacts (or potential impacts) of a peacebuilding intervention. As Paffenholz (2006: 10) suggests, 'current practice goes too quickly into the assessment of effectiveness of impacts of a programme, rather than first analysing whether it is worth doing the specific intervention at all'. If the goals and objectives of a peacebuilding intervention do not (directly or indirectly) address drivers of conflict, then it is likely to have only limited effects in terms of peacebuilding (or 'peace writ large') – even if the intervention effectively achieves its own stated objectives.

In our experience, however, many conflict analysis methods do not permit a robust analysis of relevance in the context of evaluation. Such analysis methods are often biased or narrowly focused on particular sectors, target beneficiaries or favourite intervention methods. Or they can be too comprehensive, providing long lists of factors without prioritisation (Ricigliano and Chigas 2011), making determination of relevance difficult. A systems analysis identifies key driving factors of conflict and provides a basis for assessing whether programmes are addressing things that will make a difference. Rather than identifying a single 'root' cause or listing a multitude of factors influencing conflict, a systems analysis looks at the interactions and causal connections among factors, permitting a wider understanding of multiple causes, as well as more complex chains of attribution that can take account of multiple factors and programmes affecting the evolution of a conflict (Woodrow and Chigas 2011).

A systems mapping of conflict in Ghana helped to identify how and to what degree UNDP Ghana's conflict prevention and resolution portfolio was relevant to the drivers of conflict.[10] The systems mapping helped the evaluation team to develop a nuanced understanding of the degree of relevance of the portfolio. The evaluation assessed whether the desired outcomes would be significant for peace and whether the intervention was timely and appropriate, especially given the potential of significant delays before effects could be detected and of forces that would resist positive change in the context. The evaluation, which was conducted in 2009 and covered the period 2006–2009,[11] had the following objectives:

- To assess the outputs and impacts of UNDP support in the areas of conflict prevention and resolution in the period of 2004 to mid 2009, including the overall intervention strategy, concrete programme achievements and their sustainability.
- To learn lessons and derive recommendations from five years of designing and implementing conflict prevention and resolution initiatives to ensure their continued relevance, effectiveness and ongoing contribution to key national priorities in conflict prevention and peacebuilding.

(Draman et al. 2009: 2, 51)

The evaluation included, therefore, an 'assessment of the overall conflict prevention/peacebuilding strategy design and continuous development of the strategy' (Draman et al. 2009: 2). The evaluators conducted an extensive desk review of documentation related to UNDP's conflict programs for the period under review, as well as conflict analyses and other reports providing information on the causes, dynamics and evolution of conflicts in Ghana.[12] In addition, the team interviewed UNDP staff, government and civil society partners, community members and beneficiaries, in each case posing questions regarding the types and origins of conflict in Ghana.

As early as 2004, UN documentation underscored that while 'Ghana has remained an oasis of peace and stability' in a conflict region, '[i]t is however becoming apparent that Ghana faces security threats emanating from chieftaincy rivalries and land disputes' (United Nations Development Group 2004: 47). The UN Development Assistance Framework (UNDAF) for 2006–2010 reiterated this concern and called for 'strengthening of capacities to manage national, regional and local conflicts' (United Nations Development Group 2006: 16). Based on the extensive information gathered through interviews, the evaluation team produced its own systems map of conflict in Ghana[13] (see Figures 9.1 and 9.2) and tested this understanding with several local peace practitioners. These interviews reaffirmed the UN analysis, but emphasised politicisation and polarisation along party lines – factors raised in other analyses – as one of the primary drivers of conflict in the country, as it infected, distorted and magnified all other conflicts, including chieftaincy disputes (Draman et al. 2009: 9).

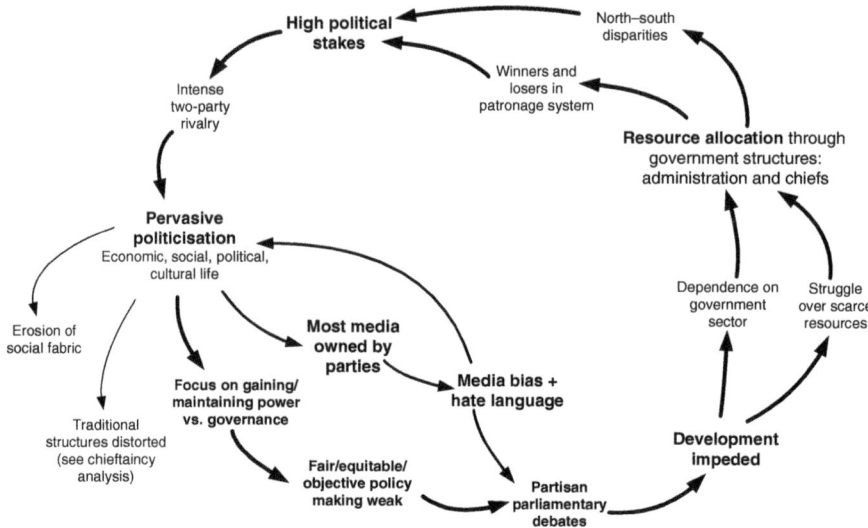

Figure 9.1 Polarisation and politicisation of public life in Ghana

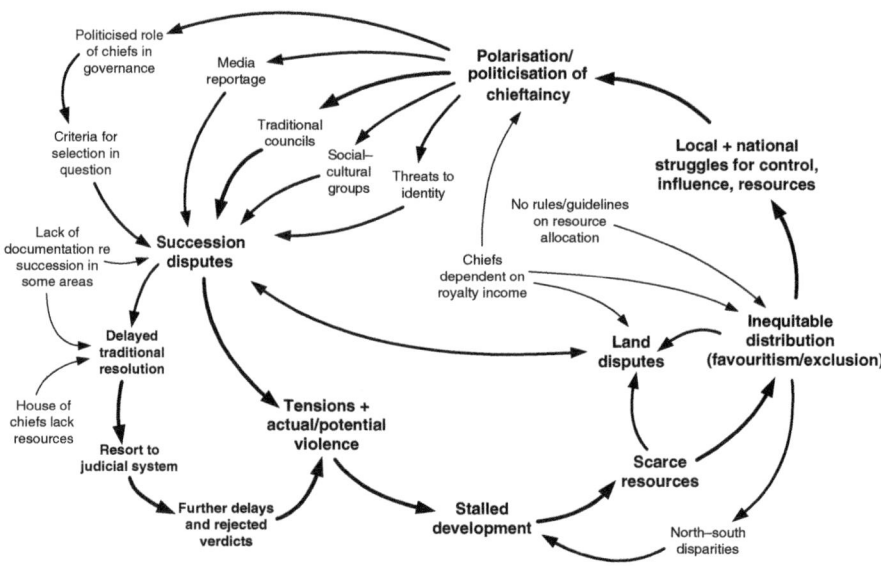

Figure 9.2 Chieftaincy conflicts in Ghana

CDA's conflict analysis, presented in Figure 9.1, identified several dynamics that created a potential for violence. Politicisation and polarisation were identified as key factors (shown in bold text) underlying and amplifying the disparities between north and south, struggles for power and control of resources, the dynamics between winners and losers in the patronage system in the country, distortion of traditional structures (especially chieftaincies) and political control of media outlets (Draman et al. 2009: 9). High political stakes in control of government and resource allocation lead to polarisation and media bias and are intensified by them in a reinforcing dynamic. While politicisation by itself was not likely to lead to widespread violence, when interacting with other factors – especially chieftaincy disputes – the potential for violence emerged.

A further systems-based analysis of chieftaincy issues, depicted in Figure 9.2, helped to identify the interactions between the key factors in Figure 9.1 in another self-reinforcing dynamic. The analysis of chieftaincy disputes linked many of the kinds of conflicts identified in other studies (e.g., land disputes, ethnic disputes, religious disputes), and shed light on the difficulty of tackling any one of them alone.

The evaluators then examined the goals and theory of change of the UN programme portfolio in relation to the systems-based conflict analyses shown above. As in many programmes, the theory of change was not explicit, but could be deduced from an examination of the activities carried out and through conversations with UNDP staff, partners and beneficiaries. Activities and programme initiatives ranged from national and regional efforts to stop immediate threats of violence to efforts to develop sustainable institutions and policies for conflict preventions. Essentially, the theory of change was identified as the following:

> The creation of functional, credible and relatively neutral institutions at the national, regional and district levels will provide the capacity to identify and respond to emerging threats of violence. These neutral institutions (National Peace Councils, regional Peace Advisory Councils, etc.) can identify longer term structural problems that, if not addressed, will result in eventual violence – and then mobilize policy makers and resources for mitigating such problems.
>
> (Draman et al. 2009: 40)

Examining the programme portfolio, the team found that UNDP's choice of interventions and partners did engage many of the important sources of conflict in the country, and thus was highly relevant. The programme was particularly focused on reducing factors that exacerbate or are exacerbated by political polarisation, such as media standards, election processes, peace councils, local conflict resolution mechanisms and mediation of difficult land and chieftaincy issues. Yet the systems analysis suggested that, while the programme addressed short-term dimensions of these factors, the deeper structural factors and dynamics, such as the culture of politicisation and polarisation or unequal distribution of resources between north and south, were unlikely to be addressed by the programme as designed (Draman et al. 2009: 41). In other words, the programme *slowed* the reinforcing dynamic of the main feedback loops shown in Figures 9.1 and 9.2, and created new feedback loops that balanced escalating dynamics at critical junctures, but it would not transform the fundamental dynamics. The systems analysis allowed for a more nuanced judgement of *relevance*, both through identification of peacebuilding needs, by analysing what might transform the dynamic among the key factors, and through analysis of whether the programme would make a logical contribution to catalysing those changes (see Rogers 2012: 4).

5 Using systems thinking in evaluation of effectiveness and impacts of peacebuilding programmes: evaluations in Guinea-Bissau and Kosovo

Analysing conflict as a complex system has also influenced how we have approached evaluation of effectiveness and impact of peacebuilding programmes. First, we have taken the conflict analysis, rather than the intervention itself, as the point of departure for the evaluation. A systems view of conflict sees the intervention as a part of the conflict context – rather than something separate from it. In this sense, a systemic approach resembles 'realist evaluation', which views programmes as embedded in social systems and assesses changes in light of 'the different layers of social reality which make up and surround programmes' (Pawson and Tilley 2004: 4). Because, as Ramalingam and Jones (2008: 54) have noted, 'Agents continuously influence and are influenced by their environment in a reciprocal fashion that changes the interacting environment and the agents themselves', the evaluation design must try to capture *system* dynamics, interdependencies and conditions; otherwise, it will likely miss important aspects of the intervention and the context that affect its potential success (Patton 2006; Hargreaves 2010). Therefore, as we have conducted evaluations, we have asked what changes in the conflict occurred, why and how, and then ask how the intervention interacted with these factors and dynamics to create that change in the conflict system.

This systemic perspective has implications for the scope of the evaluation as well. Given the interconnectedness of the elements of a system, it is important to look at the larger picture and to inquire into the interaction of the project with the context beyond the project's own boundaries.[14] Because the definition of the boundary of the system being evaluated will in part drive how we see the system and the results of a programme, focusing too narrowly on the project or programme can overemphasise the programme's influence and value (see Williams and Imam 2007), and miss important insights about the nature and mechanisms of influence.

Second, as described above, a systems-based evaluation is grounded in an understanding of causality as non-linear, recursive and multi-directional (see Patton 2006; Ramalingam and Jones 2008; Rogers 2008; Ricigliano and Chigas 2011). For example, the trajectory of a project's impact might be like a J-curve (things get worse before they get better), a step function (long periods of apparent stasis then a tipping point), diminishing returns (high impact early on that fades over time) or an S-curve (slow initial uptake, rapid improvements, then plateau) (Woolcock 2009: 5–6). Programmes are also likely to evolve, as they are themselves influenced by and respond to the context (Stern et al. 2012). In these cases, it may not be possible – or it may be misleading – to evaluate against predetermined SMART objectives,[15] unless the nature and timing of the trajectory are well known.[16] Rather, an evaluation may need to focus on whether the programme is producing outcomes of a general type in relation to the conflict dynamics. It would also document and interpret whether and how effects may be non-linear and follow the adaptations of the programme to the context (see Parsons and Hargreaves 2009; Patton 2011). The evaluation will also need to look for unintended effects, how the system adapts to, resists, or amplifies the effects of the intervention, and the responses of the programme to those changes (see Patton 2011: 119).

Third, because of the multi-directionality of cause and effect in systems and the often unpredictable outcomes from the interactions between elements, 'attribution' of results or impacts to a specific programme is difficult. Causality has a 'systemic character', in the sense that any programme becomes part of a larger web of variables whose interaction and feedback 'causes' change. Thus it is harder to credit success or blame failure on a programme, when the results are the product of interactions with other factors and interventions in the system (Midgely 2007). Theory-based, case study and participatory approaches, and emphasis on contribution and multiple causation, can all help identify mechanisms of impact (Stern et al. 2012; see also White and Phillips 2012).

In the remainder of this section, we explore two evaluations that we undertook using systems thinking and mapping to guide the inquiry and analyse data: 1) a review of an experimental conflict prevention programme in Guinea-Bissau, the International Peace and Prosperity Project (Woodrow and Murphy 2008); and 2) an assessment of the cumulative contributions of peacebuilding programming to the prevention or mitigation of inter-ethnic violence during a two-day period of rioting in Kosovo in March 2004 (Chigas et al. 2007).

5.1 Assessing effectiveness and impact in Guinea-Bissau: the International Peace and Prosperity Project

By mapping the dynamics among different conflict factors and by integrating the intervention or intervening organisation into the analysis itself, systems analysis has also helped to identify more precisely the nature and level of impacts on 'peace writ large', both positive and negative, intended and unintended. In Guinea-Bissau, CDA was asked to evaluate the International Peace and Prosperity Project (IPPP), an experimental conflict prevention programme attempting to avert the outbreak of further cycles of violence in that country similar to the destructive civil war of 1998–1999. The terms of reference asked the evaluation '[t]o discern whether and how the IPPP has contributed to reducing the likelihood of political violence in Guinea-Bissau' (Woodrow and Murphy 2008).[17] The project had started in 2004, during a period when it appeared that the situation might deteriorate rapidly. The overall strategy of the programme was to identify individuals and groups in Guinea-Bissau who could, with small amounts of technical and financial support, undertake actions to reduce the likelihood of violence and build the basis for sustainable peace. The project was testing an approach to conflict prevention of ongoing situation analysis, identification of leverage points or points for urgent intervention, provision of small amounts of funding or technical assistance to catalyse action (usually with a strategic partner), quiet diplomacy and advocacy with international actors (Woodrow and Murphy 2008: 8).[18] The evaluation was conducted in the spring of 2008, before the renewed round of political violence and assassinations in early 2009.

As a first step, the evaluation team analysed the conflict. They examined the project's own analysis and analyses from other organisations.[19] In addition, in order to develop a deeper understanding of the conflict dynamics, the team asked multiple interviewees about their view of the causes of conflict in the country. In order to understand the 'story' of the setting and the activities undertaken there, the team relied on listening to a wide range of people representing diverse perspectives and constituencies in semi-structured interviews. Interviewees included beneficiaries or participants, as well as observers outside the programme (Woodrow and Murphy 2008: 42). From the multiple interview sources, patterns of agreement and disagreement emerged and were tested against documentation from the project and partners as well. From the information gathered in this way, the team pieced together a systemic view of the conflict dynamics and the programme's trajectory. The team was able to incorporate different perspectives in the analysis, as systems analysis avoids a single or linear explanation of causality. Before leaving Guinea-Bissau, they were able to test the analysis with several local people to make sure that their understanding was valid. The resulting conflict map is presented in Figure 9.3.

The conflict map in Figure 9.3 illustrates four major intersecting dynamics which are labelled on the diagram (with key driving factors in bold). Causal loop 1 shows the elite power struggle coupled with ingrained systems of favouritism (often called 'patron-client' systems or the 'Big Man Model'). This interacts directly with a second loop indicating cycles of injustice and impunity in a non-functioning judicial system. The third loop depicts, in broad strokes, the effects of a weak private sector economy. All three of these dynamics are shown as contributing to instability and insecurity, while a fourth loop involves the recruitment of vulnerable populations and the military to violence, also feeding into insecurity. All four of these dynamics, in combination, offer an explanation for recurrent cycles of *coups d'état*, assassinations and civil war.

The evaluation team compared the initial analyses from 2004 with the analysis presented in Figure 9.3 and performed in 2008 as part of the evaluation. They also asked interviewees how they thought the situation had changed over the previous five years, if at all. This inquiry revealed progress in openness to greater dialogue, and even public criticism of both the government and the military, greater adherence to human rights standards, greater military professionalism and less involvement in political matters (Woodrow and Murphy 2008). The inquiry

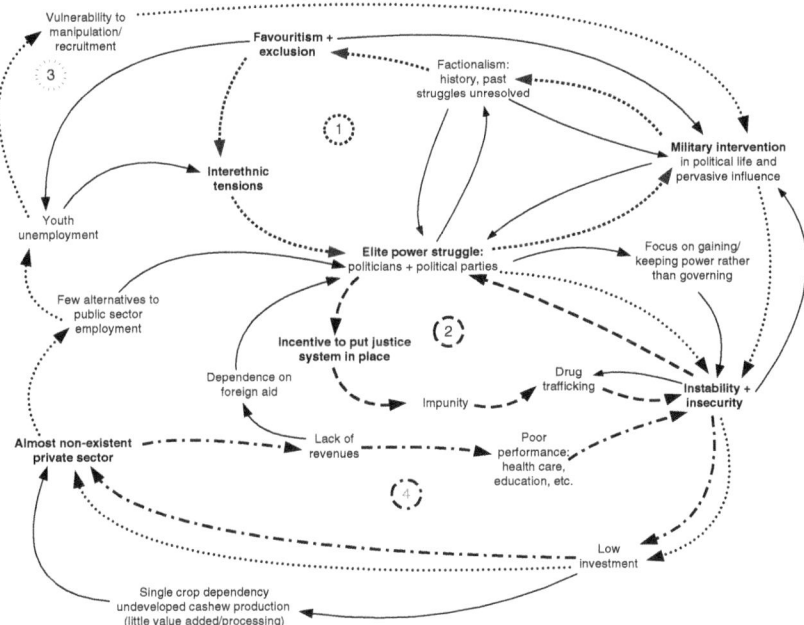

Figure 9.3 Conflict analysis of Guinea-Bissau

included examination of the reasons the changes came about, which ranged from international pressure to increase in civil society voices and reconciliation within the military.

The evaluators then examined the project's initiatives and activities in relation to these changed conflict dynamics. Which of the changes were associated with IPPP activities? How much 'credit' could the project take, and which changes would have happened anyway? It was difficult to discern with specificity the shorter-term objectives of the program, beyond the broadly stated goal of 'preventing violence' in Guinea-Bissau (Woodrow and Murphy 2008: 22–23). The evaluators analysed the narratives of how change in the conflict dynamics came about and the project's chronology, mapping the project's activities and their (implicit) theories of change onto the systems map, and gathering a wide range of people's perceptions of the project's contribution to the conflict changes. Based on this, they were able to develop a picture of the nature of the project's contribution to violence prevention. In some cases, the project was able to catalyse efforts by other actors (e.g., the international community's attention to security sector reform) or reinforce and strengthen existing efforts by providing assistance at the right time (e.g., military reform).

The systems analysis made clear that patron–client systems represent a core dynamic that lies at the heart of the political struggle in Guinea-Bissau, and that until this syndrome is changed, there will likely be a series of dangerous struggles for power among the elite political class, spilling over into overt violence on occasion (as it subsequently did in 2009 with two high-profile assassinations). In this situation, IPPP was doing a good job assisting local political leaders to forestall a range of potentially dangerous circumstances, effectively interrupting or at least mitigating vicious cycles of conflict escalation by weakening links between causal factors. For instance, the project worked to build relationships with key military leaders to break the link between 'vulnerability to recruitment' and 'military intervention' (see Figure 9.3). In addition, the IPPP provided crucial support to a group promoting violence-free elections, addressing, at least in the short term, elements of the elite power struggle. Other efforts included initiation of discussions of security sector reform, support for a series of dialogue processes with key stakeholder groups and promotion of a national reconciliation process. However, the systems analysis of the conflict also revealed that, while the interventions were effective in mitigating the short-term dynamics of the problem, the project's longer-term strategy for addressing deeper structural issues was less effective, as its shift to economic programming was less productive and the programme was not able to address the underlying dynamics of the political culture.

The systemic approach to evaluation was able to identify the nature of the contribution IPPP had made in relation to other factors, and, importantly, its relation (or lack of relation) to significant factors that affected violence in the longer run. Given the experimental, innovative nature of the programme, which was constantly being tested, refined and improved, and the political nature of the intervention, with high-level peacebuilding goals, the systems thinking approach was well-suited to the evaluation. Despite these advantages, the systemic evaluation approach was not able to assess the degree of contribution the IPPP made to the reduction of violence.

The highly dynamic and politicised nature of the context, as well as the diverse and evolving activities of the programme, made traditional evaluation approaches difficult (see Stern et al. 2012). Systems mapping allowed the evaluation team to situate the intervention within the evolving context. Indeed, the funder commented that the evaluation (and the systemic analysis of conflict within it) deepened his own understanding of what the conflict was about. The programme team also gained this understanding. The systems approach also helped it to synthesise multiple perspectives on how and why the conflict had changed and what role IPPP played in it. The systems mapping of the conflict and the findings about relevance also provided a solid basis for the subsequent discussion within the programme team about where to focus further efforts and how to adapt the programme approach to the evolving context.

5.2 Testing theories of change and accounting for systems pushback: assessment of cumulative impacts in Kosovo

A theory of change describes a programme's assumptions about how and why an initiative will contribute to desired changes in the conflict situation. While not necessarily systemic, theories of change are also closely associated with a systems perspective because the theories can be seen as essentially about how to induce change in a system (Weiss 1995; Church and Rogers 2006). Many evaluation frameworks, including the DAC Guidance (OECD 2012: 59; see also Leeuw and Vaessen 2009; Stern et al. 2012; White and Phillips 2012) encourage the use of theories of to assess effectiveness and impact and underscore the importance of evaluating theories of change and their underlying assumptions. Most theories of change remain quite linear, even if the actual impact trajectory is not (Woolcock 2009). Systems thinking can help practitioners and evaluators develop more plausible and contextualised theories of change, and in the evaluation process it can provide an analytic lens for assessing how and why they may or may not be appropriate and valid in a particular context.[20]

In 2006, CDA was asked to assess whether a range of peace programmes had contributed to the absence of violence in some communities during the riots that had engulfed Kosovo during March 2004 (Chigas et al. 2007). The study arose due to a paragraph and footnote in the International Crisis Group's highly respected analysis of the March 2004 riots, which stated that some communities in which CARE International had implemented peacebuilding programming had either resisted or experienced little violence (International Crisis Group 2004: 16). CARE International commissioned the assessment to understand whether this was, in fact, the case. The study was not limited to CARE's programmes but assessed the effects of a broad array of local and international NGOs, as well as international organisations and municipal governments.

The general approach to the assessment was similar to that used in Guinea-Bissau. First, a broad conflict analysis of Kosovo was conducted and supplemented by an in-depth analysis of the type of and trends in inter-ethnic violence in Kosovo. The team analysed statistics relating to inter-ethnic violence (from the Kosovo Police and the OSCE) from 2002 to 2005 to assess trends and the nature of violence in each of the regions of Kosovo. They also conducted several workshops with practitioners from local and international NGOs, the United Nations mission field offices, and the OSCE. The purpose of the workshops was to refine their understanding of the definition and forms of violence in Kosovo and how it was experienced in communities, and to begin to develop some hypotheses, based on practitioners' experience, about the possible factors contributing to the presence/absence of violence.

Second, we analysed the programmes and attempted to identify the theories of change underlying them. As this study did not focus on specific projects or programmes, we identified types and density of peacebuilding programmes and their underlying theories of change. The workshops were used to develop, inductively, a typology for peacebuilding work and the underlying theories of change, building on practitioners' actual work and assumptions.

The team continued to refine the typology and the theories of changed through interviews with agency staff in communities where case studies were carried out, as well as in Pristina. A significant proportion of the programming consisted of joint (inter-ethnic) projects and institutions, designed to improve relations and

188　*Diana Chigas and Peter Woodrow*

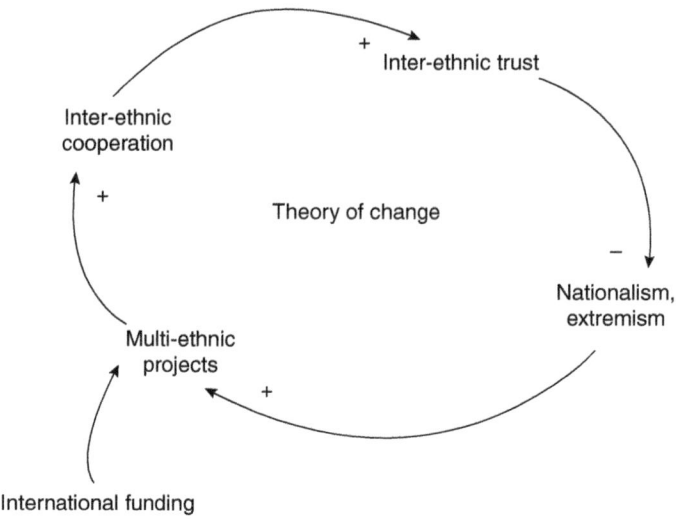

Figure 9.4 Theory of change of peacebuilding programming in Kosovo

cooperation, reduce hostility and eventually build support for coexistence in a multi-ethnic Kosovo. The basic theory of change was that peacebuilding programming would promote positive interactions that would then improve attitudes and relationships, making it more likely that Kosovo Albanians and Serbs would support and engage in peaceful resolution of conflicts (see Babbitt et al. 2013). We represented the (often implicit) assumptions of the theory of change underlying these programmes in a systems map (Figure 9.4). By providing rewards and incentives for cross-ethnic contact and activities, international agencies could induce Kosovar Albanians and Serbs to develop bridges that would reduce cross-ethnic distrust, build willingness and capacity to work together, and create interdependence between ethnic groups that would restrain them from violence. This would create a 'virtuous cycle' of cooperation and trust-building that would reduce nationalism to a desired (low) level and lead the parties to be more willing and able to reach and implement a political agreement on the status of Kosovo.

Third, we undertook seven case studies, which were chosen to allow comparison across several variables: high/low levels of peacebuilding support, high/low historical levels of violence, violence/no violence in March 2004. Multiple data-collection methods were used, including document review, one-on-one semi-structured interviews and small group discussions.

Finally, the study analysed the interaction of programming with the violence specifically and the key drivers of conflict more generally, with a focus on analysis of the relevance of the programming and the validity of the theories of change in relation to the factors for absence of violence. Comparative analysis of the cases was conducted to identify common patterns and themes, as well as differences, across the cases, regarding 1) reasons identified for community resistance to or prevention of violence in 2004; and 2) peacebuilding activities (goals, theories of change, targeting and choice of participants, coordination, reports of impacts, etc.). The team also convened several consultations with local practitioners and analysts to do the same, then coded the cases for those themes.

The study found that the programming did have some positive results; some people were in fact cooperating across ethnic lines. The projects often had powerful effects on participants and played an important role in providing opportunities for inter-ethnic contact that otherwise would not have occurred after 1999. Participants reported that they developed good communication skills through dialogue and training programmes, and that the joint projects helped build some lasting ties across conflict lines. 'The relationships are better. There was much more business, a higher frequency,' as one beneficiary commented (Chigas et al. 2007: 38). The scale of multi-ethnic participation in the cultural events, such as festivals, also suggests that there was interest in cross-community contact beyond participation in inter-ethnic projects. In fact, many individuals took action, even in communities that experienced violence and often at significant personal risk, to help or protect their Kosovo Serb neighbours during the March 2004 violence (Chigas et al. 2007: 26).

However, these improved relationships did not explain the lack of violence in some of the communities (including those in which CARE and others implemented peacebuilding programmes). Communities that had extensive inter-ethnic contact, and had been held up as 'good' or 'models' in terms of inter-ethnic relations, also had some of the higher rates of inter-ethnic violence, including in March 2004 (Chigas et al. 2007). At the same time, communities in which peacebuilding programmes had encountered difficulties had not experienced violence in March 2004. The case studies suggested that strong intra-ethnic social networks, which allowed communities to organise, had contributed to the prevention of violence, where there was strong Kosovo Albanian motivation to demonstrate adherence to international standards to gain independence. In addition, leadership, access to information that allowed communities realistically to address threat levels, and location of the community all also were significant factors (Chigas et al. 2007).[21]

What were the implications of these findings for peacebuilding programming? The limited role that peacebuilding programmes played in the prevention of violence did not mean that the programming was ineffective or that the theory of change was invalid. Through a systems analysis, we were able to understand how the system had adapted to these and other interventions in ways that counteracted or limited the programmes' effectiveness and maintained nationalism and hostility. Those insights served as a basis for agencies to adjust their strategies to anticipate and address the ways in which the system resisted change (often referred to as system 'push back').

For example, a systemic view of the trends and patterns of violence over a several-year period allowed us to see that violence had not actually diminished over time. Reduced physical violence (e.g., assaults) and greater freedom of movement had masked a rise in other forms of more targeted violence (property and

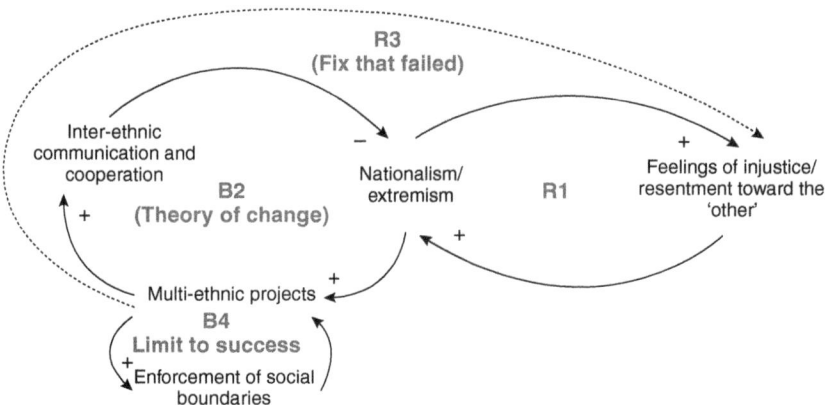

Figure 9.5 What actually happened in Kosovo

psychological), strategically aimed at intimidation of Serbs and encouragement of their departure from strategic areas (Chigas et al. 2007). This had not been understood by most agencies, and therefore not addressed in programming.

More generally, mapping what actually happened with regard to the theory of change also helped participating agencies to understand how the system resisted change, and how their own interventions had generated unintended negative effects that undermined their impacts.

As depicted in Figure 9.5, these included:

- Contextual dynamics that limited the growth or spread of cooperation across ethnic groups. In both Kosovo Albanian and Kosovo Serb communities, implicit rules of social interaction across ethnic lines were enforced through social networks; these and intra-community pressure restricted the boundaries of permissible interaction to generally non-visible business dealings. These 'simple rules' (Eoyang and Berkas 1999; Rogers 2008) that everyone followed generated system-wide patterns of behaviour. The greater the volume of multi-ethnic projects and interactions, the greater the enforcement of these boundaries. This operated as a constraint (B4 in Figure 9.5) in the system, ultimately limited the number and scope of multi-ethnic contacts that were possible and, consequently, undermined the potential of the programmes to increase communication and trust significantly.
- Negative unintended consequences of a focus on involving different ethnicities in programmes. Even (or especially) when the multi-ethnic projects were successful (R3 in Figure 9.5), they had secondary effects on other dynamics that ultimately undermined the achievement of the goal of reducing nationalism and extremism. International focus on multi-ethnic communities and projects led more 'hard line' constituencies, including Kosovo Liberation Army veterans, living largely in mono-ethnic areas, to feel excluded from the

process. Consequently, the international policy of promoting multi-ethnicity had an inadvertent negative consequence of worsening, not improving, coexistence and inter-ethnic hostility (R3 and R1). In other words, it became a 'fix that failed' (Senge 1990; Meadows 2008). Moreover, international donors' assumptions (in B2) that their support for multi-ethnic projects and minority rights would provide an incentive for cross-ethnic communication and collaboration proved to be wrong, as members of both groups, especially Kosovo Albanians, viewed this as a condition for funding, not a benefit, and resented it.

The systems maps (with accompanying narrative) provided a visual tool for communicating the findings in a digestible form and facilitating strategic planning on how to improve effectiveness. In particular, several agencies addressed three aspects that were identified as significant and adjusted their programming to deal with them. This included shifting focus within their programming (to the extent possible) away from facilitation of returns exclusively to addressing key drivers of conflict, especially feelings of injustice and the past and the question of the status of Kosovo; engaging more with key/influential constituencies in mono-ethnic areas that were hard to reach; and supporting to a greater extent *intra-ethnic* processes to deal with constraints on multi-ethnic cooperation.

6 Conclusion: potential of a systems approach for evaluating peacebuilding interventions

As illustrated by the three case examples described above, systems thinking can be useful for evaluations in complicated and complex contexts where it is important to identify what is working (and what is not working), how and why. Systems tools support both learning and adaptation of programming and help identify what aspects of a programme might be transferable to other context or not. In conflict-affected and fragile contexts, in which causes are interacting and influencing each other, there are multiple perspectives and multiple, often interconnected, ways to achieve peacebuilding goals. Systems thinking can fill gaps in approaches to conflict analysis and programme logic that are critical to understanding *relevance*, *effectiveness* and *impact*. Systems thinking concepts and tools have also proven valuable in evaluation processes, to understand the complex nature of the conflicts in which programmes are intervening and the relevance of programming to those dynamics, as well as the ways in which they influence 'peace writ large'.

In all the systems-based evaluations we have conducted, a systemic analysis of the conflict has resulted in a more nuanced assessment of relevance. Systems mapping has permitted identification of points of leverage where interventions might have the biggest effect, given system push back (resistance to change). Systems analyses have also have provided a useful tool for testing the broader theory of change of a programme: the assumed pathway by which it will address drivers of conflict and peace. A systemic map of the theory of change was used in Kosovo to test the theory of change, and was implicit in the analysis of the relation of programming to the conflict analyses in Guinea-Bissau and Ghana. This represents an advance over linear models often used in theories of change; they account for interactions among conflict causes and between the programme and the conflict context, as well as for the ways in which the conflict system will resist attempts at positive change.

It should be noted that systems thinking is not a panacea. It is neither necessary nor desirable for all analytic, planning or evaluation processes. Systems mapping, of the type we have used in our evaluations, is not well-suited to identifying degrees of contribution and causality. Computer-based systems dynamics or agent-based modelling (see Forrester 1968, 1969, 1971; Sterman 2000; Bonabeau 2002) do allow quantification and testing of the degree and sensitivity of causal relationships and feedback processes identified in systems maps; however, they may require financial and human resources and expertise not readily available in many situations. This may limit the usefulness of such a highly technical process.

Moreover, a systems approach may not be needed or appropriate for all interventions, or even for all aspects of a peacebuilding intervention. Most interventions have elements that are simple, complicated and complex. In other words, not all aspects of all peacebuilding interventions are complex. Linear and 'reductionist' analysis (breaking a problem down into its component parts) and evaluation methods are good for 'simple' problems (i.e., those that are discrete and known), where there is a degree of certainty about outcomes and how change comes about (see Patton 2011). In a development context, this might include building a school or organising an election. In the peacebuilding field, more traditional evaluation processes might suffice for understanding whether training in conflict resolution skills did in fact result in expected knowledge, skills, attitude and behaviour changes anticipated by the programme. Or whether inter-group contact and cooperation did lead to greater trust, cooperation and more positive attitudes about the 'other'. For these kinds of problems, 'best practice' evidence can identify steps for achieving desired outcomes with a fair degree of confidence, even if the steps are difficult and complicated. Fairly straightforward evaluations can determine whether those outcomes were in fact achieved.

Systems thinking shows great promise in providing the basis for evaluating programmes that operate in a flexible and adaptive mode under uncertainty as, we believe, most peacebuilding activities should. Classic evaluation methods look at a programme's original stated goals and objectives and examine the extent to which the programme has achieved them. Systems-based evaluations look for changes in patterns of individual and group behaviour, shifts in causation (X no longer leads clearly to Y), weakening or strengthening of key conflict factors, and the reverberations through the system of any such changes, including surprises, intended and unintended consequences. Systems evaluations focus less on causal attribution for individual programmes, and more on how programmes contribute to 'peace writ large' and on how changes are leveraged in the system. In this sense, in peacebuilding evaluations, systems approaches have been particularly helpful for interventions that have (implicitly or explicitly) goals at the level of the whole system, such as contributing to peace or conflict mitigation. Systems approaches are not 'project-centric'; they ask how important or significant the benefits of a programme are in relation to everything else that is going on in participants' or beneficiaries' lives. In other words, they ask how worthwhile it is in the grand scheme of things (Fugita 2010: 70). Systems approaches help us understand how actions at micro or local levels can influence patterns at the macro level, and for answering the kind of question the Kosovo study described in this chapter tackled: what difference did the intervention make, rather than solely whether the programme achieved its goal. This is crucial for evaluations focused on helping programme teams and donors learn and improve their practice.

Notes

1 The Reflecting on Peace Practice Program (RPP) is part of CDA (formerly CDA Collaborative Learning Projects). CDA is a non-profit organisation based in Cambridge, Massachusetts.
2 'Peace writ large' refers to the long-range goals of peace work at the broad level of society: ending cycles of violence and addressing political, economic and social grievances that may be driving conflict (Anderson and Olson 2003: 12).
3 A thorough explanation of systems thinking is beyond the scope of this chapter. For an accessible introduction to systems thinking, see Senge (1990) or Meadows (2008).
4 Dynamic and dynamical interactions are distinguished in complex systems. Dynamical change refers to evolving systems where the interactions within, between and among parts are volatile, turbulent, and cascading rapidly and unpredictably. Dynamic change, by contrast, while also describing a system's change over time, assumes a smooth trajectory (Patton 2011: 8, 139).
5 The first phase of RPP's learning on peacebuilding effectiveness took place from 1999 to 2003. Twenty-six case studies of peacebuilding activities were developed and analysed collaboratively in a number of consultations bringing the authors together with practitioners, academics and policymakers, in order to identify cross-cutting themes and findings. The preliminary findings were shared and discussed in 35 feedback workshops held around the world. Anderson and Olson (2003) summarise the lessons from this phase.
6 We define 'impact' as 'the results or effects of any peacebuilding intervention that lie beyond its immediate programme activities or sphere and constitute broader changes in the conflict' (Anderson et al. 2007).
7 See Church (2011); Rogers (2012).
8 Paffenholz and Reychler (2007) propose assessment of the 'peacebuilding relevance' of an intervention by assessing the viability of the interventions goals by comparing the objectives and main activities of the intervention with the peacebuilding needs and examining how they are consistent with those needs using a 'relevance scale'. The peacebuilding needs are based on a conflict analysis and a 'peacebuilding deficiency and needs analysis' (i.e., identification of the vision and comparison of the vision to the current situation).
9 Rogers (2012) identifies five dimensions of 'relevance': based on conflict analysis, needs/goals appropriateness, timeliness, adaptability/responsiveness, stakeholder perception of relevance and strategic policy alignment. He proposes standards evaluation of each dimension.
10 The evaluation was conducted by Peter Woodrow of CDA, in cooperation with national consultants Janet Adama Mohammed and Dr Rasheed Draman.

11 The evaluation Terms of Reference called for a review of the programme from 2003 onwards, but the evaluators were able to collect data only from 2006 onwards, with some references to activities in 2004 and 2005 (Draman et al. 2009).
12 The programme did not have a written conflict analysis. Based on document review and conversations with the Peace and Governance Advisor, however, the team concluded that UNDP did work with an implicit analysis through ongoing monitoring of the situation, team discussions and regular engagement with the Bureau for Crisis Prevention and Recovery's Conflict Prevention Team and the Framework Team Secretariat (Draman et al. 2009: 36). This analysis, however, was not developed or shared with partners or other donors.
13 These systems 'maps' are known as 'causal loop diagrams' in systems thinking terms. See Senge (1990) and Meadows (2008) for further explanation of the methods used.
14 The DAC Guidance implicitly recognises this possibility in its discussion of the criterion of effectiveness, by suggesting that an evaluation must look beyond whether a programme as designed met its predetermined objectives to examine the outcomes in relation to peacebuilding and conflict dynamics (OECD 2012: 66)
15 SMART refers to Specific, Measurable, Attainable, Relevant and Time-bound. Other formulations of these criteria exist.
16 It may even be difficult to specify outcomes in advance. A programme may have clear long-term objectives, but as the Guinea-Bissau example suggests, find it hard to determine specific intermediate outcomes in advance because they are developed as part of a consultative process with local constituencies and in response to an evolving context. Or, as in Kosovo, where at the time of the evaluation the question of Kosovo's status was still contested, the long-term goals may be emergent, but shorter term goals much clearer (see Funnell and Rogers 2010: 76–80).
17 The evaluation also was to provide recommendations on further IPPP engagement in Guinea-Bissau, as well as identify lessons about the approach and methodology of the project that might be relevant to subsequent efforts to prevent violence elsewhere in West Africa (Woodrow and Murphy 2008: 41).
18 Points of leverage comprise situations where the project hypothesised that small amounts of resources could have larger effects. In the IPPP, these included situations where something was 'stuck' and needed an injection of resources or ideas to become 'unstuck', efforts to bring together the right people for dialogue to promote resolution, and initiatives to address urgent circumstances in a timely and flexible manner (Woodrow and Murphy 2008: 9).
19 The project staff had engaged in on-going analysis, although it had been unrecorded and not easily accessible. In addition, the project had facilitated a conflict analysis by local stakeholders from a wide range of perspectives that was written (Woodrow and Murphy 2008).
20 Systems thinking can help practitioners develop a more realistic theory of change that reflects how change occurs in the particular context, taking into account potential forces of resistance to change. See Babbitt et al. (2013).
21 Inter-ethnic interdependence did play a role, but mainly in relation to shared infrastructure, and not inter-ethnic relationships (Chigas et al. 2007).

Bibliography

Anderson, M. B. and Olson, L. (2003) *Confronting War: Critical Lessons for Peace Practitioners*. Cambridge, MA: CDA Collaborative Learning Projects.

Anderson, M. B., Chigas, D. and Woodrow, P. (2007) 'Encouraging Effective Evaluation of Conflict Prevention and Peacebuilding Activities: Towards DAC Guidance', *OECD*

Journal on Development 8(3). www.oecd-ilibrary.org/development/oecd-journal-on-development/volume-8/issue-3_journal_dev-v8-3-en, accessed 26 March 2013.

Anderson, M. B., Brown, D. and Jean, I. (2012) *Time to Listen: Hearing People on the Receiving End of International Aid*, Cambridge, MA: CDA Collaborative Learning Projects.

Babbitt, E., Chigas, D. and Wilkinson, R. (2013) *Theories and Indicators of Change: Concepts and Primers for Conflict Management and Mitigation*. Washington, DC: USAID.

Bonabeau, E. (2002) 'Agent-based Modelling: Methods and Techniques for Simulating Human Systems', *Proceedings of the National Academy of Sciences of the USA* 99(3): 7280–7287. www.ncbi.nlm.nih.gov/pmc/articles/PMC128598, accessed 17 May 2013.

Chigas, D. et al. (2007) *Has Peacebuilding Made a Difference in Kosovo? A Study of the Effectiveness of Peacebuilding in Preventing Violence: Lessons Learned from the March 2004 Riots in Kosovo*, Prishtinë/Pritina: CARE International and CDA Collaborative Learning Projects.

Church, C. (2011) *The Use of Reflecting on Peace Practice (RPP) in Peacebuilding Evaluation: Review and Recommendations – Final Report*, Cambridge, MA: CDA Collaborative Learning Projects. www.cdainc.com/cdawww/pdf/other/rpp_use_in_evaluation_scharbatke_church_05232011_Pdf.pdf, accessed 26 March 2013.

Church, C. and Rogers, M. (2006) *Designing for Results: Integrating Monitoring and Evaluation in Conflict Transformation Programs*, Washington, DC: Search for Common Ground. www.sfcg.org/programmes/ilt/ilt_manualpage.html, accessed 26 March 2013.

Draman, R., Mohammed, J. and Woodrow, P. (2009) *The Conflict Prevention and Resolution Portfolio of UNDP Ghana: Evaluation Report*, New York: UNDP. http://erc.undp.org/evaluationadmin/downloaddocument.html?docid=4036, accessed 26 March 2013.

Eoyang, G. H. and Berkas, T. H. (1999), 'Evaluating Performance in a Complex Adaptive System', in M. R. Lissack, and H. P. Gunz (eds) *Managing Complexity in Organizations*, Westport, CT: *Quorum Books*, pp. 313–335.

Forrester, J. W. (1968) *System Dynamics*, Waltham, MA: Pegasus Communications.

——(1969) *Urban Dynamics*, Waltham, MA: Pegasus Communications.

——(1971) *World Dynamics*, Cambridge, MA: Wright-Allen.

Fugita, N. (2010) *Beyond Logframe: Using Systems Concepts in Evaluation*, Issues and Prospects for International Developlment Series IV, Tokyo: Foundation for Advanced Studies on International Development.

Funnell, S. and Rogers, P. (2010) *Purposeful Program Theory: Effective Use of Theories of Change and Logic Models*, San Francisco: Jossey-Bass.

Goldwyn, R. and Chigas, D. (2013) *Monitoring and Evaluating Conflict Sensitivity: Methodological Challenges and Practical Solutions*, Practice Product Series, Conflict, Crime and Violence Reduction Initiative, London: DFID.

Hargreaves, M. (2010) *Evaluating System Change: A Planning Guide*, Methods Brief. Cambridge, MA: Mathematica Policy Research.

International Crisis Group (2004) *Collapse in Kosovo*, ICG Europe Report No. 155, Pristina, Belgrade and Brussels: International Crisis Group. www.crisisgroup.org/~/media/Files/europe/155_collapse_in_kosovo_revised, accessed 26 March 2013.

Leeuw, F. and Vaessen, J. (2009) *Impact Evaluations and Development*, Nonie Guidance on Impact Evaluation. http://siteresources.worldbank.org/EXTOED/Resources/nonie_guidance.pdf, accessed 5 October 2012.

Meadows, D. (2008) *Thinking in Systems: A Primer*, White River Junction, VT: Chelsea Green Publishing Company.

Midgely, G. (2007) 'Systems Thinking for Evaluation', in B. Williams and I. Imam (eds) *Systems Concepts in Evaluation: An Expert Anology*, Point Reyes, CA: EdgePress/American Evaluation Association, pp. 11–34.

OECD (2012) *Evaluating Peacebuilding Activities in Settings of Conflict and Fragility: Improving Learning for Results*, DAC Guidelines and Reference Series, Paris: OECD Publishing. doi: 10.1787/9789264106802-en.

Paffenholz, T. (2006) *Third-Generation PCIA: Introducing the Aid for Peace Approach*, Berghof Dialogue Series No. 4: New Trends in Peace and Conflict Impact Assessment (PCIA), Berlin: Berghof Foundation. www.berghof-handbook.net/documents/publications/dialogue4_paffenholz.pdf, accessed 26 March 2013.

Paffenholz, T. and Reychler, L. (2007) *Aid for Peace: A Guide to Planning and Evaluation for Conflict Zones*, Baden-Baden: Nomos.

Parsons, B. and Hargreaves, M. (2009) *Matching an Evaluation to the Dynamics of a Complex System and the Nature of the Intervention*, professional development workshop presented at the American Evaluation Association Conference, Orlando, FL, 15 November 2009.

Patton, M. Q. (2006) 'Evaluation for the Way We Work', *The Non-profit Quarterly* 13(1): 28–33.

——(2011) *Developmental Evaluation: Applying Complexity Concepts to Enhance Innovation and Use*, New York: Guilford Press.

Pawson, R. and Tilley, N. (2004) *Realist Evaluation*, paper funded by the British Cabinet Office. www.communitymatters.com.au/RE_chapter.pdf, accessed 26 March 2013.

Ramalingam, B. and Jones, H. (2008) *Exploring the Science of Complexity: Ideas and Implications for Development and Humanitarian Efforts*, Working Paper 285, London: Overseas Development Institute.

Ricigliano, R. and Chigas, D. (2011) *Systems Thinking in Conflict Assessment: Concepts and Application*, Washington, DC: USAID. https://dec.usaid.gov/dec/content/Detail.aspx?ctID=ODVhZjk4NWQtM2YyMi00YjRmLTkxNjktZTcxMjM2NDBmY2Uy&rID=MzIxNDMz&sID=Mg==&bckToL=VHJ1ZQ==&qcf=&ph=VHJ1ZQ, accessed 26 March 2013.

Rogers, M. (2012) *Evaluating Relevance in Peacebuilding Programs*, Working Papers on Program Review and Evaluation # 1, CDA Collaborative Learning Projects, Cambridge, MA: CDA.

Rogers, P. (2008) 'Using Programme Theory to Evaluate Complicated and Complex Aspects of Intervention', *Evaluation* 14(1): 29–48.

Senge, P. (1990) *The Fifth Discipline: The Art and Practice of the Learning Organization*, New York: Doubleday.

Smith, D. (2004) *Towards a Strategic Framework for Peacebuilding: Getting Their Act Together: Overview Report of the Joint Utstein Study on Peacebuilding*, Oslo: Royal Norwegian Ministry of Foreign Affairs.

Spurk, C. (2008) 'Forget Impact: Concentrate on Measuring Outcomes – Lessons from Recent Debates on Evaluation of Peacebuilding Programmes', *New Routes* 13(3): 11–14.

Sterman, J. D. (2000) *Business Dynamics: Systems Thinking and Modelling for a Complex World*, Boston: Irwin/McGraw Hill.

Stern, E., Stame, N., Mayne, J., Forss, K., Davies, R. and Befani, B. (2012) *Developing a Broader Range of Rigorous Designs and Methods for Impact Evaluations*, report of a study commissioned by the Department for International Development (DFID), London:

Department for International Development. www.dfid.gov.uk/Documents/.../design-method-impact-eval.pdf, accessed 26 March 2013.

United Nations Development Group (2004) *Common Country Assessment: Ghana*. www.preventionweb.net/english/policies/v.php?id=10490&cid=67, accessed 26 March 2013.

——(2006) *United Nations Development Assistance Framework 2006–2010*. www.unfpaghana.org/page.php?page=425&section=42&typ=1, accessed 26 March 2013.

Weiss, C. (1995) 'Nothing as Practical as a Good Theory: Exploring Theory-based Evaluation for Comprehensive Community Initiatives for Children and Families', in J. Connel, L. Kubisch, B. Schoor and C. Weiss (eds) *New Approaches to Evaluating Community Initiatives: Volume 1: Concepts, Methods and Contexts*, New York: Aspen Institute.

Williams, B. and Hummelbrunner, R. (2011) *Systems Concepts in Action: A Practitioner's Toolkit*, Stanford: Stanford University Press.

Williams, B. and Imam, I. (eds) (2007) *Systems Concepts in Evaluation: An Expert Anthology*, Point Reyes, CA: EdgePress/American Evaluation Association.

White, H. and Phillips, D. (2012) *Addressing Attribution of Cause and Effect in Small n Impact Evaluations: Towards an Integrated Framework*, Working Paper 15, New Delhi: International Initiative for Impact Evaluation.

Woodrow, P. (2006) *Advancing Practice in Conflict Analysis and Strategy Development*, CDA Collaborative Learning Projects, Cambridge, MA: CDA. www.cdainc.com/cdawww/pdf/article/RPP%20Article%20Conflict%20Analysis%2020060101.pdf, accessed 26 March 2013.

Woodrow, P. and Chigas, D. (2011) 'Connecting the Dots: Evaluating Whether and How Programmes Address Conflict Systems', in D. Korppen, N. Ropers and H. Giessman (eds) *The Non-linearity of Peace Processes – Theory and Practice of Systemic Conflict Transformation*, Opladen and Farmington Hills: Barbara Budrich Verlag.

Woodrow, P. and Murphy, S. (2008) *International Peace and Prosperity Project – Guinea-Bissau: Project Review*, CDA Collaborative Learning Projects, Cambridge MA: CDA. http://beforeproject.org/site/wp-content/uploads/2009/03/before_ippp_program-evaluation.pdf, accessed 26 March 2013.

Woolcock, M. (2009) *Towards a Plurality of Methods in Project Evaluation: A Contextualized Approach to Understanding Impact Trajectories and Efficacy*, BWPI Working Paper 73, Manchester: Brooks World Poverty Institute.

Index

aid effectiveness 42, 154, 170; Paris Declaration on Aid Effectiveness 9, 42, 58
Afghanistan 8, 105–29, 138, 158, 165, 172
Anderson, M. B. 2, 16, 24–5, 176–7, 193
attribution 24, 30, 38, 41, 68–9, 81, 102, 130, 141–5, 149, 159–60, 162, 178, 192
attrition 112, 140

Bamberger, M. 17, 23, 26–8, 31, 32, 33, 51
bias 6, 24, 25, 33, 46, 56, 57, 69, 102, 112, 144–5, 178, 180, 181; cognitive 28, 101; sampling 26–29, 31, 32–3, 46, 96; selection 112, 117–18, 131, 135
biased reporting 32, 33, 40, 45, 56–7, 138

capacity-building 50, 98, 103, 106–7, 110, 111, 114
case study (approach) 26–7, 94, 97–9, 100, 102, 183
causalities 20, 24, 69, 99–101, 102, 182–4; assessing or inferring 33, 105, 120–1, 144, 192; chains of 69, 159, 163, 169; *see also* attribution
causation, establishing 26, 30, 69; 144, 183
comparison group 23, 27, 117, 130–8, 141, 144; *see also* control groups
complexity: theory 19, 31, 93, 96; dealing with 15, 20, 24, 30, 31–2, 86–7, 92–3
conflict analysis: conducting 90, 95–7, 111, 120, 193; use of in evaluation 21, 23, 39, 44–50, 55–6, 86, 92–4, 100, 102, 138, 148, 160, 162, 169, 178–91; use of in programming 23, 53, 92, 167, 194
conflict sensitivity (conflict sensitive) 25, 48, 51, 90, 94, 102, 138; *see also* 'do no harm'

control groups 27, 45, 97, 105, 137, 142, 146–8, 157; ethical concerns regarding use of 132–3, 137; natural 135
contribution: analysis of 5, 24, 30, 52–3, 94, 99–101, 167, 175, 182–3, 185–6
counterfactual 23, 31, 32, 41, 68, 73, 77, 130–49, 155–67
criteria: evaluation 3, 22, 57, 107, 177; OECD DAC evaluation 39, 42, 50, 56, 86

data collection 6, 18, 26–29, 34, 97, 119–20, 130–7, 140, 145, 148, 156–62, 168; qualitative methods for 38, 101, 159; *see also* sampling
Democratic Republic of Congo (DRC) 85–103, 132–3, 139, 142, 147, 158, 164, 169, 172
'do no harm' 8, 23, 28, 30, 32, 81, 139, 148, 177

encouragement design 136, 142
endogeneity 117, 119, 145
evaluation design 26, 56, 97, 130, 139–40, 148, 159, 163, 166, 168, 182
experiments 117, 130–1; natural 135; randomised 23; thought 157
experimental design 127

fragile states xii, 1–3, 5, 7, 9, 10, 19; Principles for Good International Engagement in 9, 21

gender: gender-based violence 98; in sampling 70, 134, 135

impact evaluation 15, 16, 17, 23–4, 31, 32, 41, 130–49, 156, 169

inside-out 69, 74, 76, 81, 145
intervention logic 18, 157, 161, 169;
  see also theory of change
Israel 132, 137, 147, 150

Liberia 3, 127, 132, 134–8, 146–8, 158, 171
logical framework (log frame) 19, 31, 176, 178
logic model 19, 51, 92

matching 23, 27, 127, 135, 142, 147
meta-evaluation 55, 159–61
mixed-methods 24, 81, 131, 156, 163, 168, 171

n: small *n* 26, 33–4, 101, 131, 141, 144–5, 149, 159, 166; large *n* 27, 32, 105, 131, 132, 141–2, 144–5

OECD DAC 7, 9, 10, 16, 21, 31, 39, 44, 50, 56, 86, 154, 167, 170; guidance on evaluating in situations of conflict and fragility 7, 31, 42, 44, 48–9, 50–2, 177, 187, 194
outputs 19, 100, 101, 130, 141, 172, 179
outside-in 69, 74, 76, 81, 145

Palestine 3, 132, 137
participatory: analysis 94, 96; approaches 17, 20, 31, 85, 86, 94–5, 102, 103, 143, 183; conflict mapping 95; methods
path dependency 69
political economy 10, 39–40, 55–6, 63, 67, 69, 75, 81
programme theory 7, 11, 18, 19, 20, 51, 91, 93, 102, 156–7, 161–2
programme design 167–70
propensity score 135

qualitative: data 69, 101, 120–2, 124, 145, 166, 171; methods 24, 27, 29, 38, 44, 62, 81, 105, 120, 127, 159, 166
quasi-experimental 23–4, 26, 31–2, 131–5, 146–8, 157, 160

randomisation 116, 131–4

randomised: experiments 23, 127, 135; randomised control trial(s) (RCTs) 23, 27, 130–1, 142, 146–7; sampling 102, 119, 137, 166
regression discontinuity design 33, 135
relevance: assessing 42, 43, 56, 85, 88, 102, 177–9, 182, 188; criterion 39, 48, 50, 57, 86, 107
Rogers, P. 11, 18–21, 31, 32, 51, 103, 178, 182, 187, 190, 193, 194

sampling; pragmatic sampling, 33, 34; purposive sampling, 26, 46–8; qualitative 112; representative sampling, 112; stratified sampling 112; *see also n*
selection bias *see* bias
social constructivism 16–18
social realism 16–17
Sri Lanka 3, 8, 32, 61–82, 132, 135, 145, 148, 158–9, 169
South Sudan 1, 3, 9, 38–58, 137, 158, 160, 162, 164, 169, 171
stakeholder mapping 29
Stern, E. 15, 20, 24, 32, 51, 54, 63, 67, 68, 85, 141, 183, 186–7
systematic review 132, 143
systems thinking 175–93

theory of change 6, 7, 18–20, 21, 23, 31, 34, 39, 51–3, 91–2, 105, 108–11, 115, 122, 127, 130, 131, 141, 144, 155–7, 161–72, 178–94
theory-based evaluation 18–19, 24, 26, 156, 183; limitations of 31, 39; sampling strategy 28
tipping points 19, 95
triangulation 29, 55, 57, 68, 145, 163, 169
turning points 69–71, 75–6, 81

unobservable characteristics 117, 135
Utstein: study 16, 30, 31, 32, 33, 171; palette 47, 50–1, 54, 57

White, H. 41, 131, 141, 156–7, 160–1, 172
White, H. and Phillips, D. 24, 28–9, 32, 33, 34, 101, 144, 183, 187